W9-CAD-014

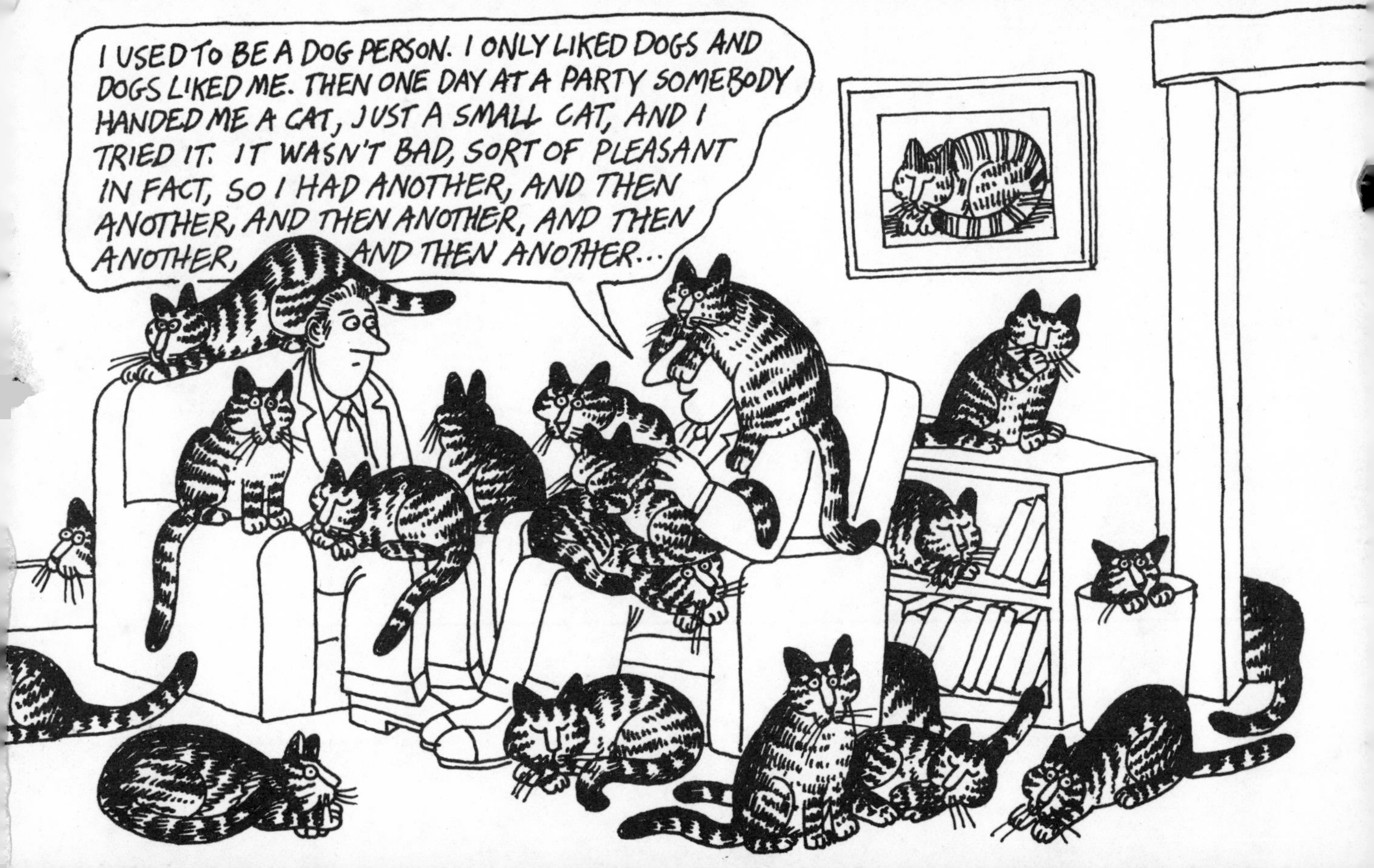
I USED TO BE A DOG PERSON. I ONLY LIKED DOGS AND DOGS LIKED ME. THEN ONE DAY AT A PARTY SOMEBODY HANDED ME A CAT, JUST A SMALL CAT, AND I TRIED IT. IT WASN'T BAD, SORT OF PLEASANT IN FACT, SO I HAD ANOTHER, AND THEN ANOTHER, AND THEN ANOTHER, AND THEN ANOTHER, AND THEN ANOTHER...

cat (kat), *n.* [*pl.* CATS (kats) AS. *catte*, akin to G. *katze* < LL. *cattus*, etc., all via Celt.; prob. IE. base **qat-*, to bear young, seen in L. *catulus*. 1. a small, lithe, soft-furred animal, domesticated since ancient times, and often kept as a pet or for killing mice. 2. . . .

By B. Kliban

Workman Publishing Co. New York

Copyright© 1975 by B. Kliban
All rights reserved. This book may not be
reproduced in whole or in part, by mimeograph
or any other means, without permission in
writing from the publisher.

ISBN: 0-911104-54-2

Design by Paul Hanson

Printed and bound by the George Banta Company

Manufactured in the United States of America

Workman Publishing Company
231 East 51st Street
New York, New York 10022

First printing March 1975

       14   15   16

Definition of cat shown on cover is printed with permission. From *Webster's New
World Dictionary*, College Edition. Copyright © 1968 by The World Publishing Company.

To Norton, Nitty and their mother Noko Marie the Snake,
and Burton Rustle, formerly unrelated but now family.

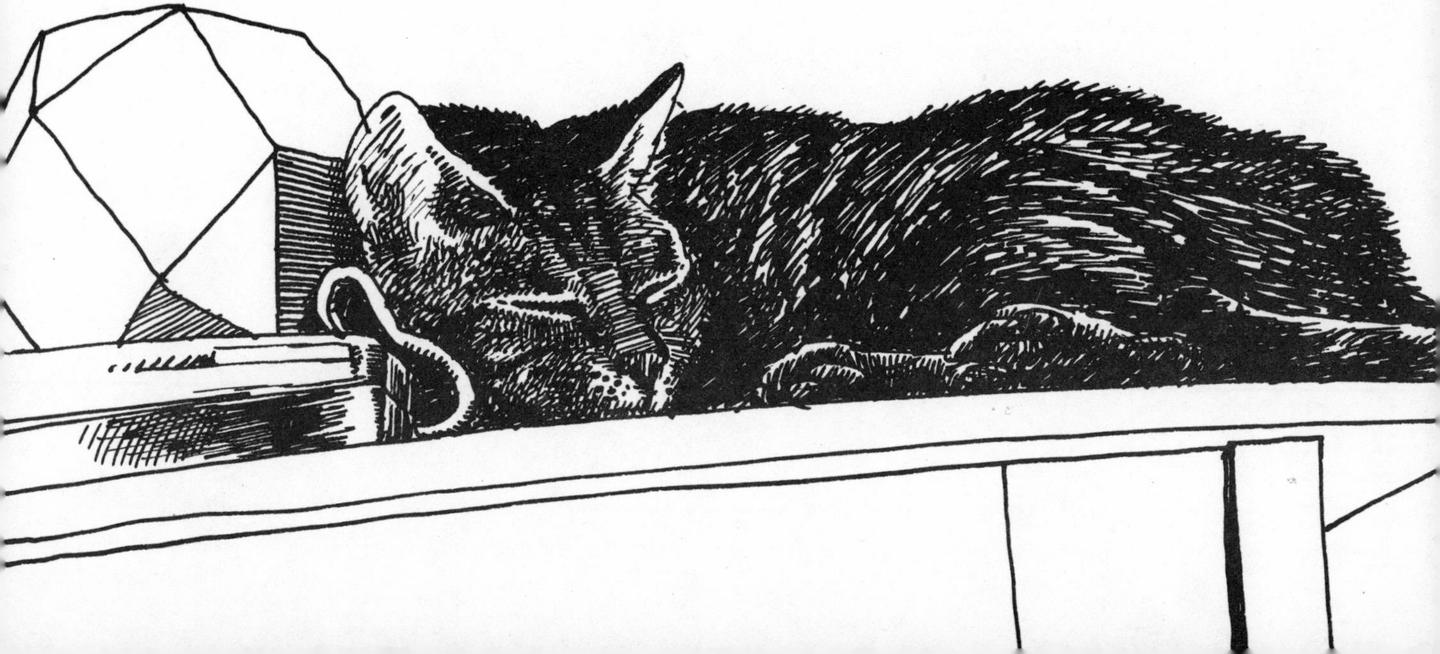

How to draw a Qat

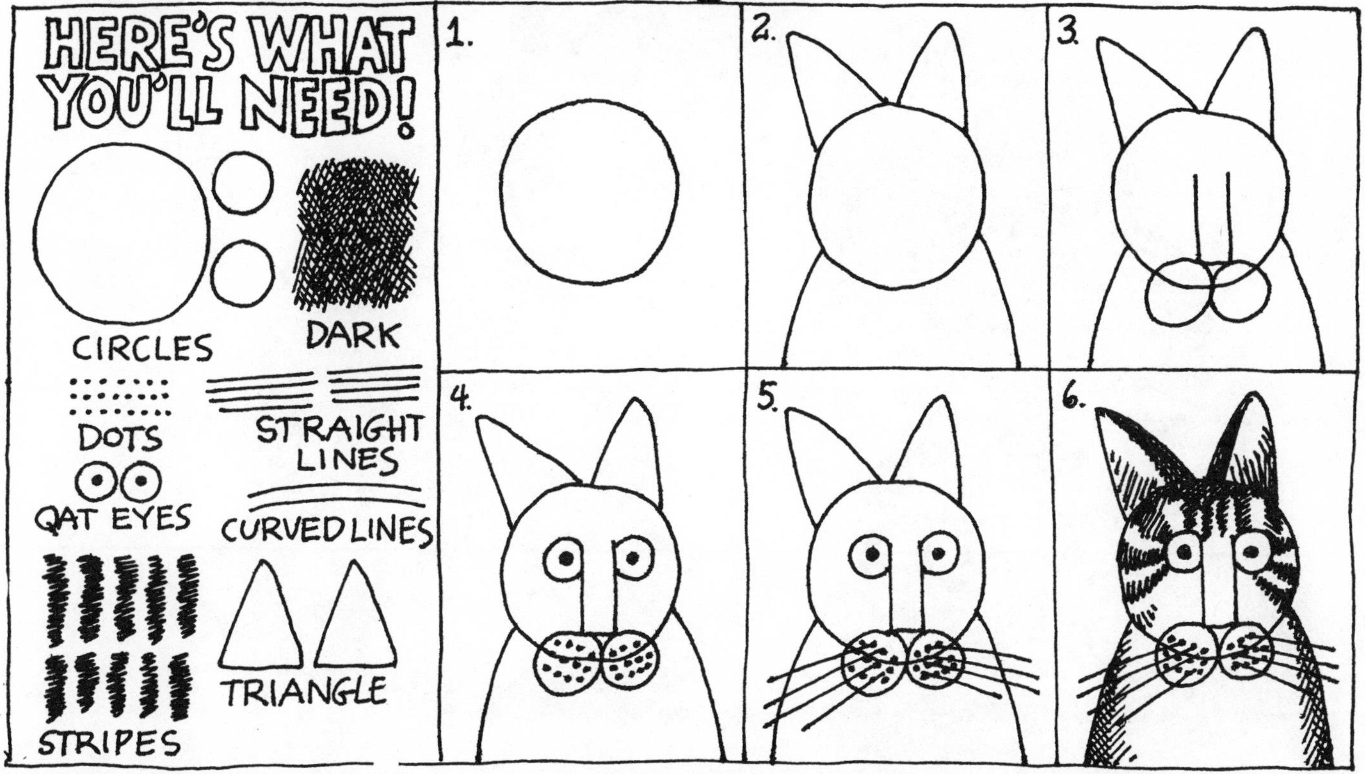
HERE'S WHAT YOU'LL NEED!
CIRCLES
DARK
DOTS
STRAIGHT LINES
QAT EYES
CURVED LINES
STRIPES
TRIANGLE
1.
2.
3.
4.
5.
6.

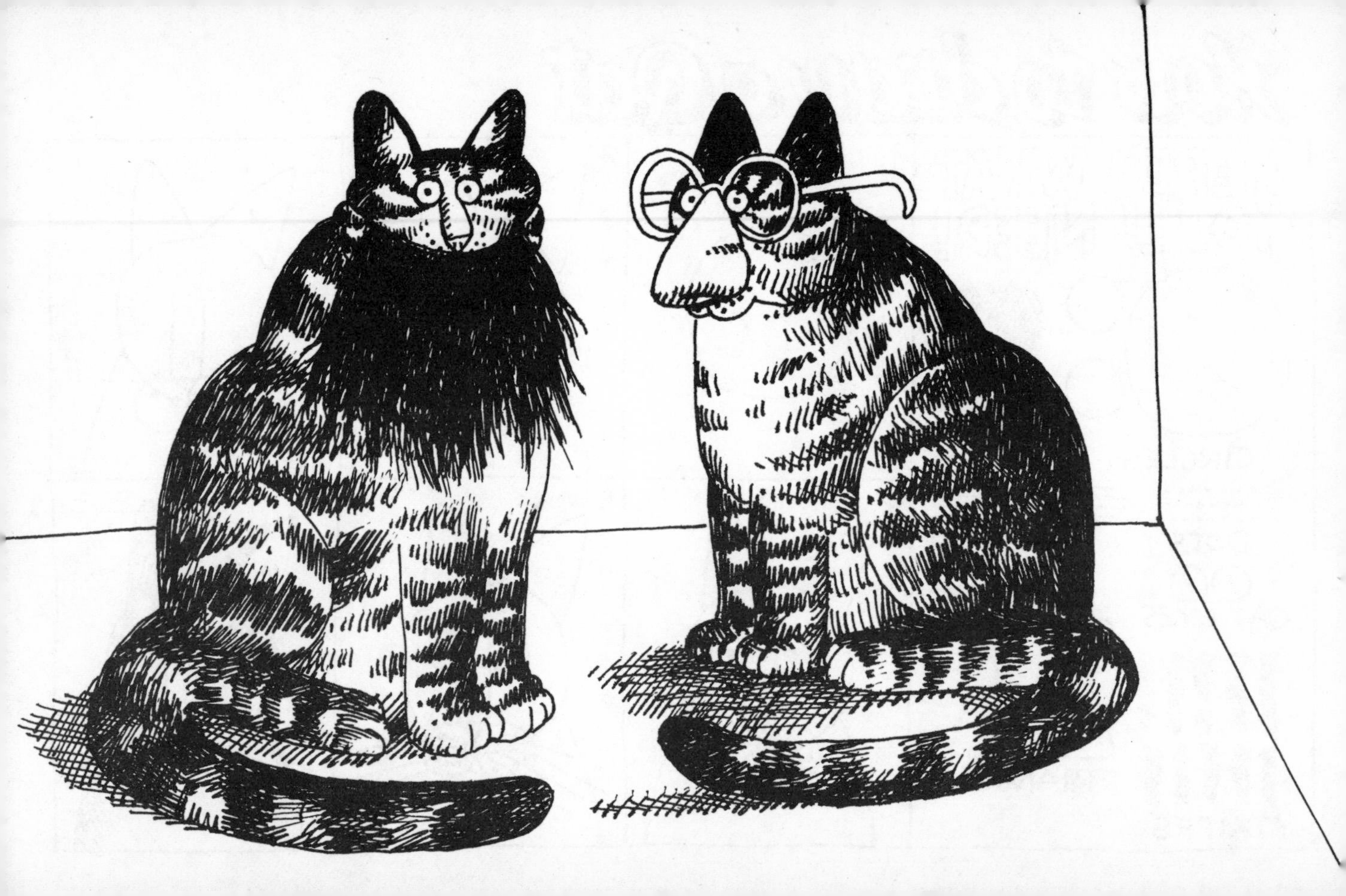

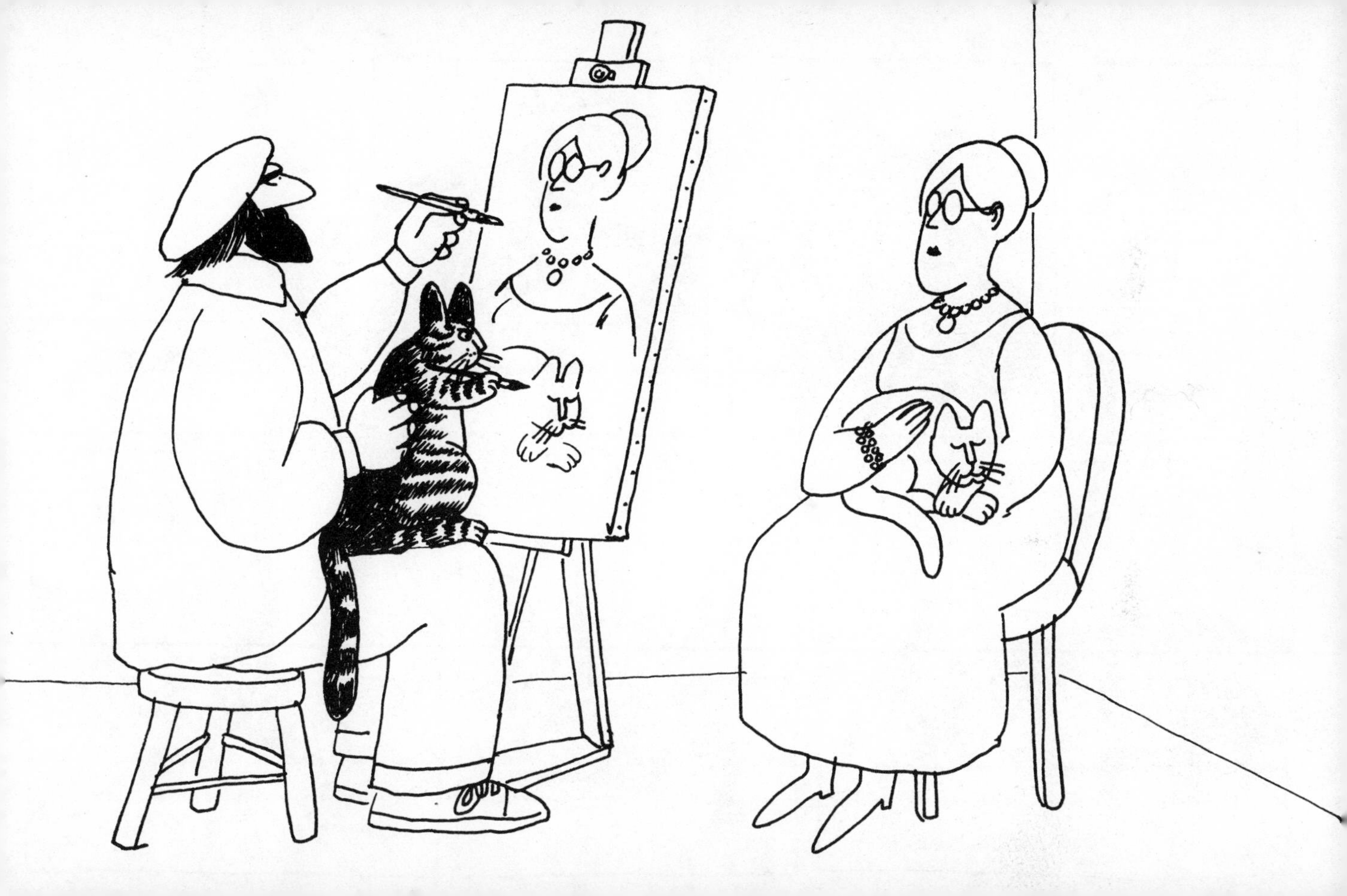

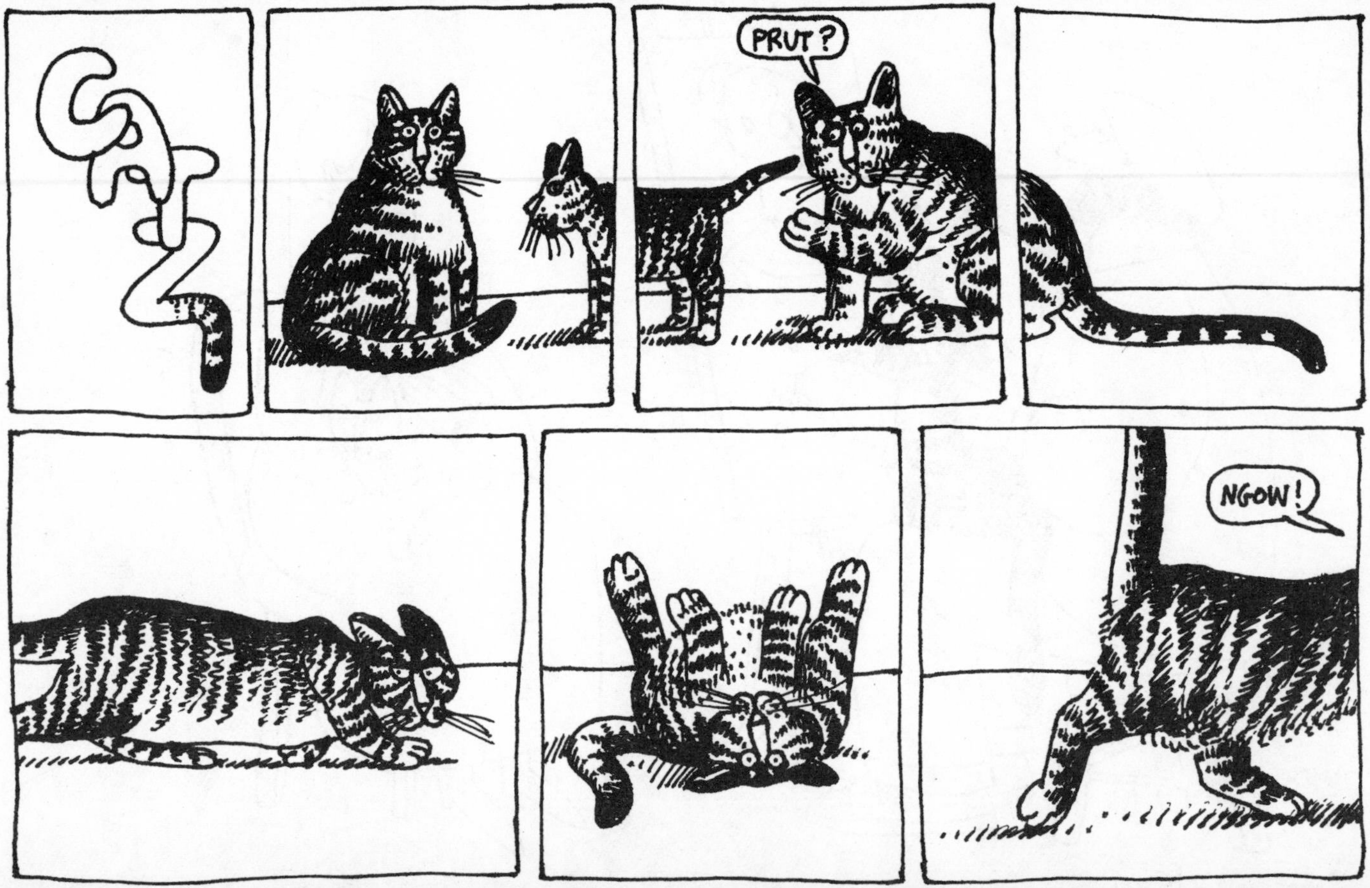
PRUT?
NGOW!

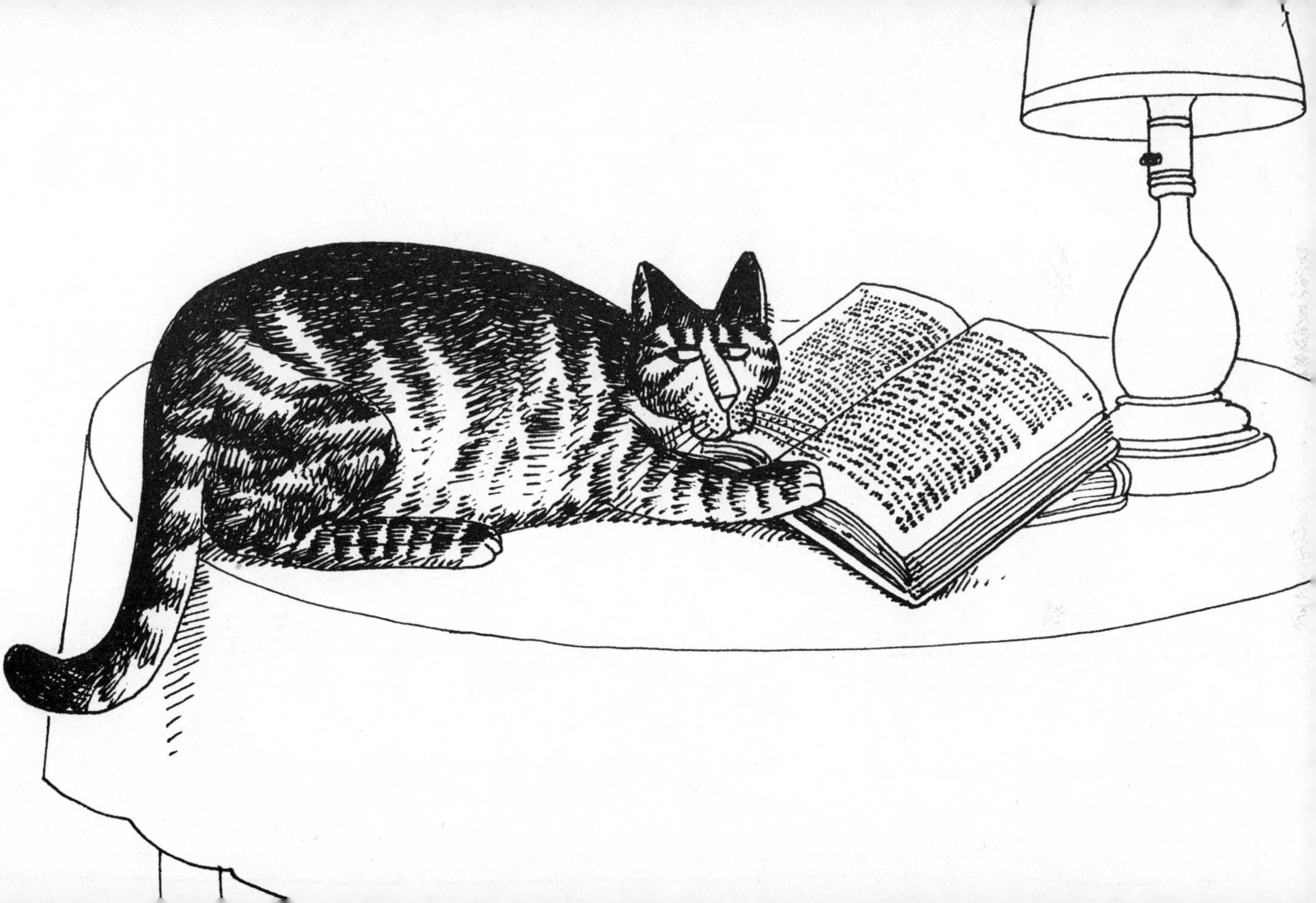

Wanda & Her Cats

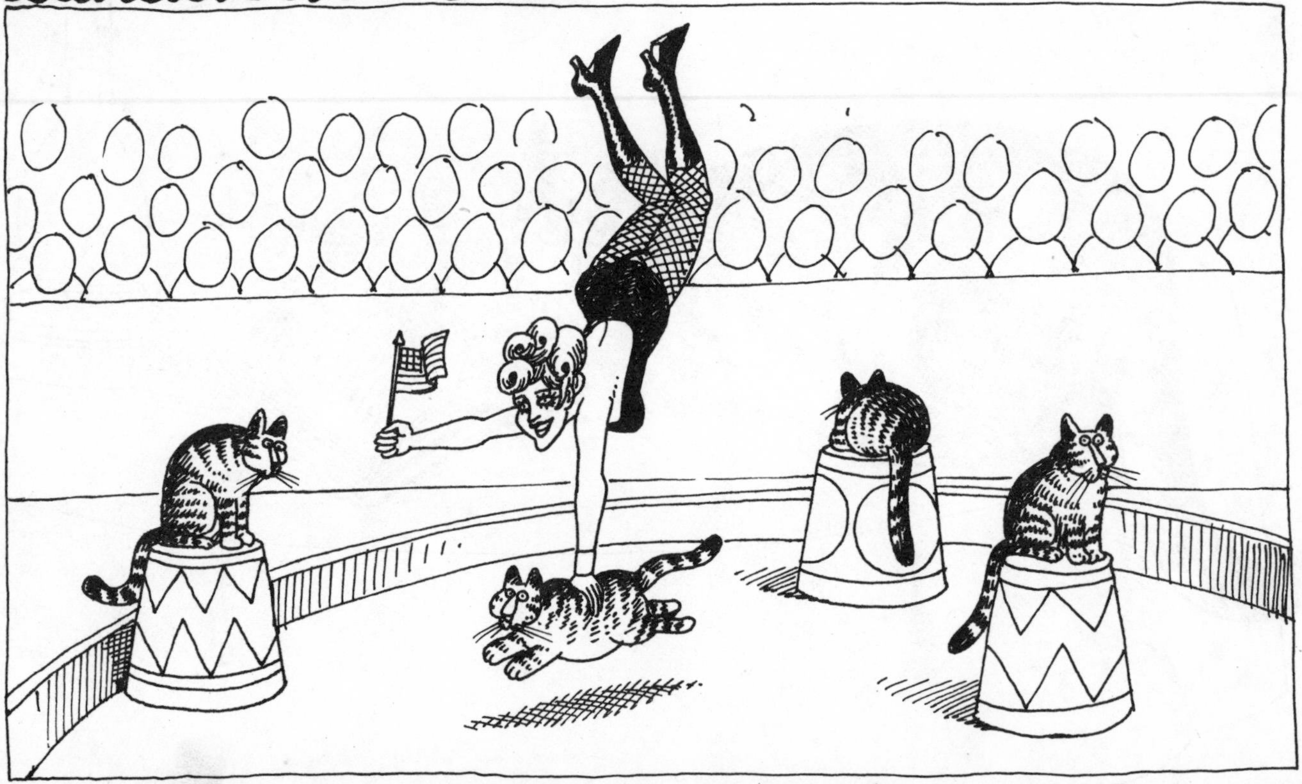

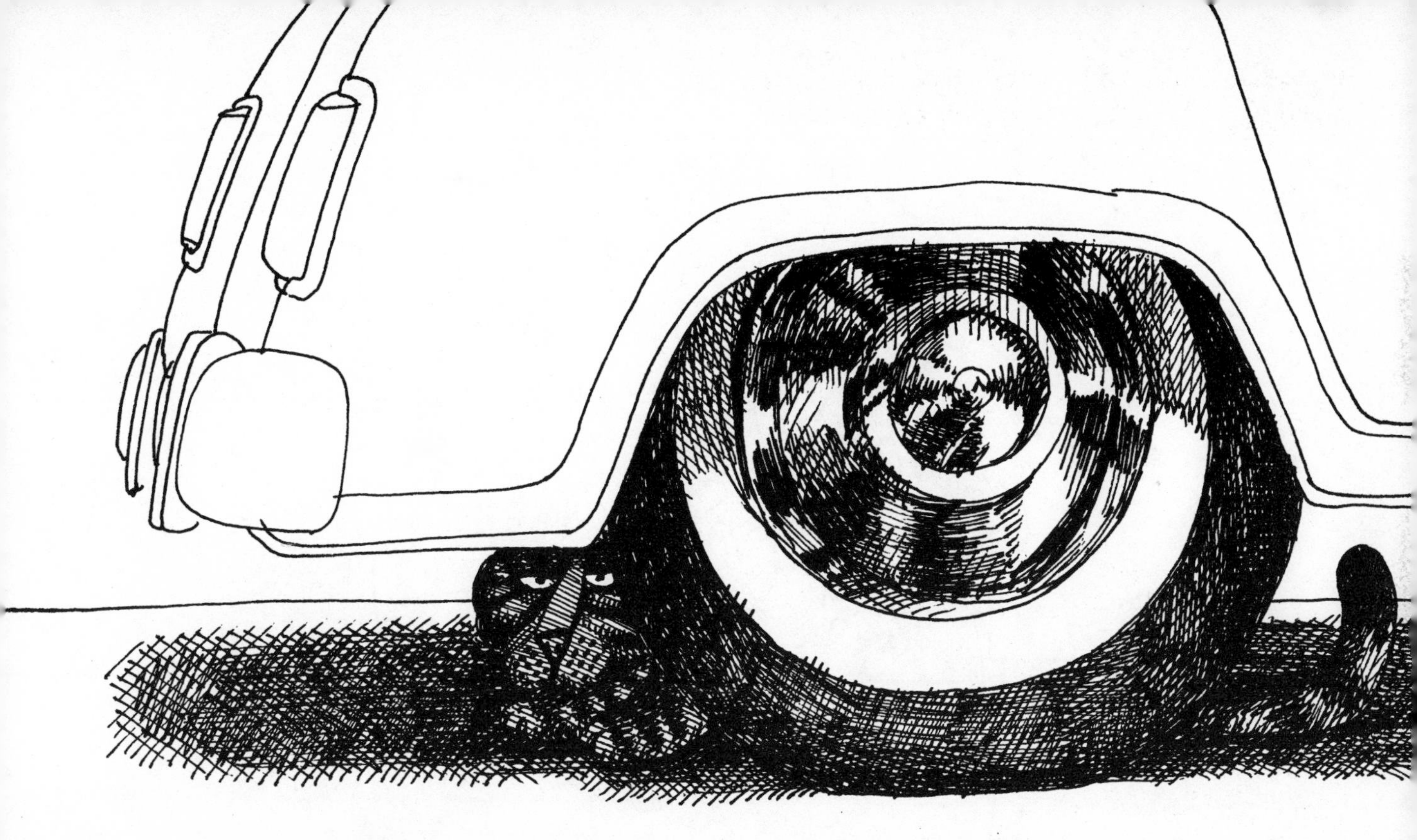

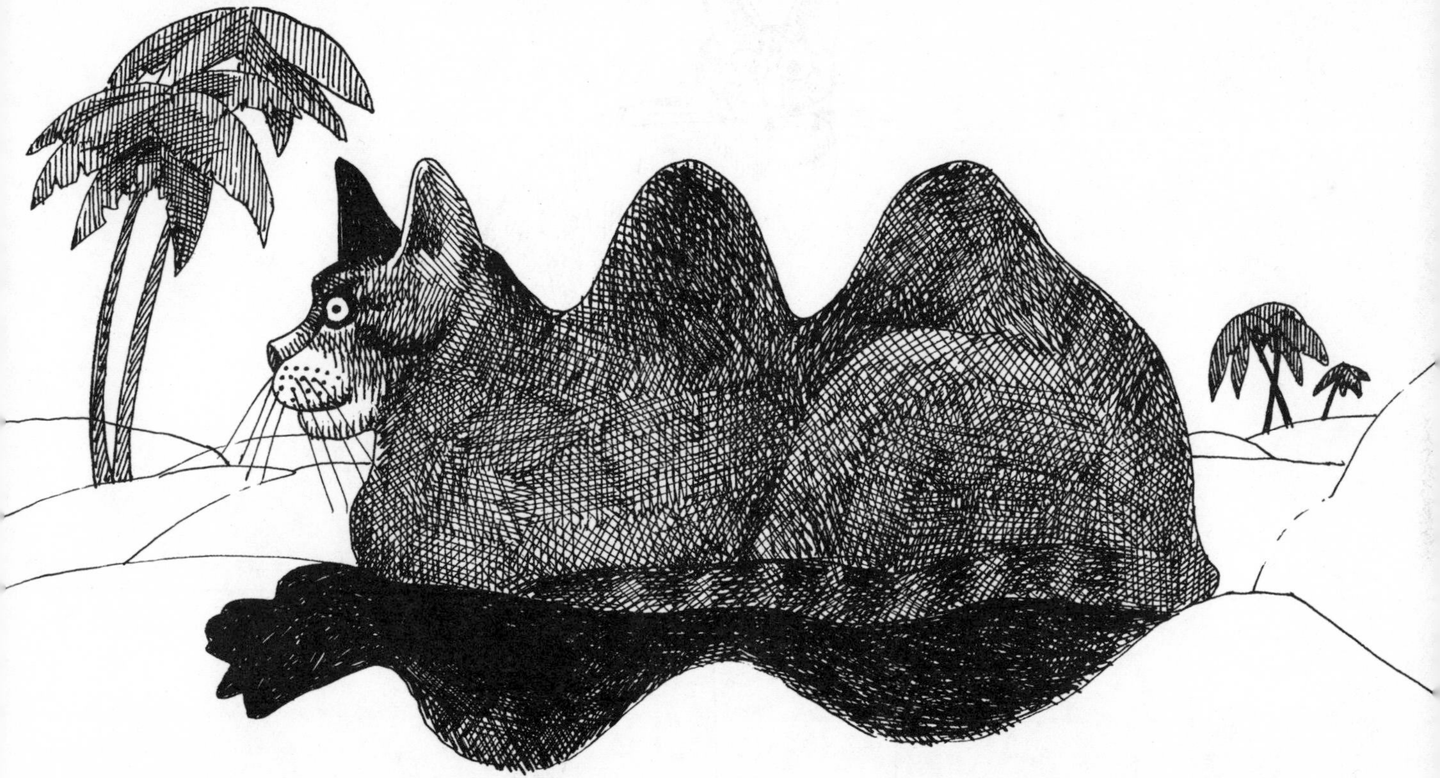

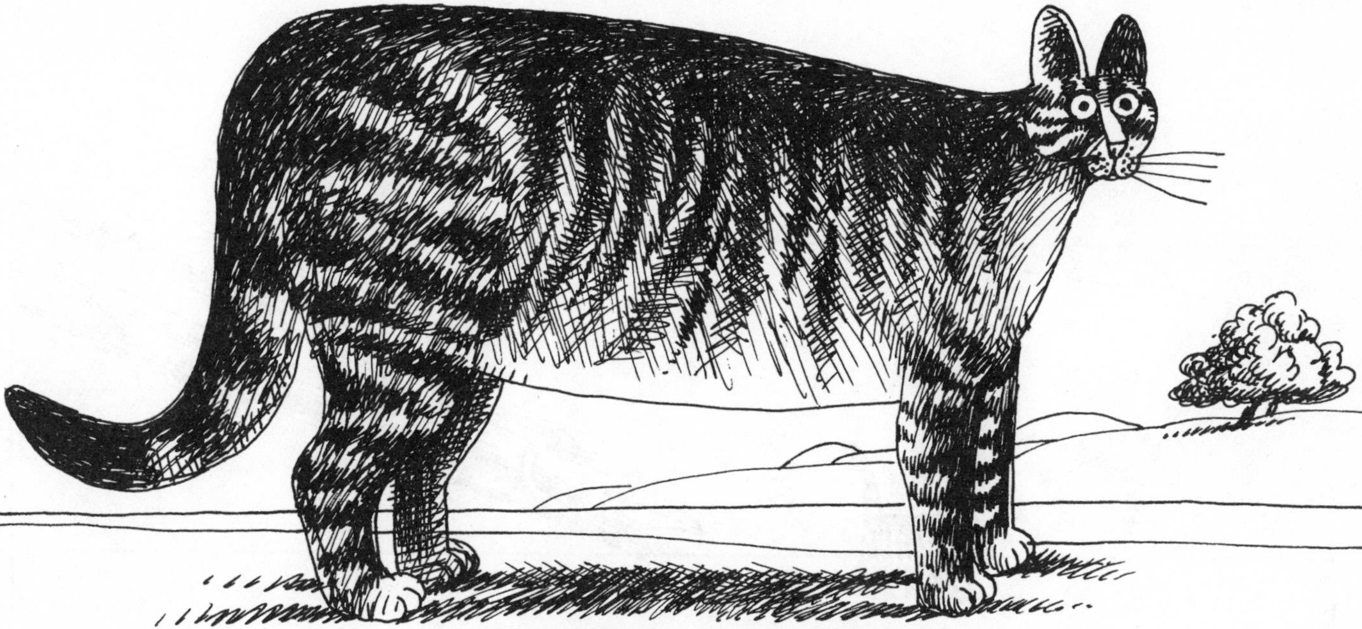

GRAND CHAMPION
Burton Rustle

Tiny Cat & Fountain Pen

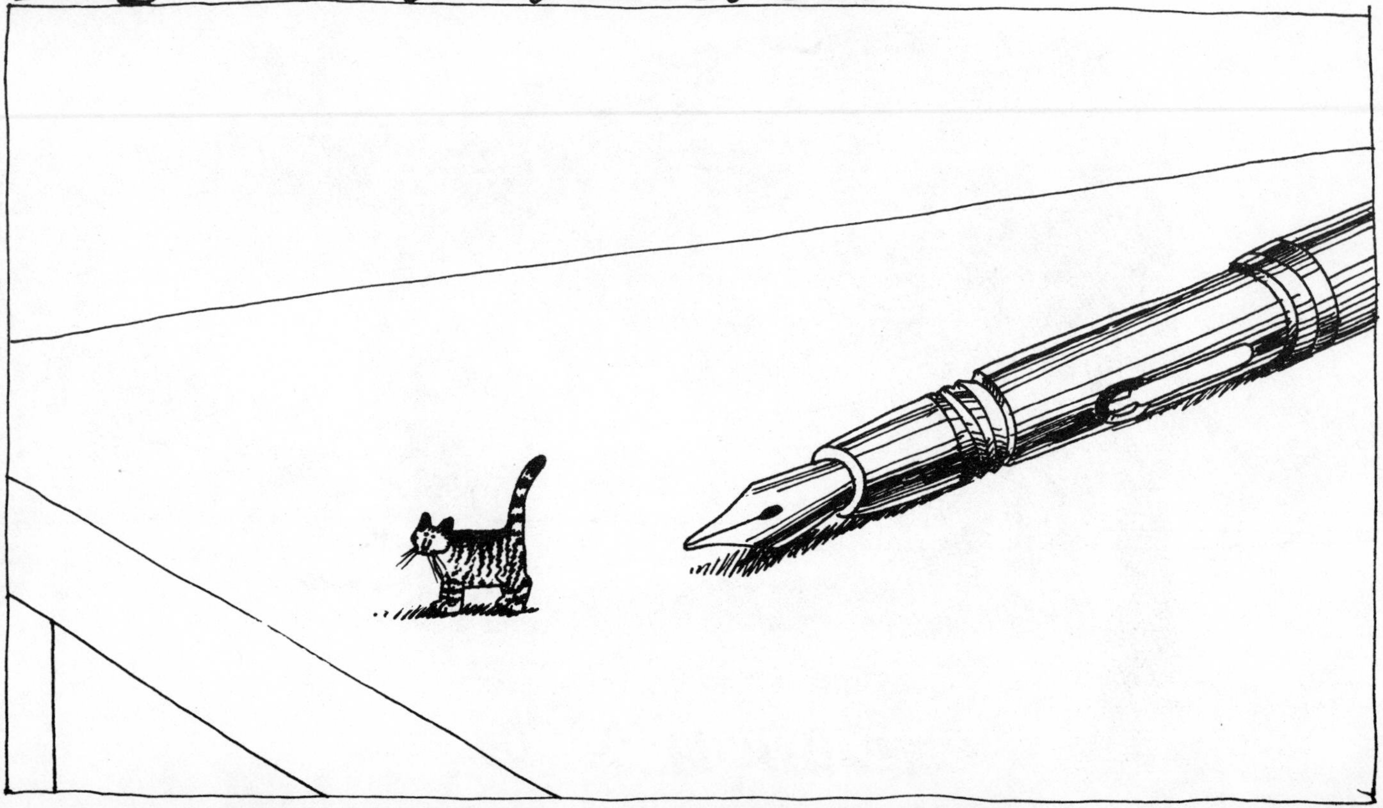

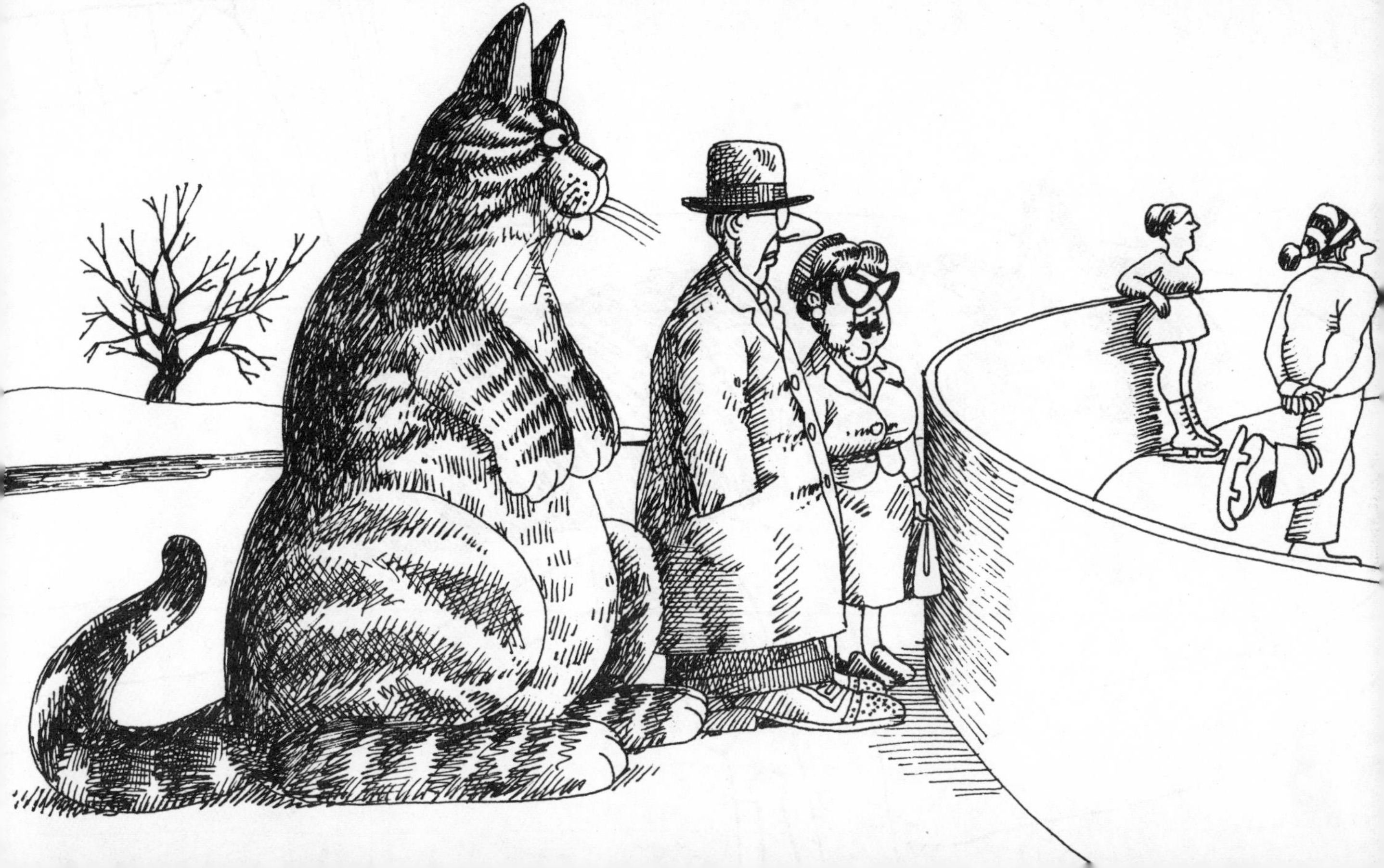

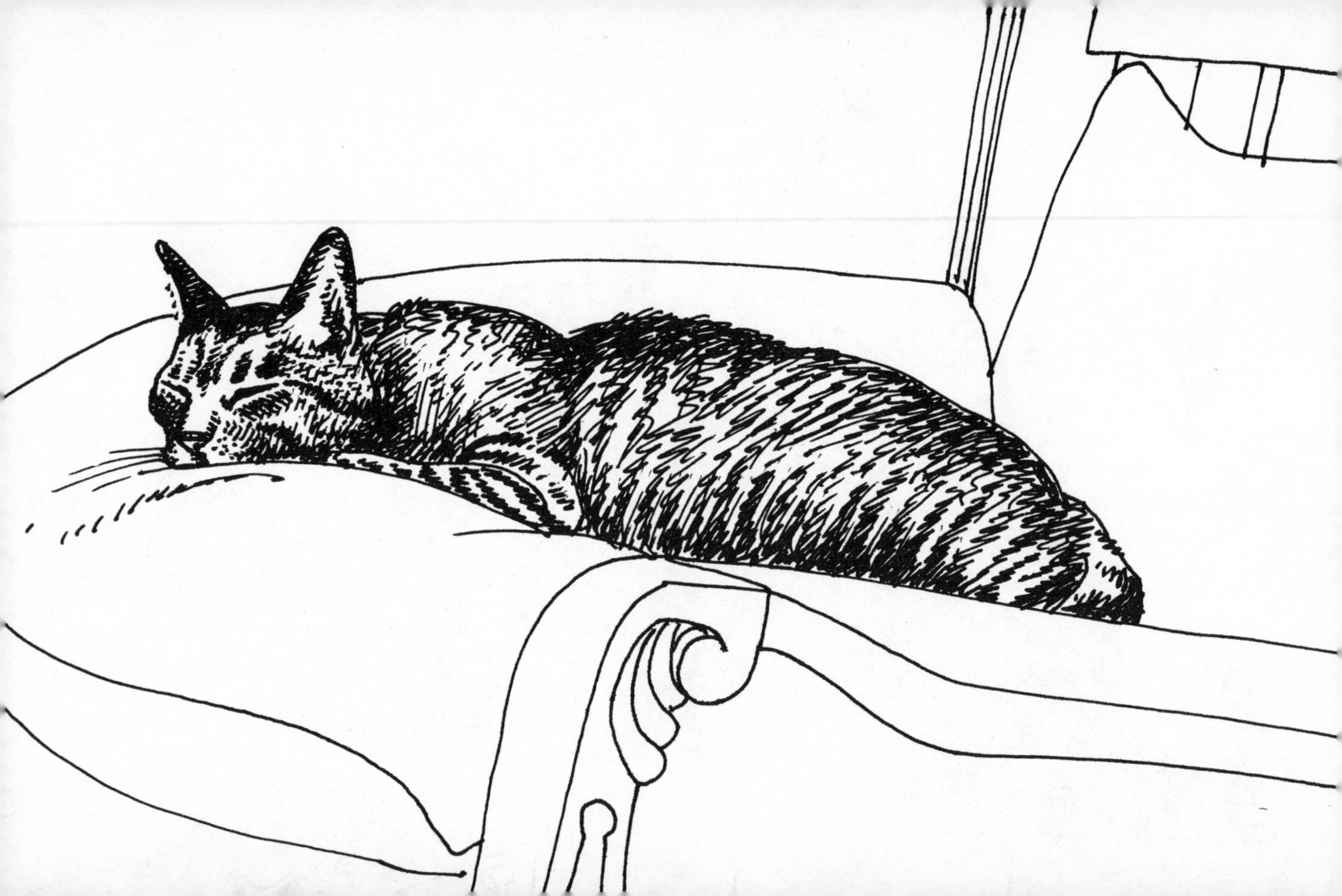

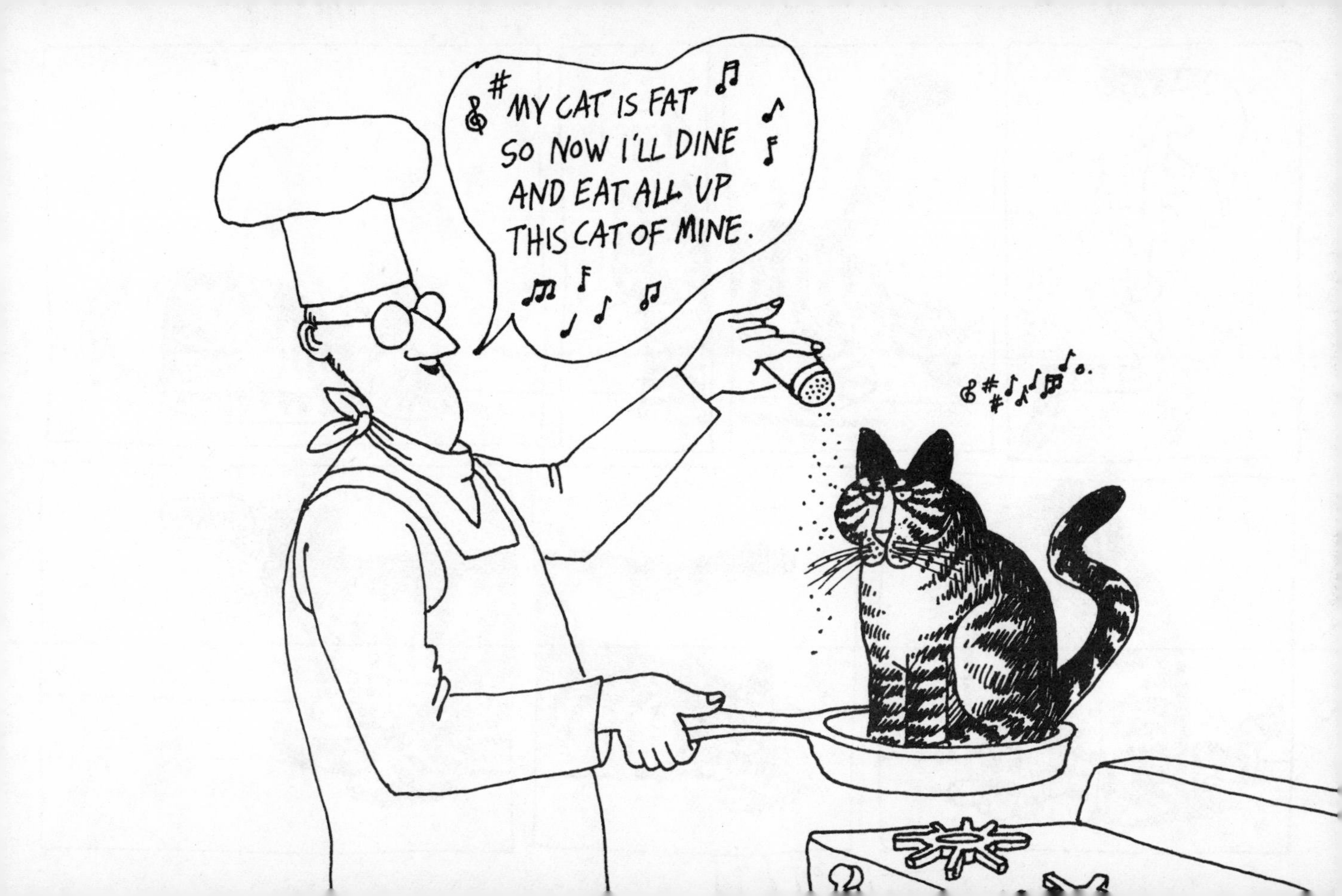
MY CAT IS FAT
SO NOW I'LL DINE
AND EAT ALL UP
THIS CAT OF MINE.

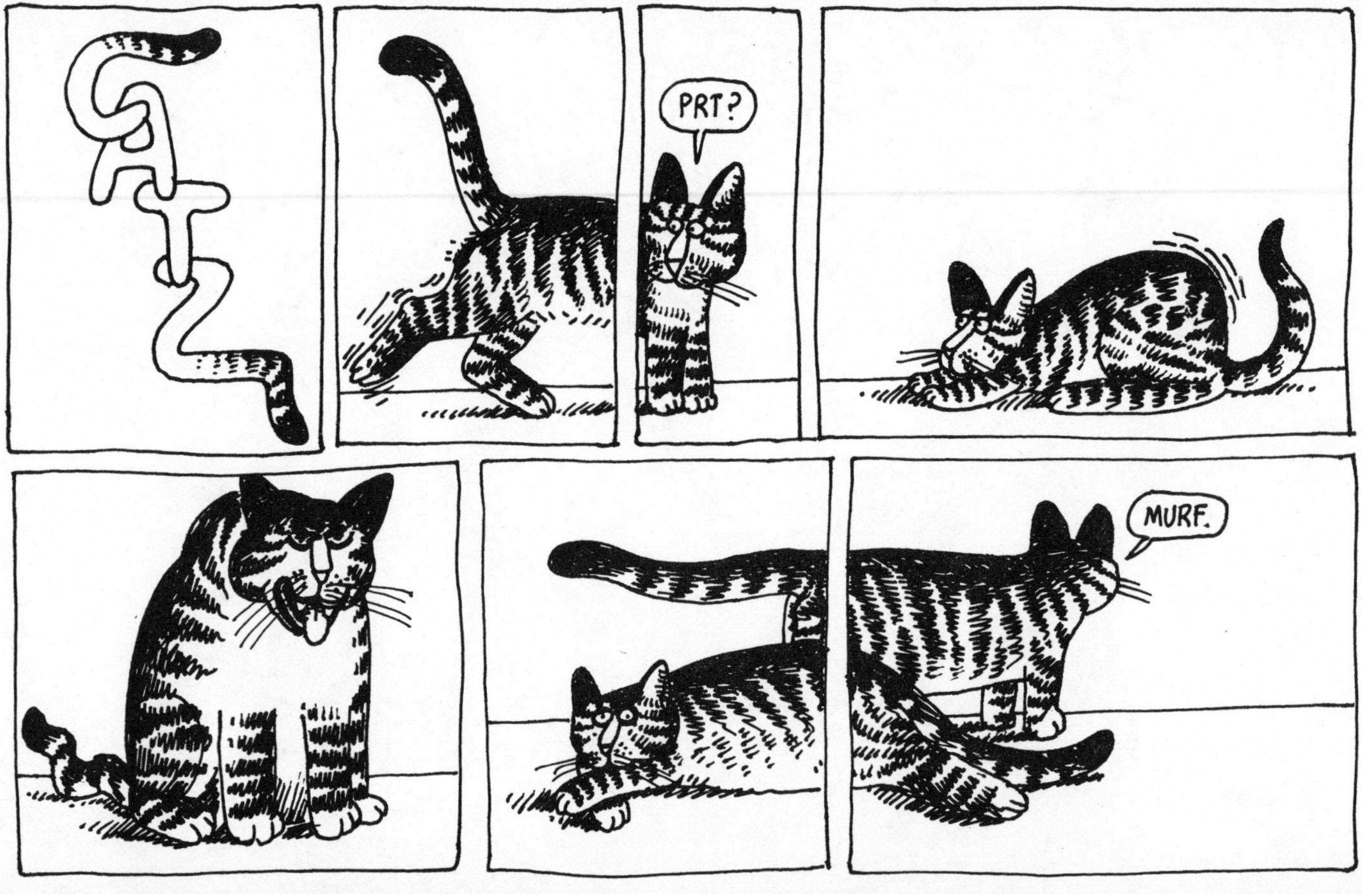
CAT
PRT?
MURF.

Cat gun

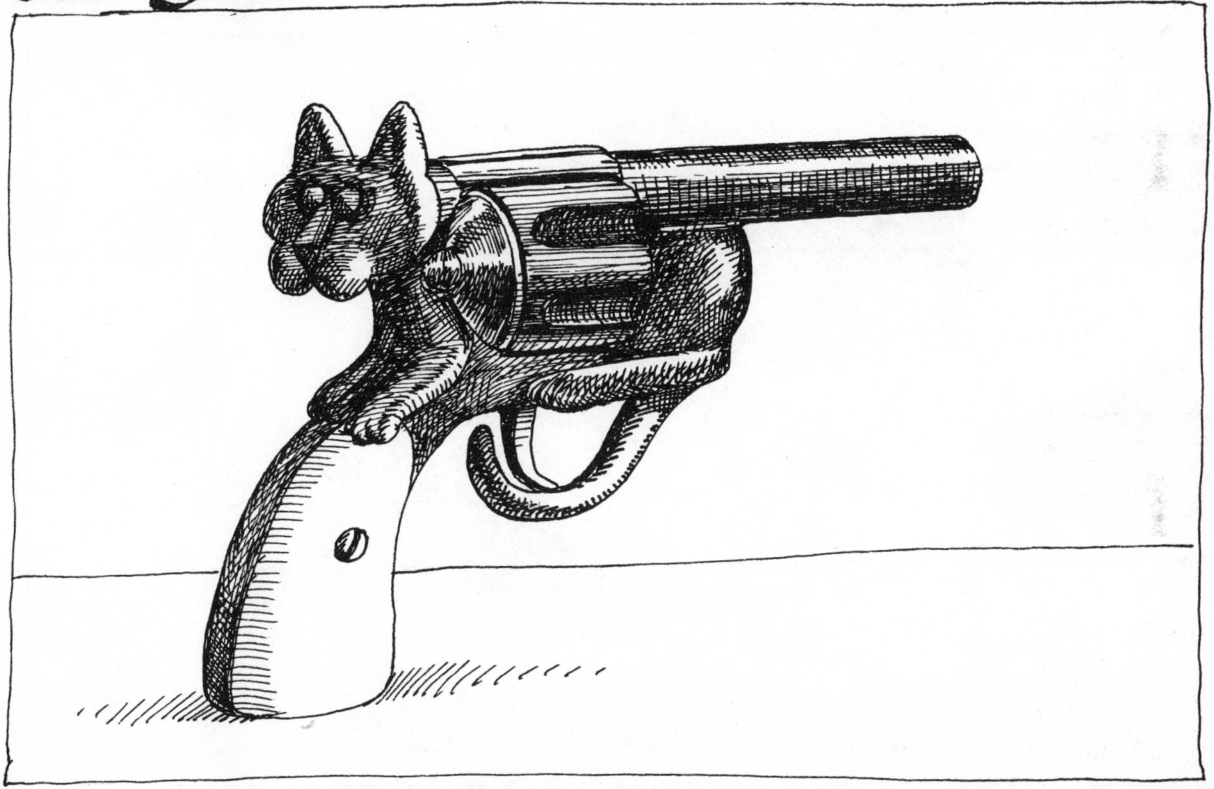

Noko Marie

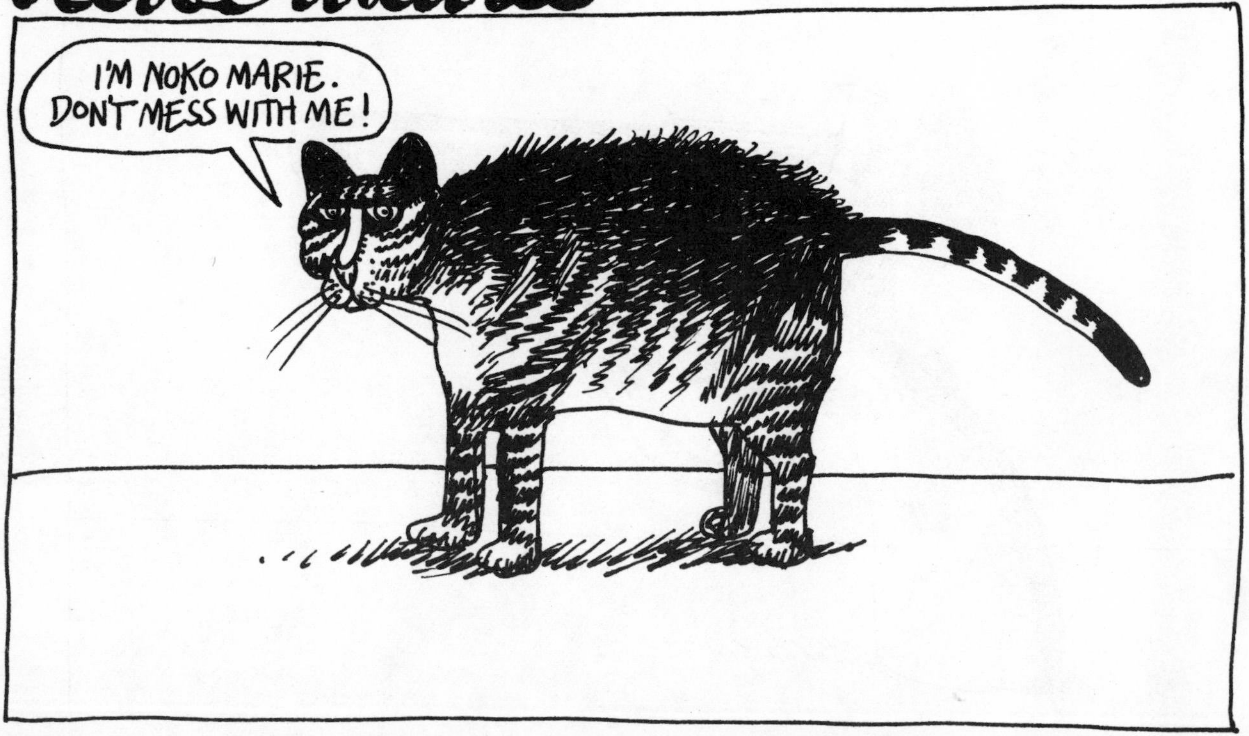
I'M NOKO MARIE. DON'T MESS WITH ME!

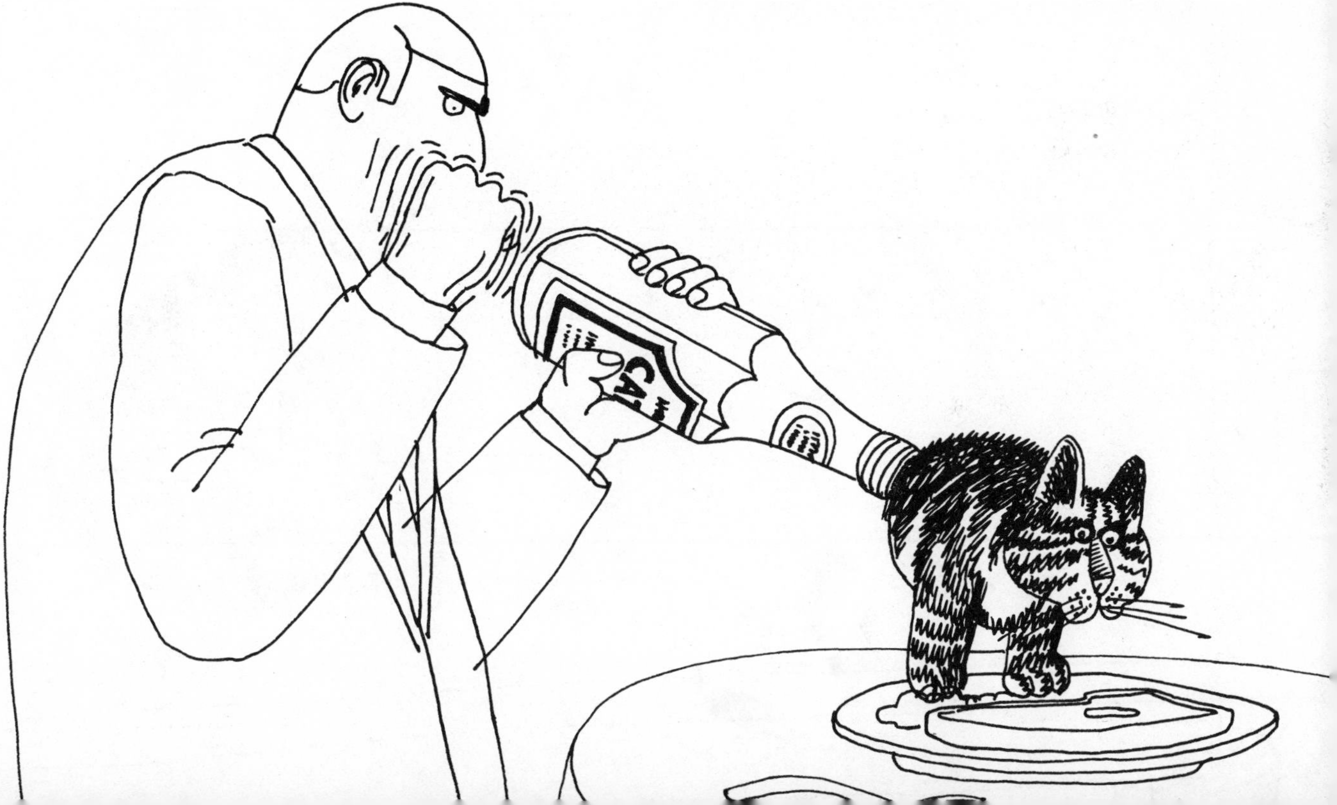

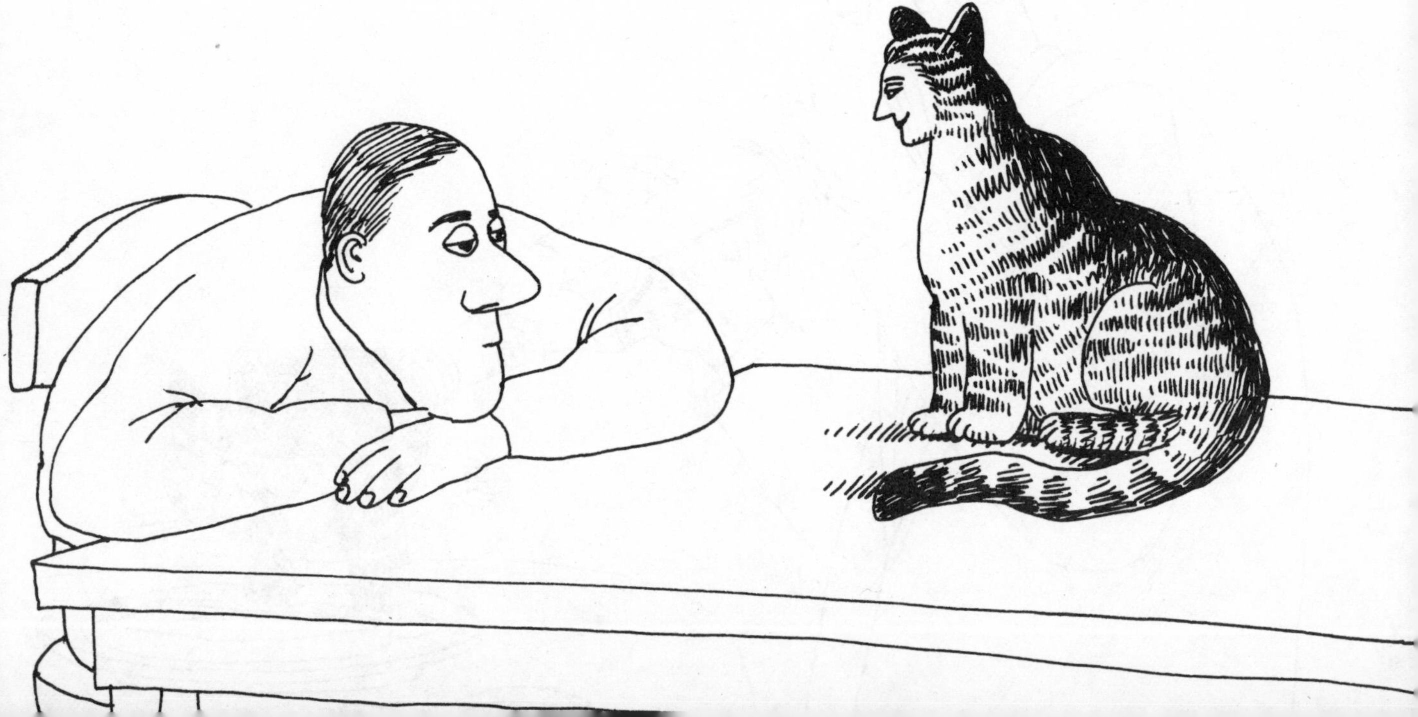

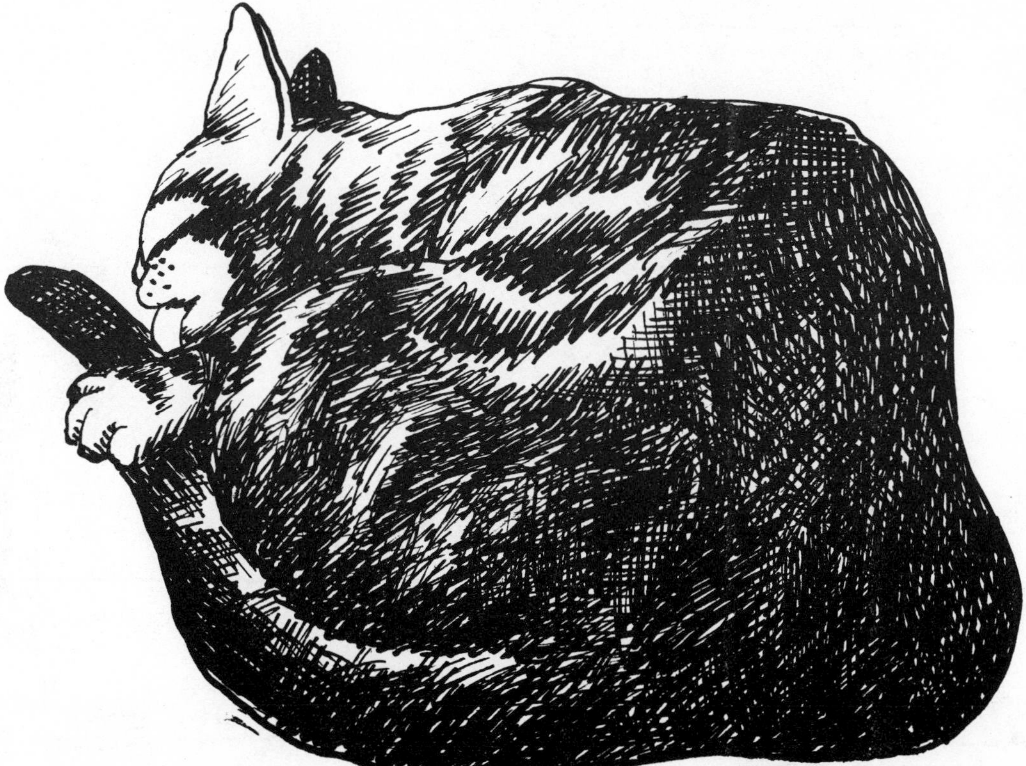

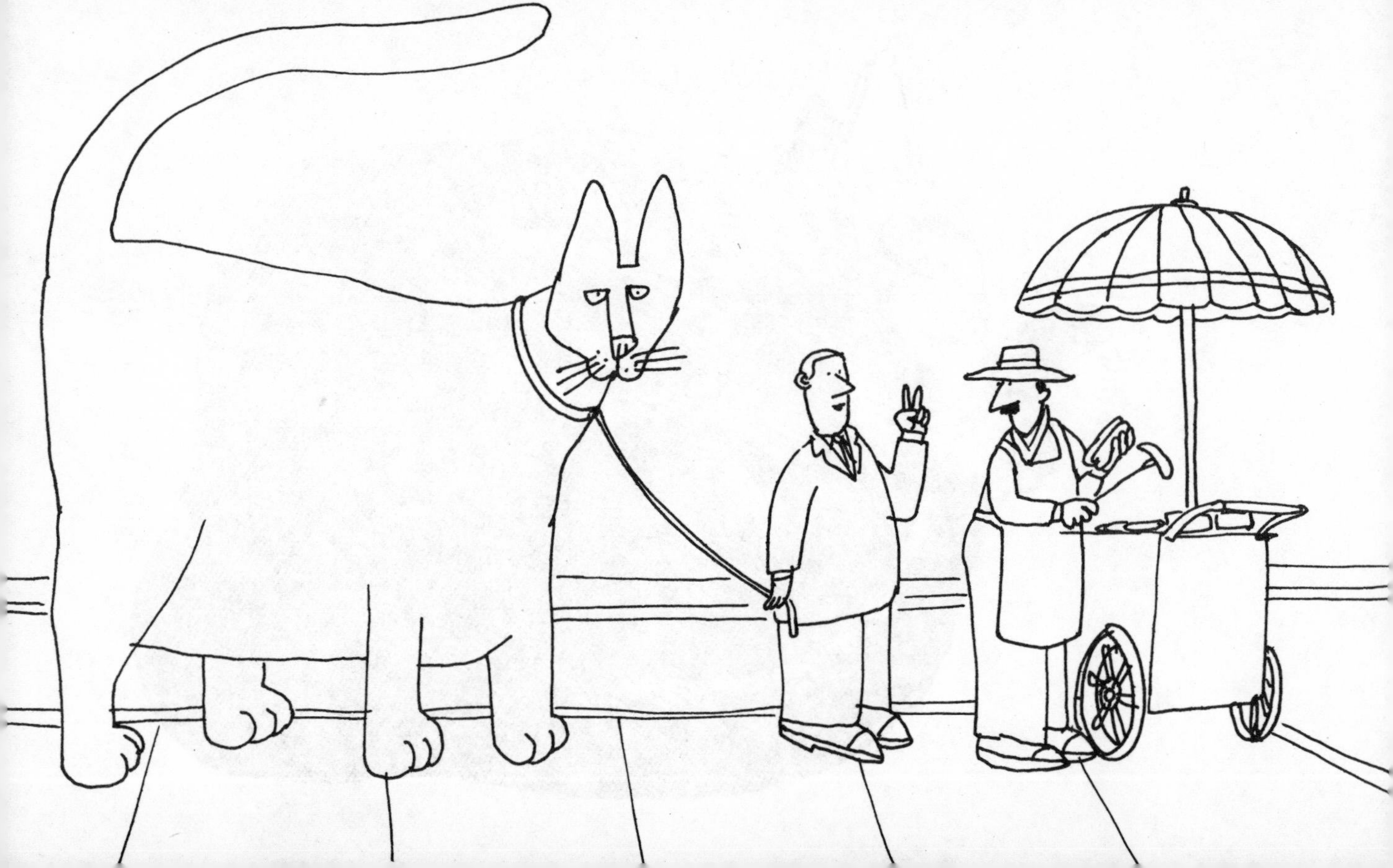

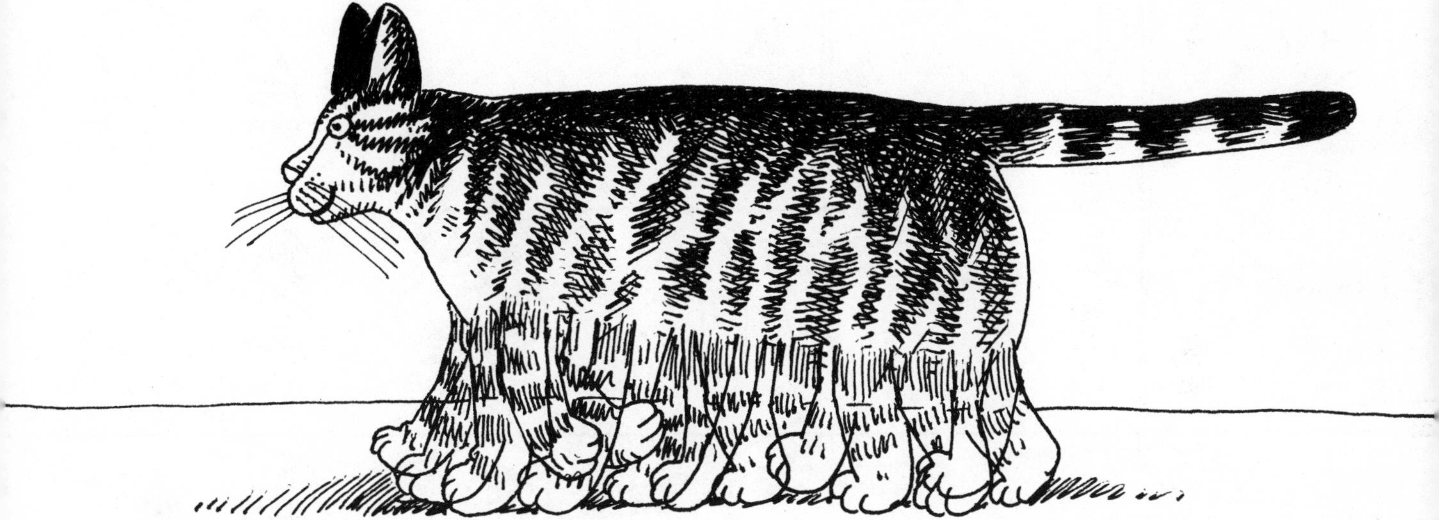

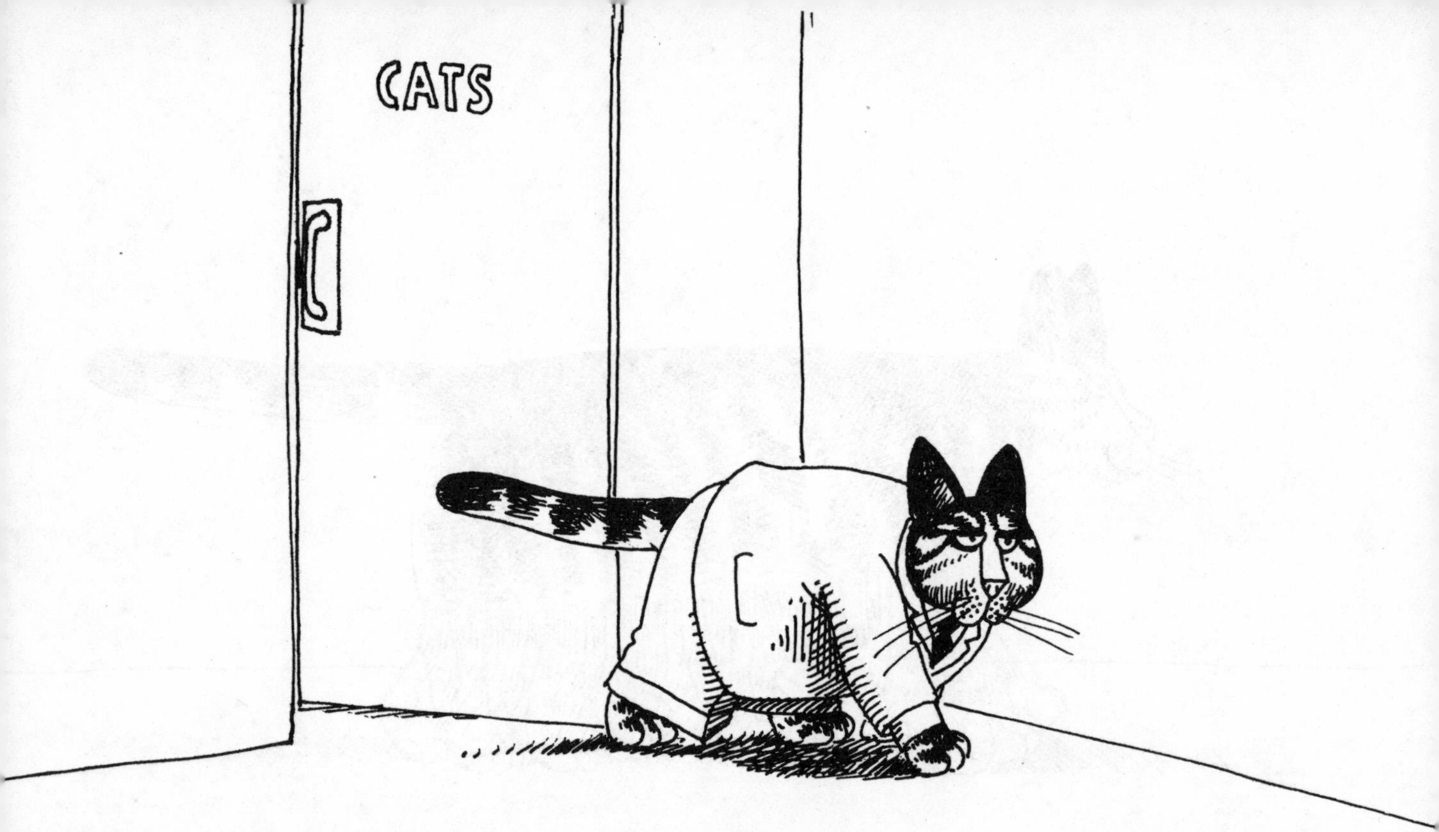
CATS

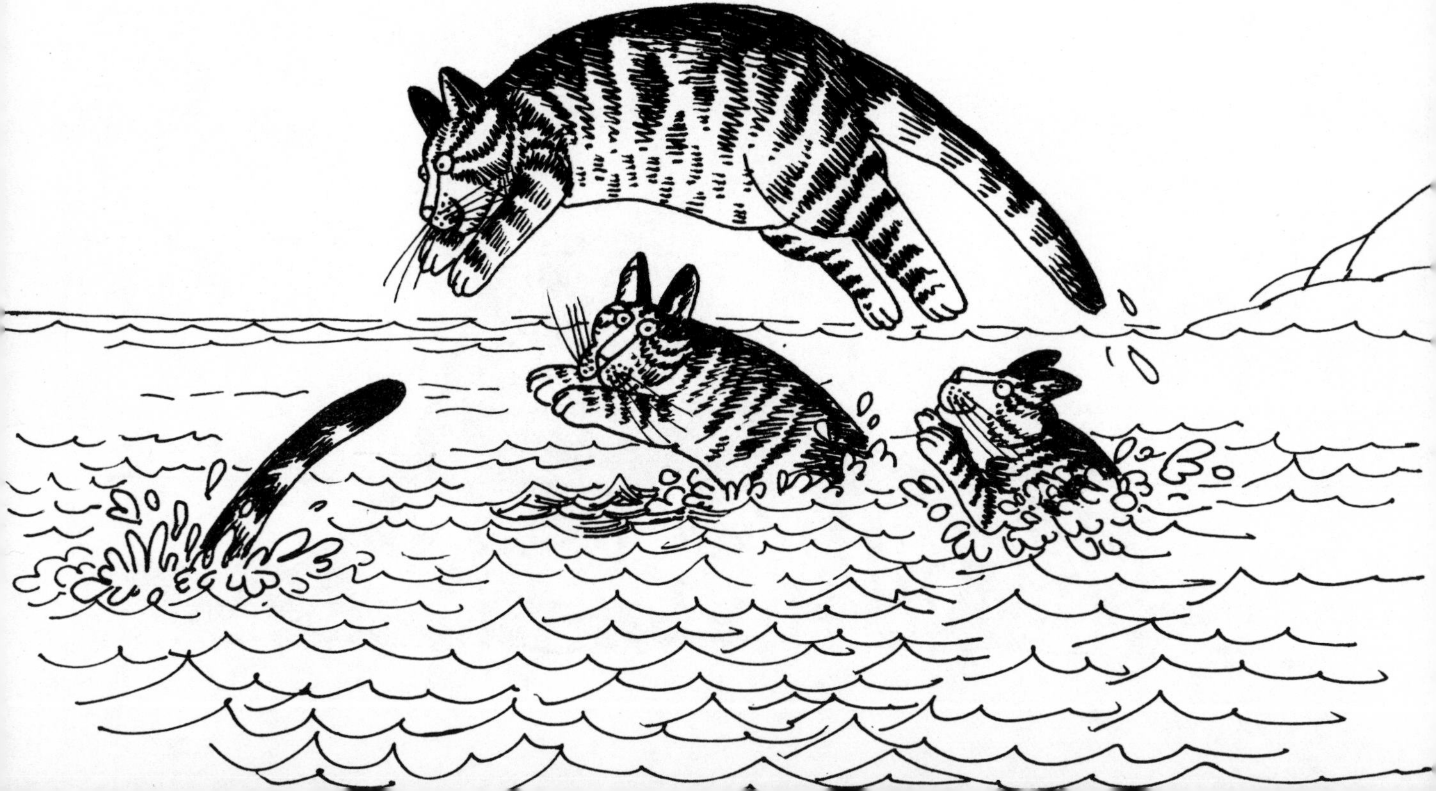

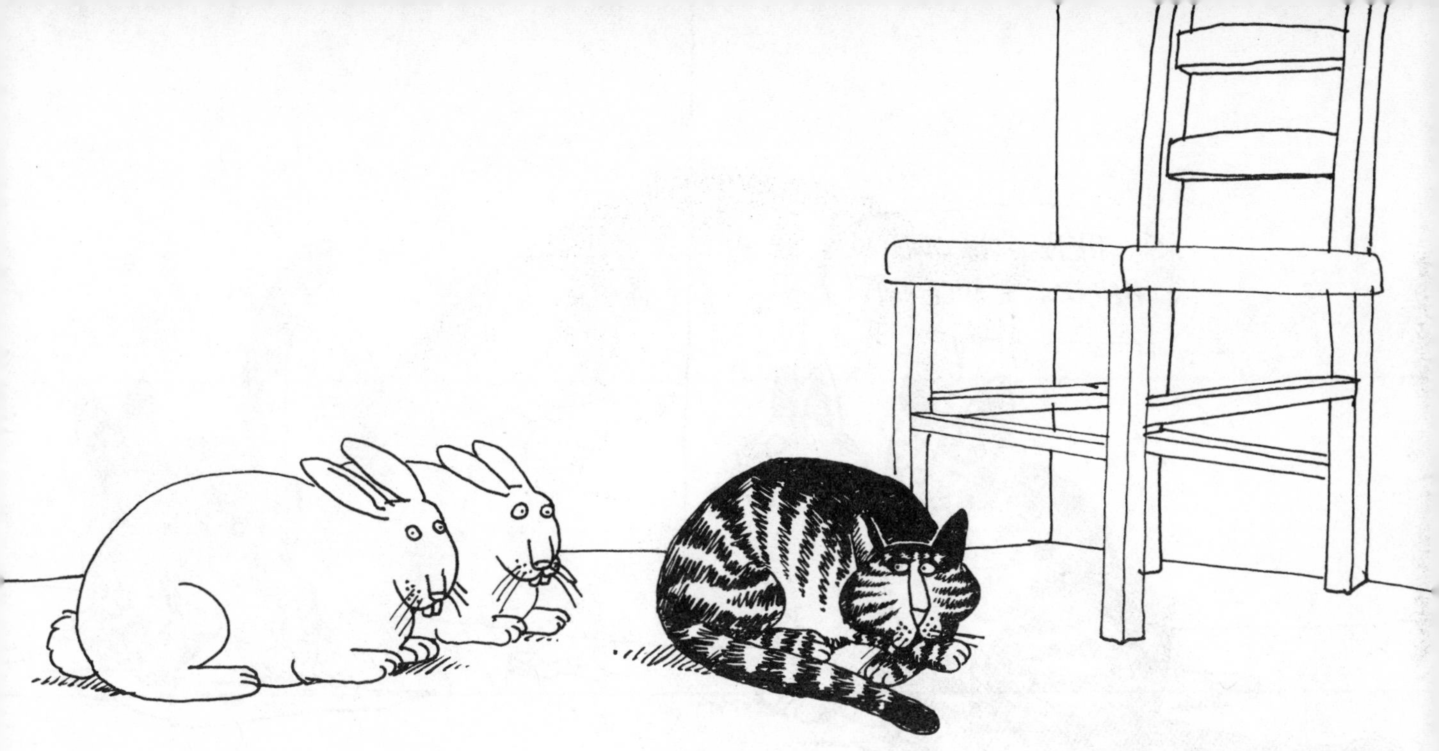

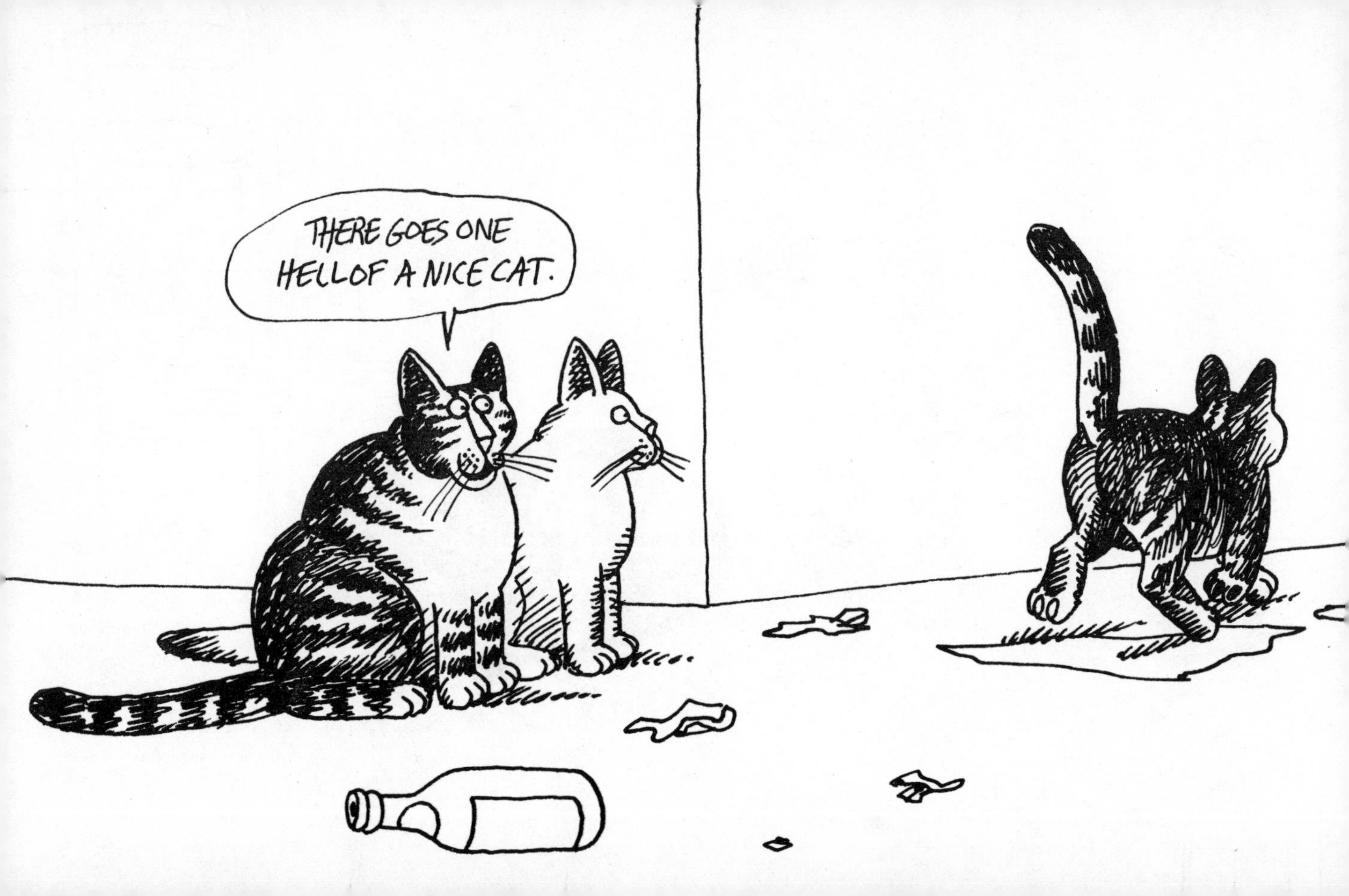
THERE GOES ONE
HELLOF A NICE CAT.

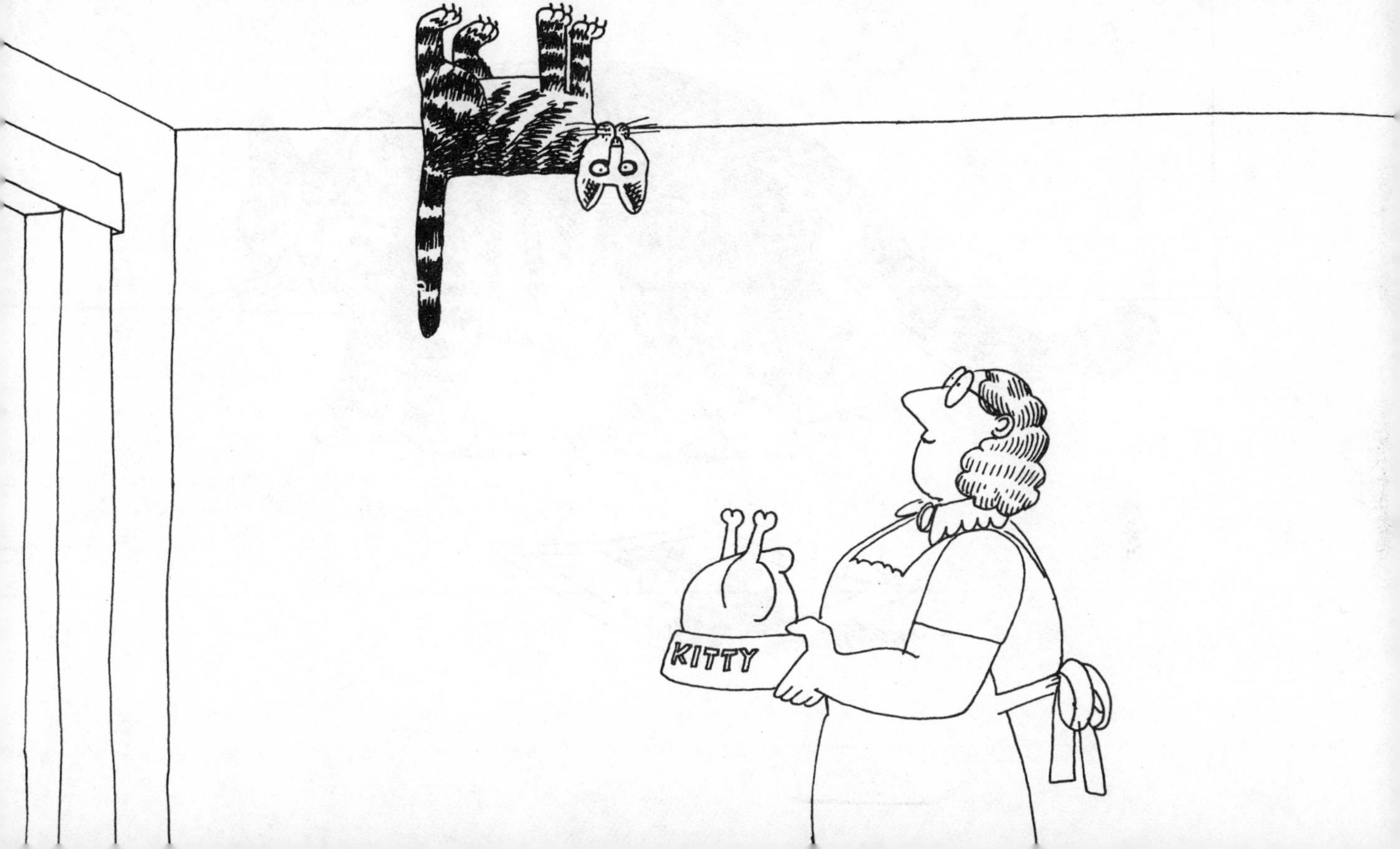
KITTY

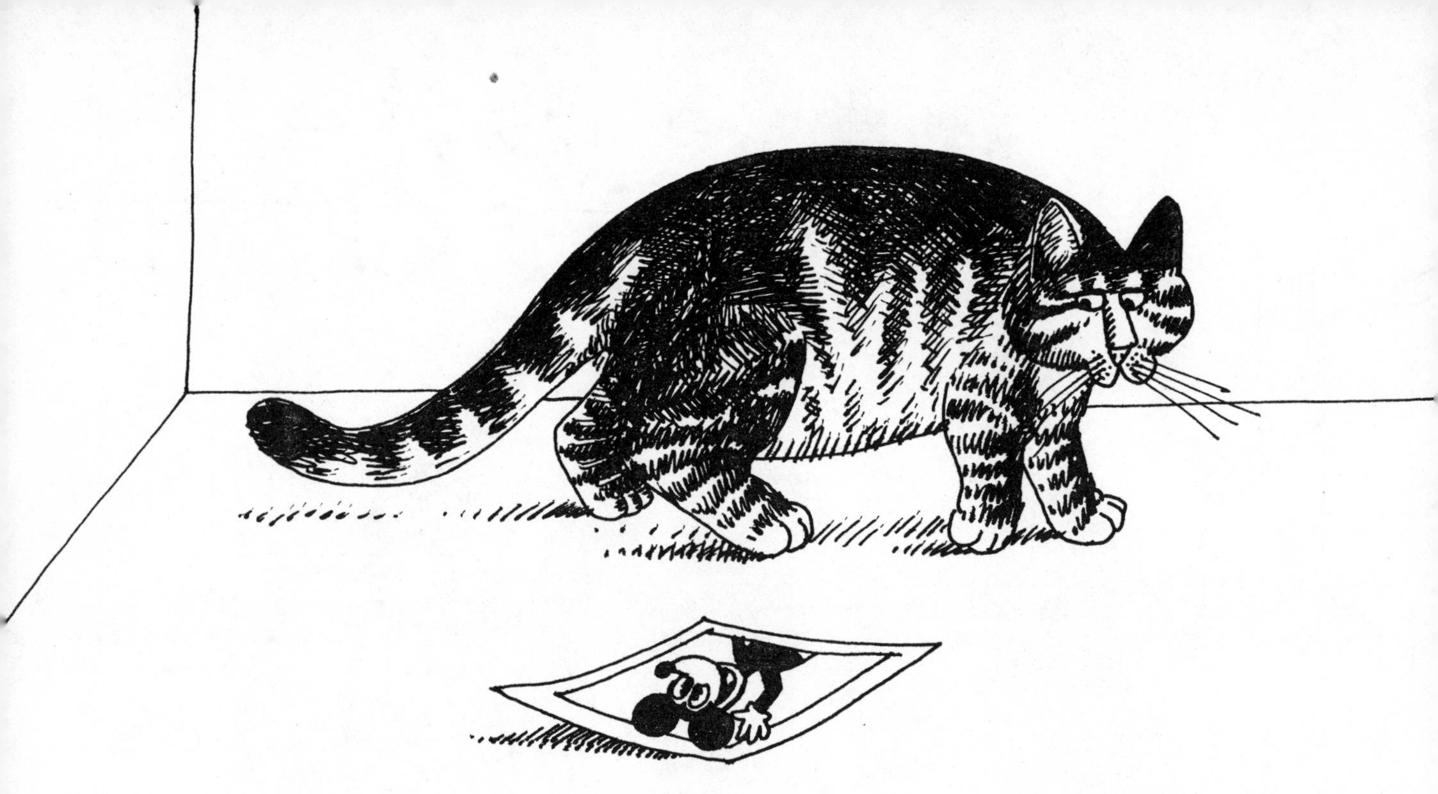

Purr Box

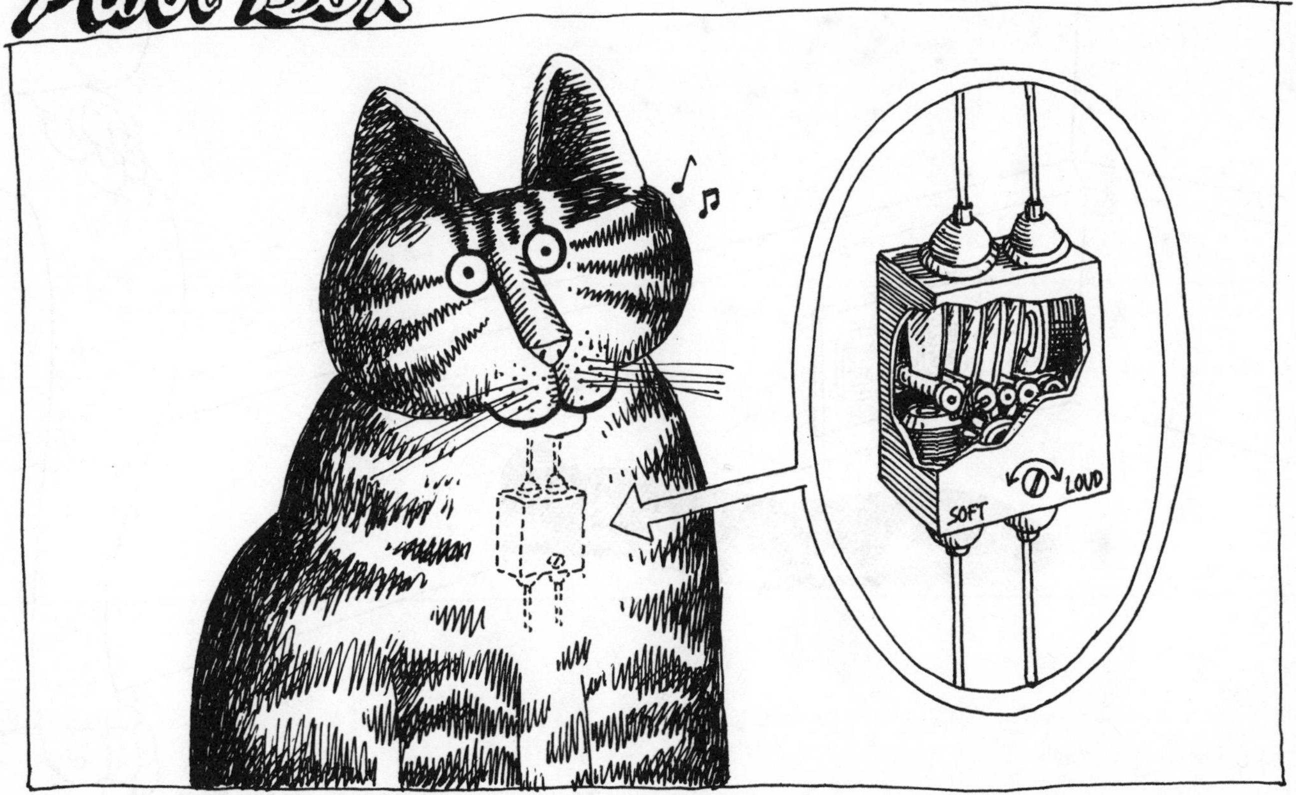
SOFT
LOUD

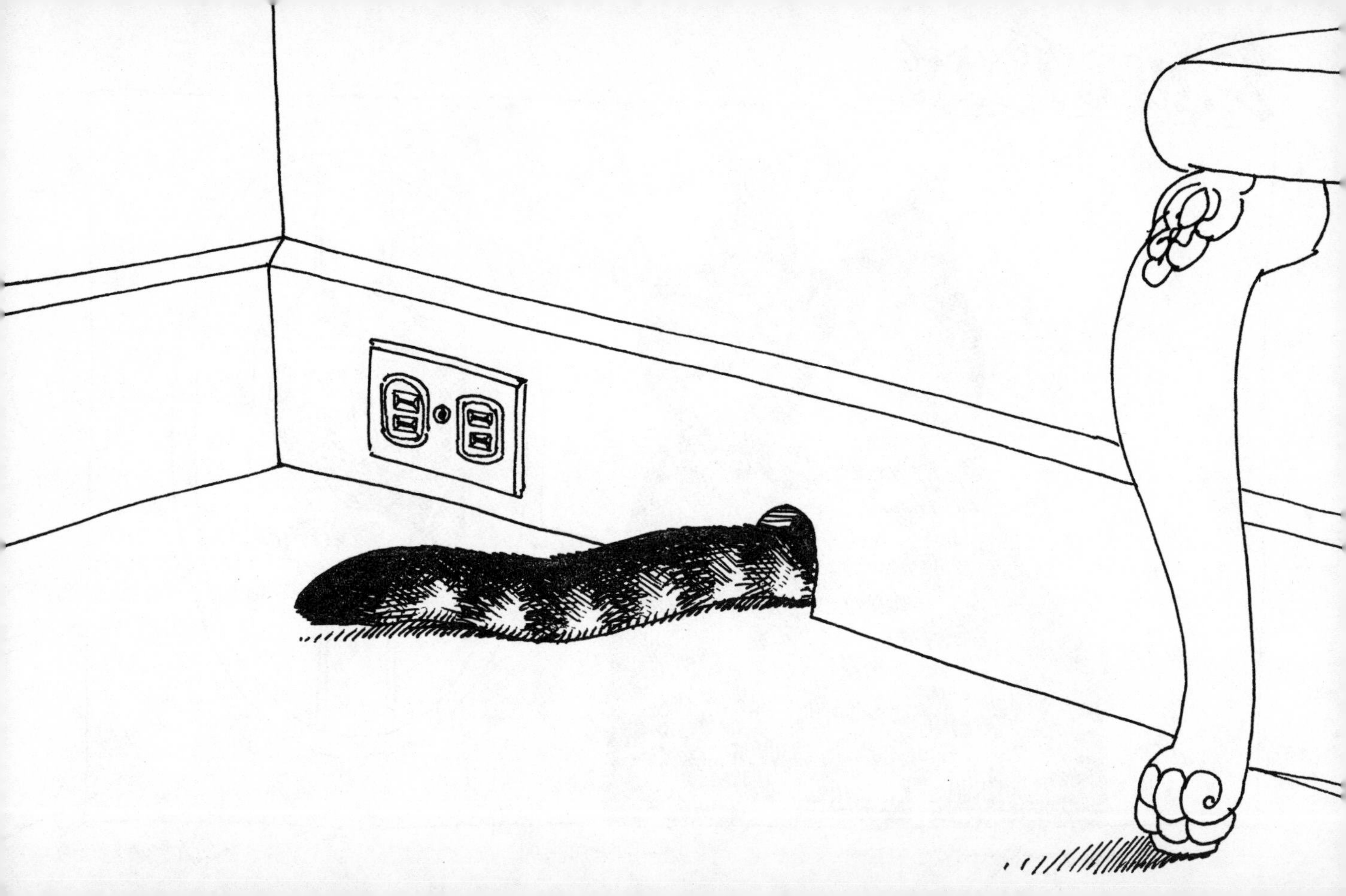

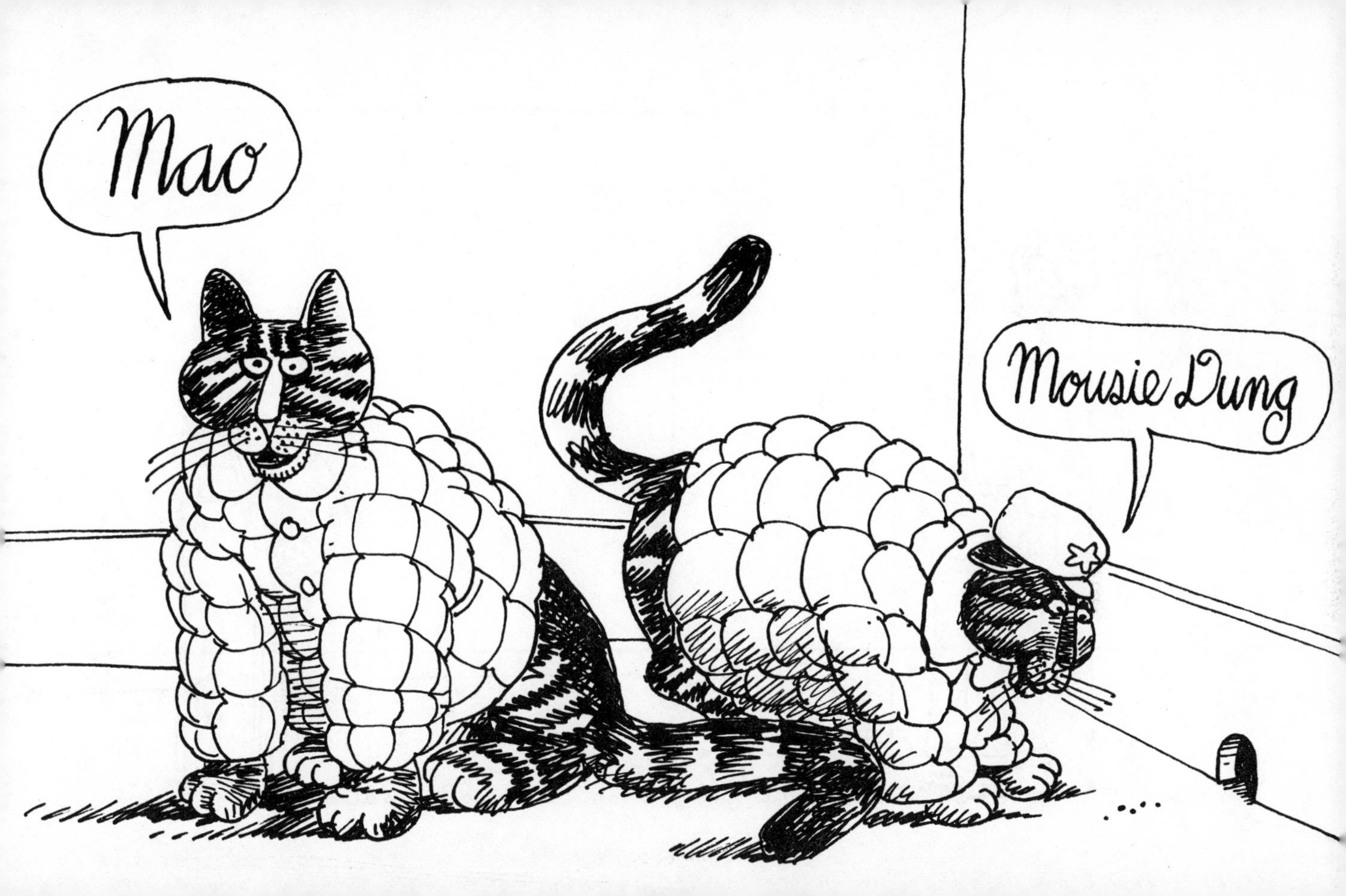
Mao
Mousie Dung

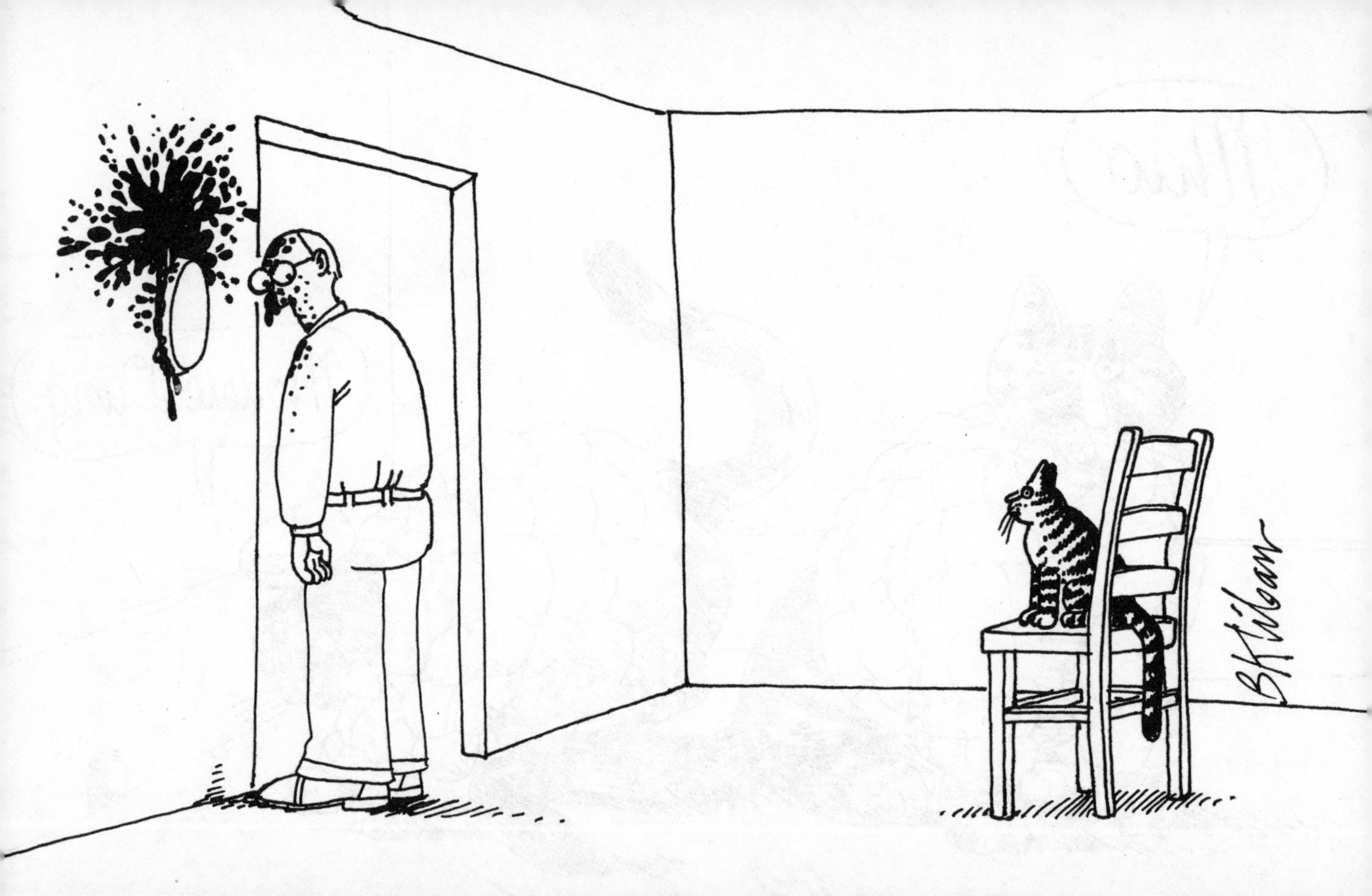
BKliban

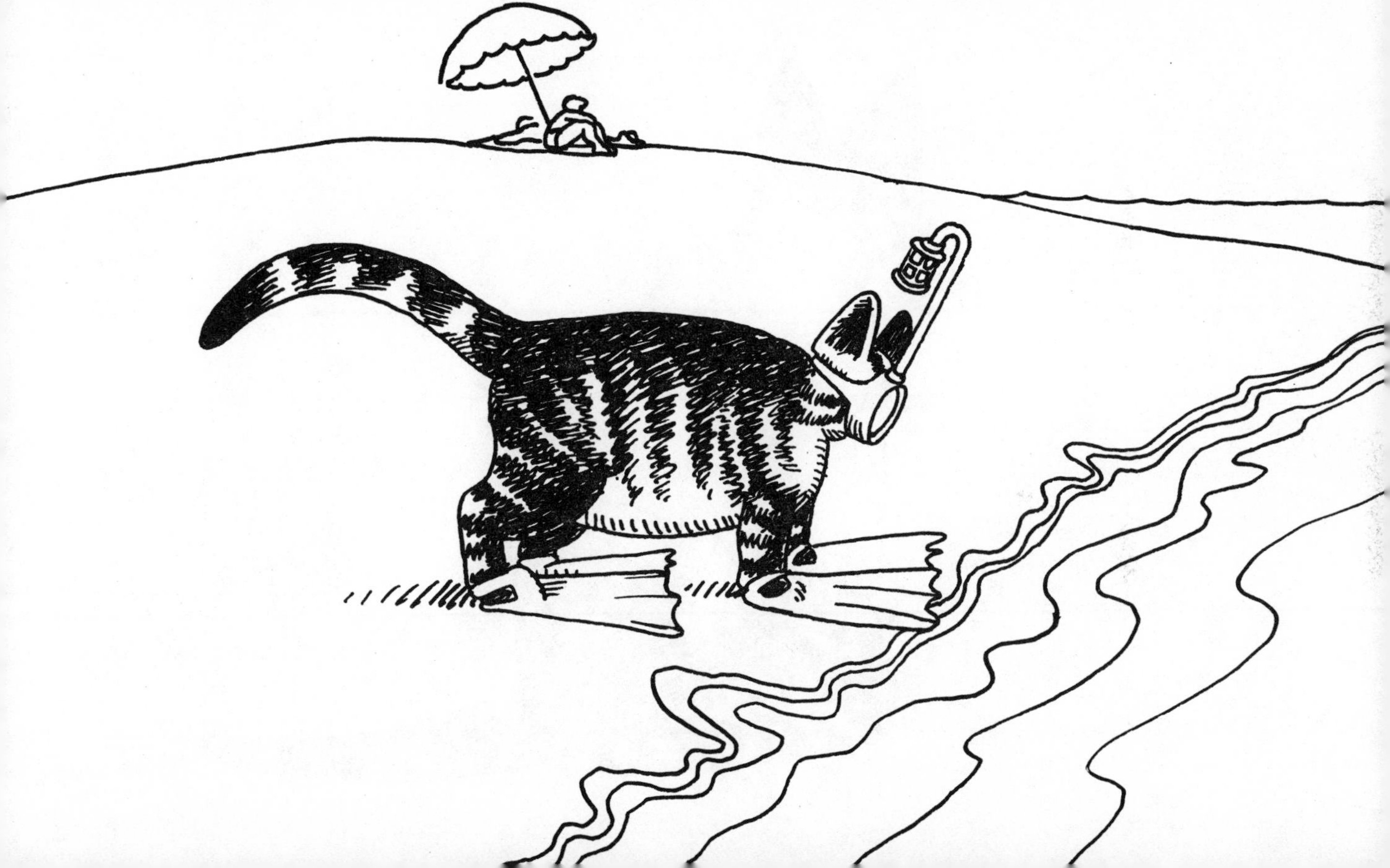

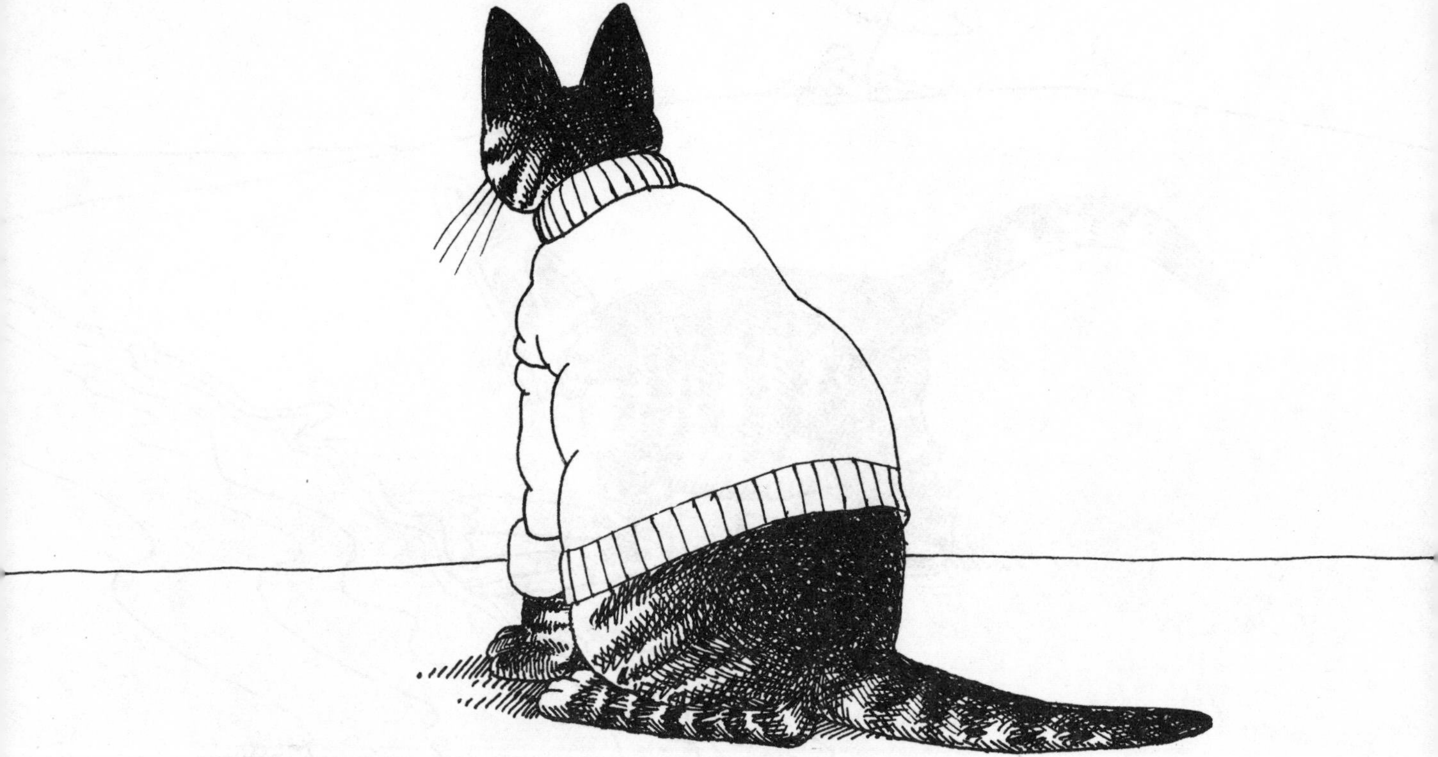

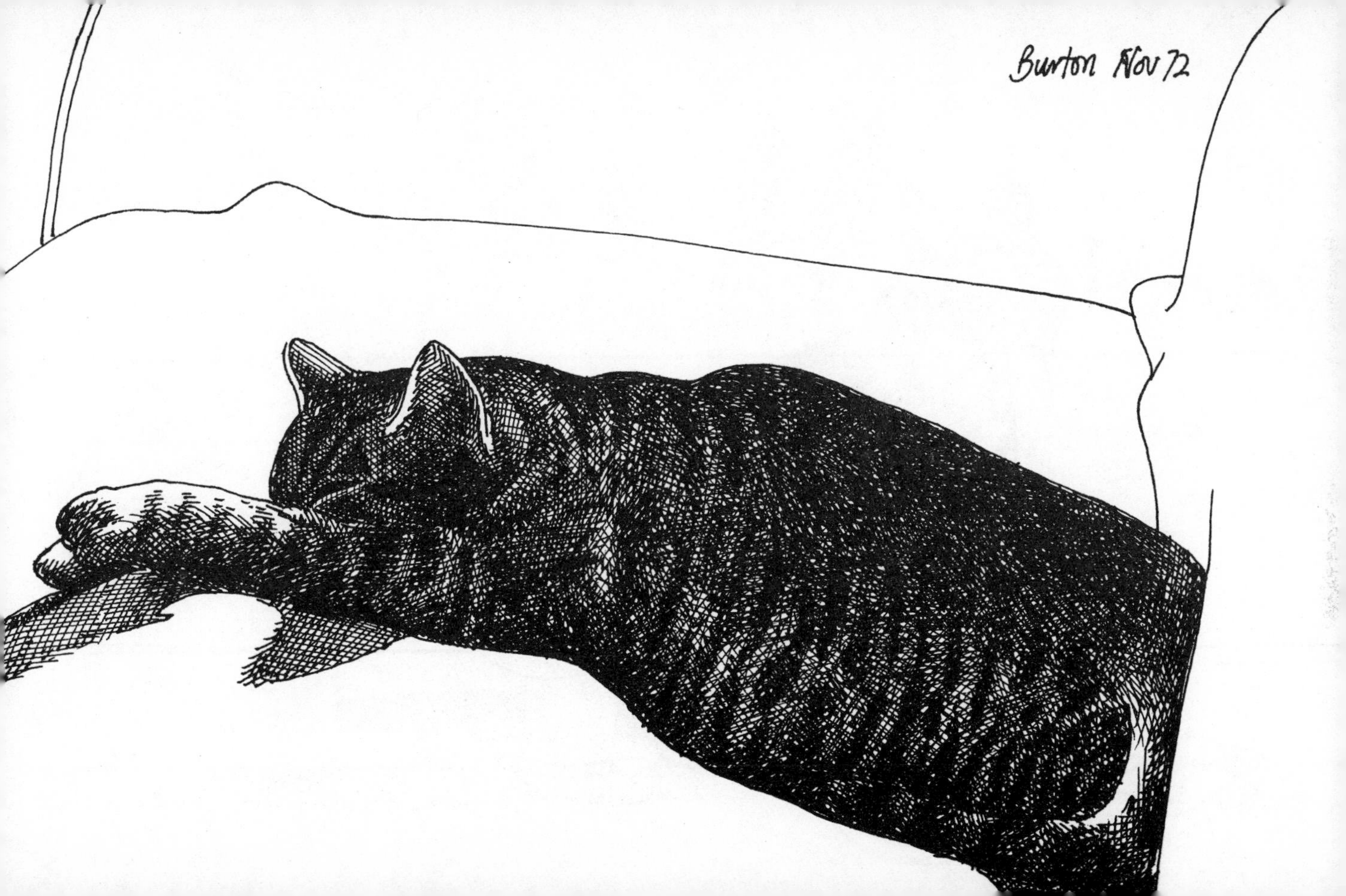
Burton Nov 72

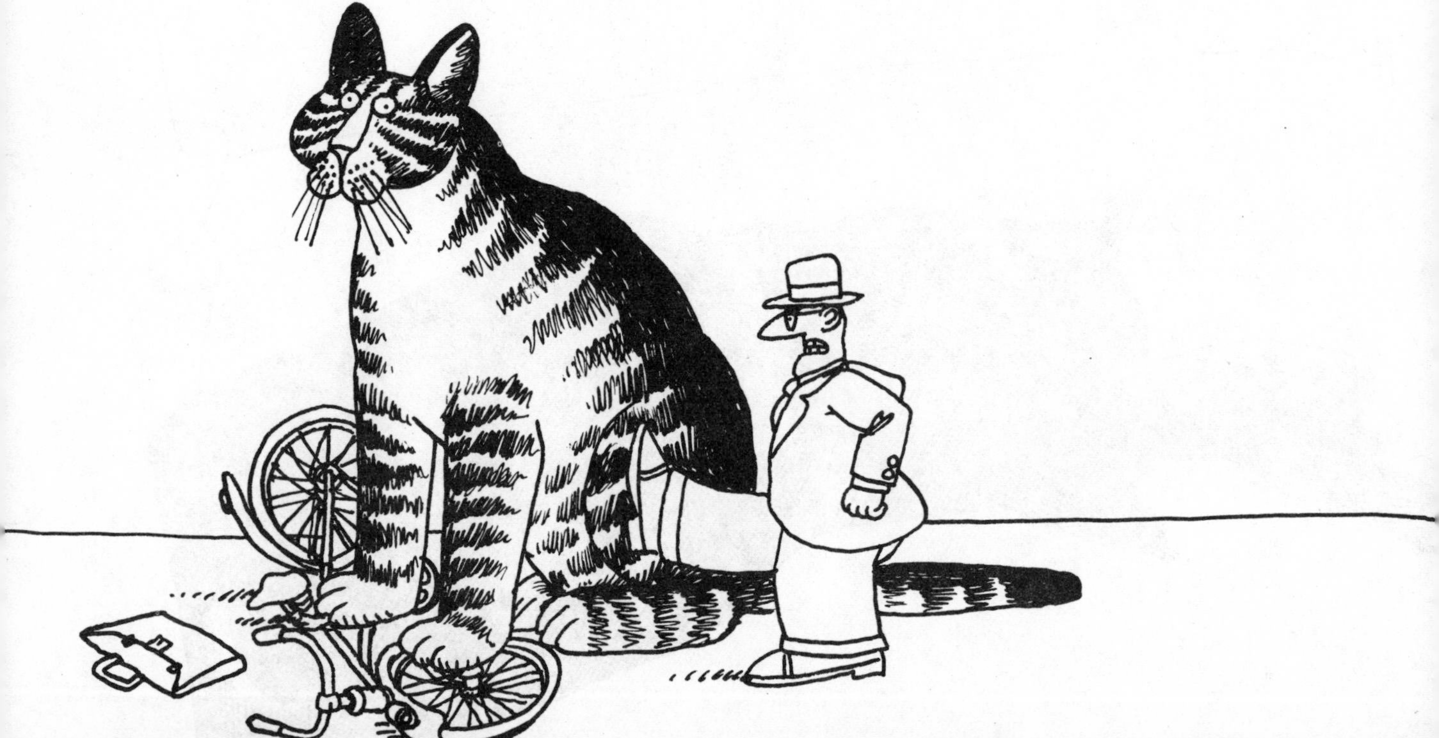

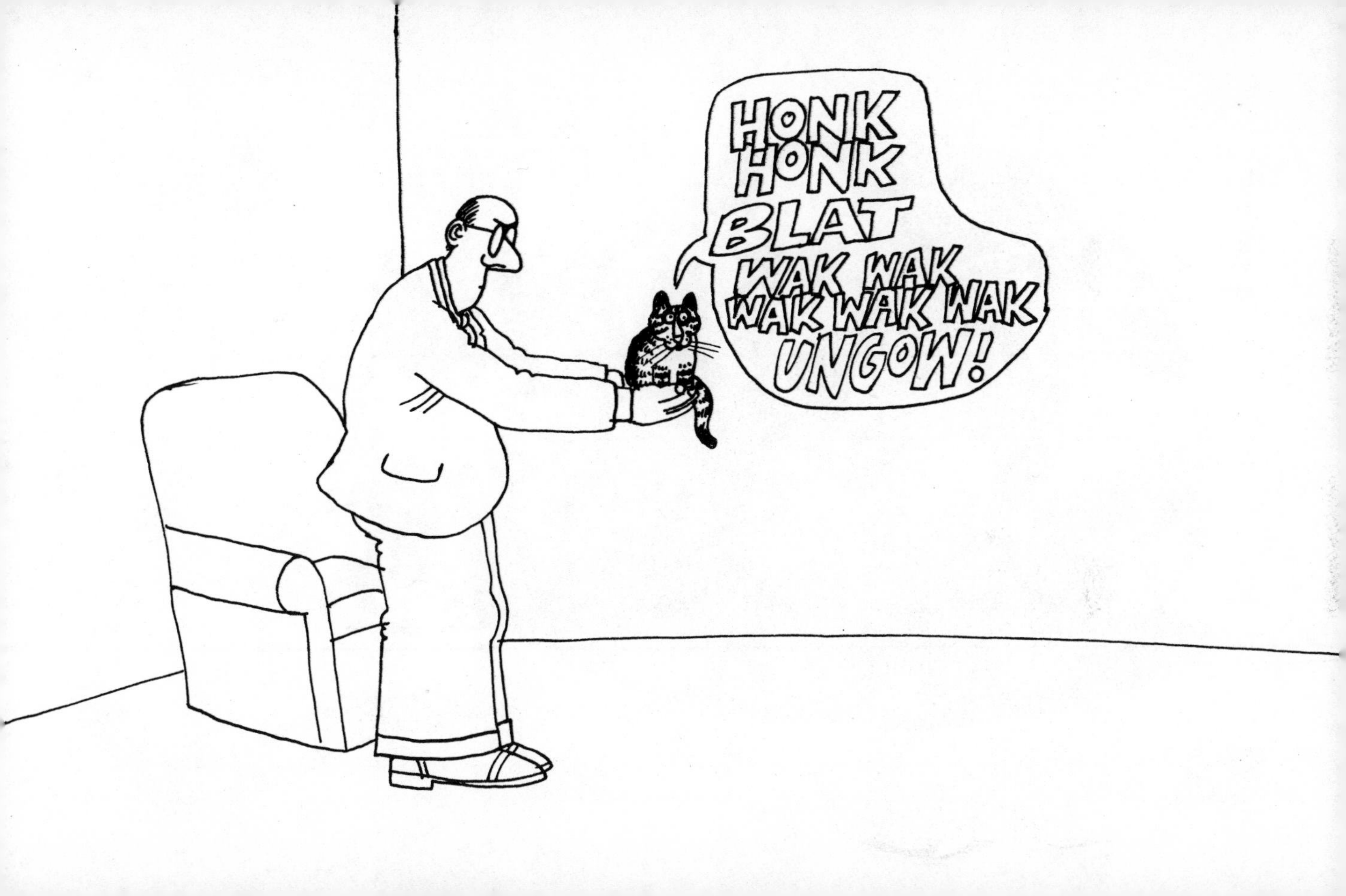
HONK
HONK
BLAT
WAK WAK
WAK WAK WAK
UNGOW!

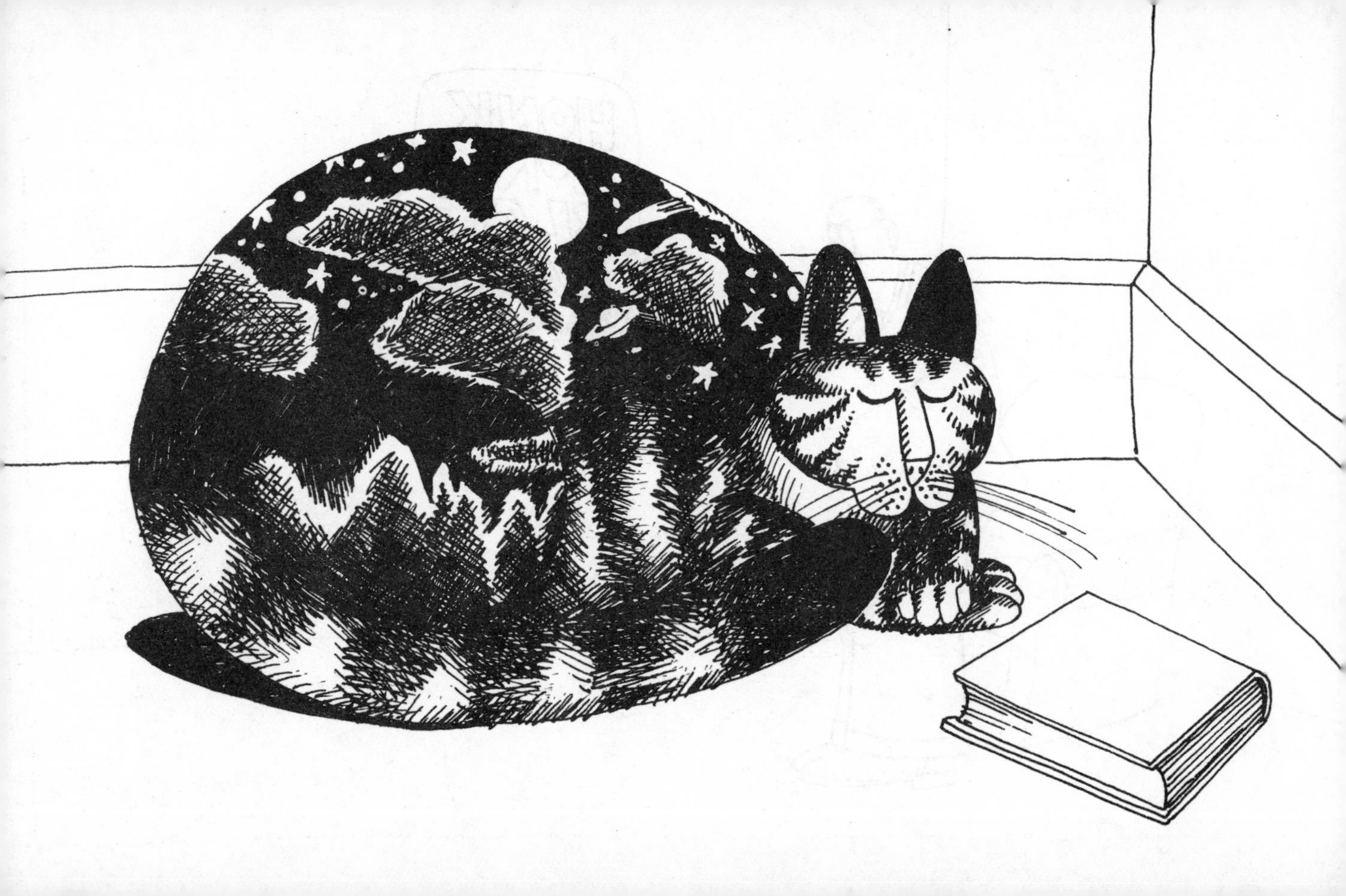

How to draw a Qat

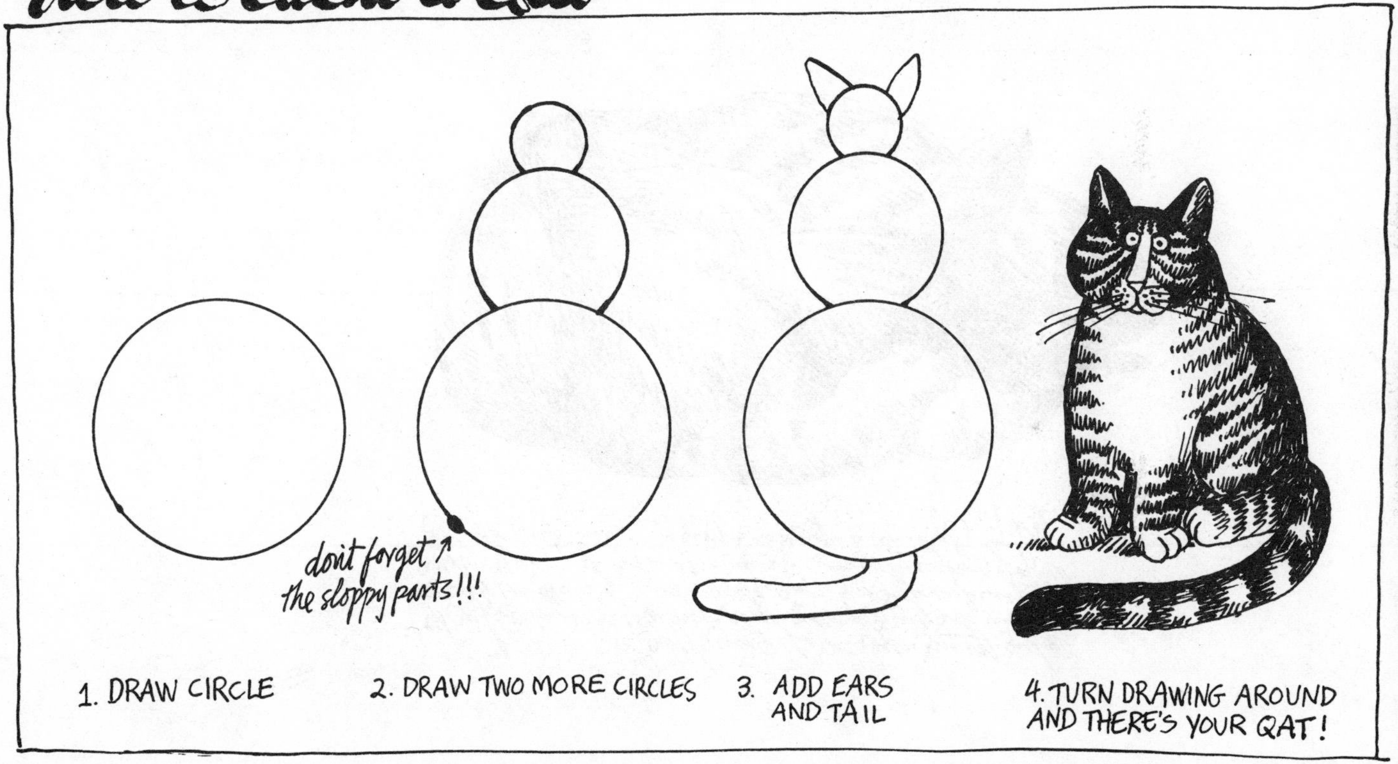
don't forget ↑
the sloppy parts!!!
1. DRAW CIRCLE
2. DRAW TWO MORE CIRCLES
3. ADD EARS AND TAIL
4. TURN DRAWING AROUND AND THERE'S YOUR QAT!

Fig 1.

MAN LYING TO A CAT

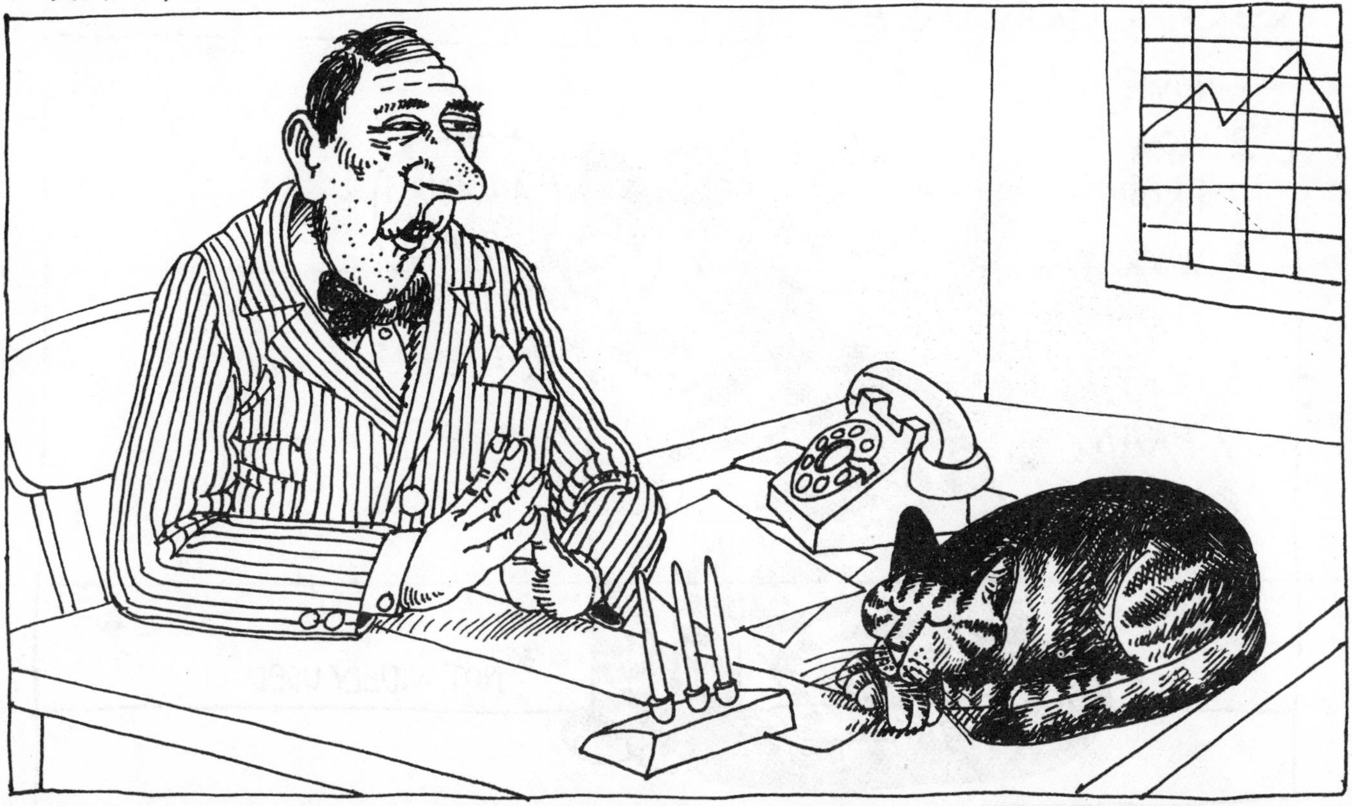

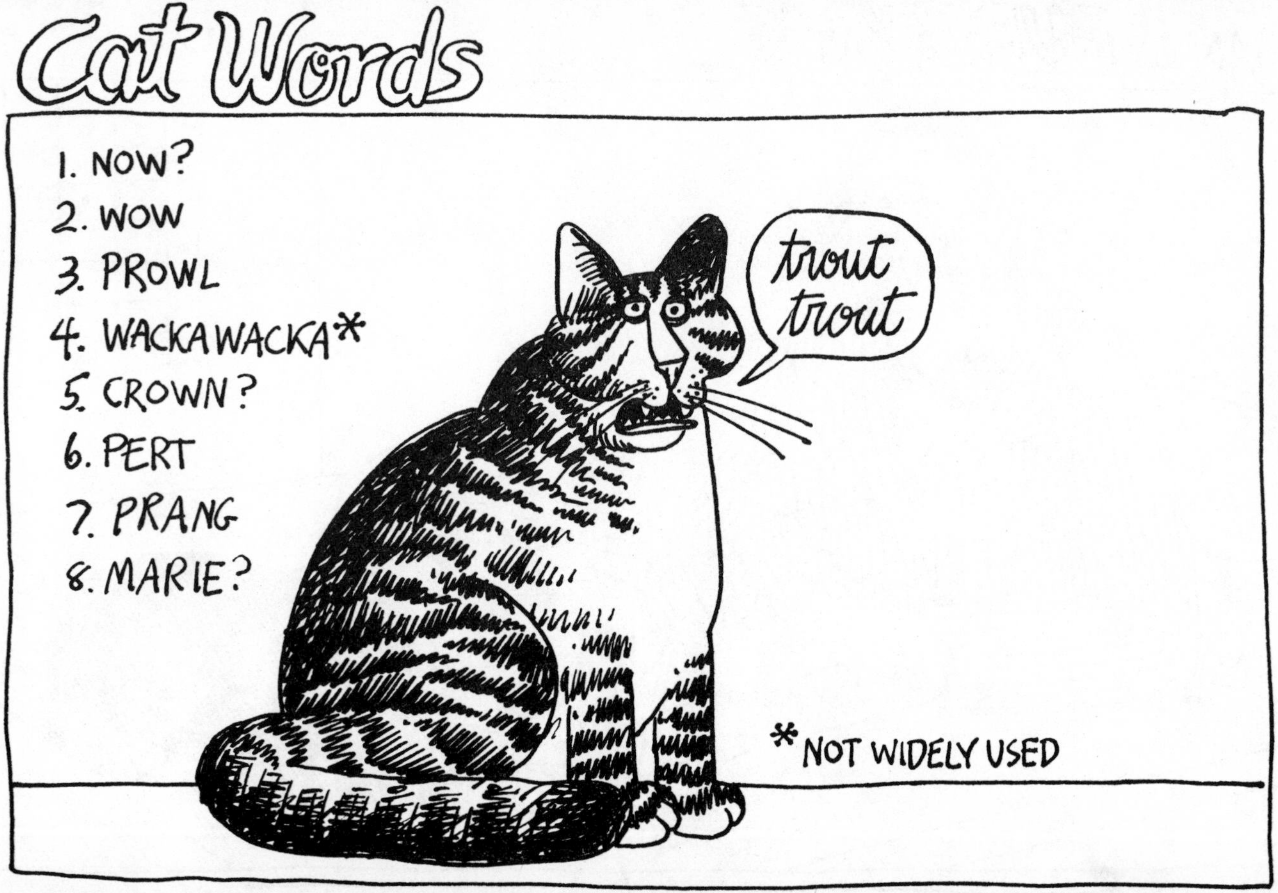
Cat Words
1. NOW?
2. WOW
3. PROWL
4. WACKAWACKA*
5. CROWN?
6. PERT
7. PRANG
8. MARIE?
trout trout
* NOT WIDELY USED

PURSEY CAT

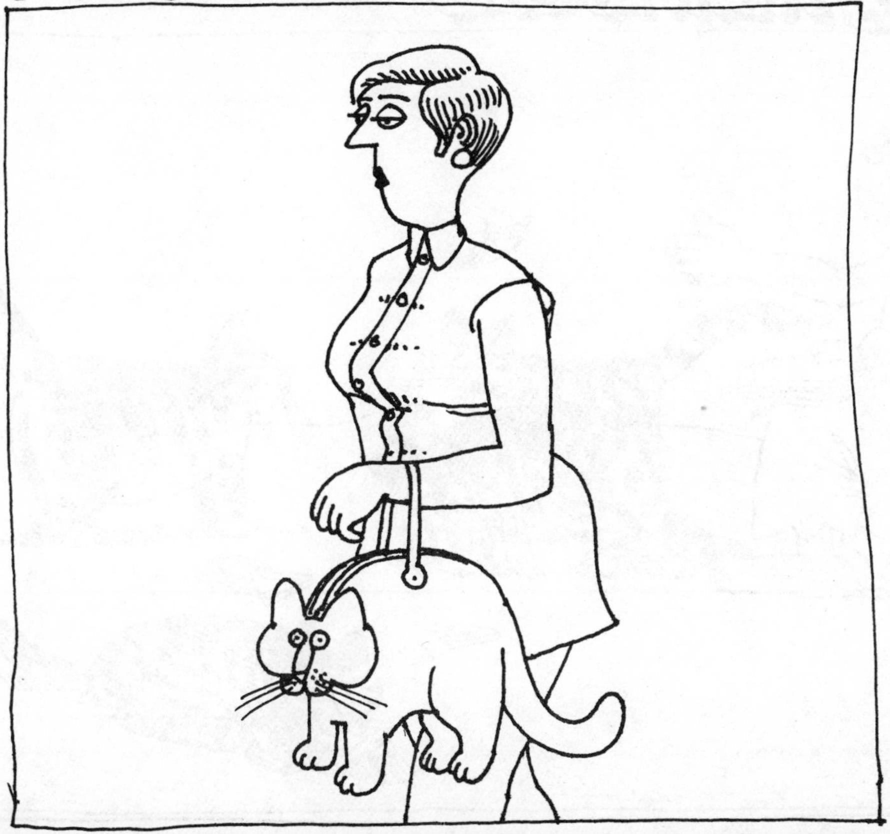

Feeding Ham to Cats

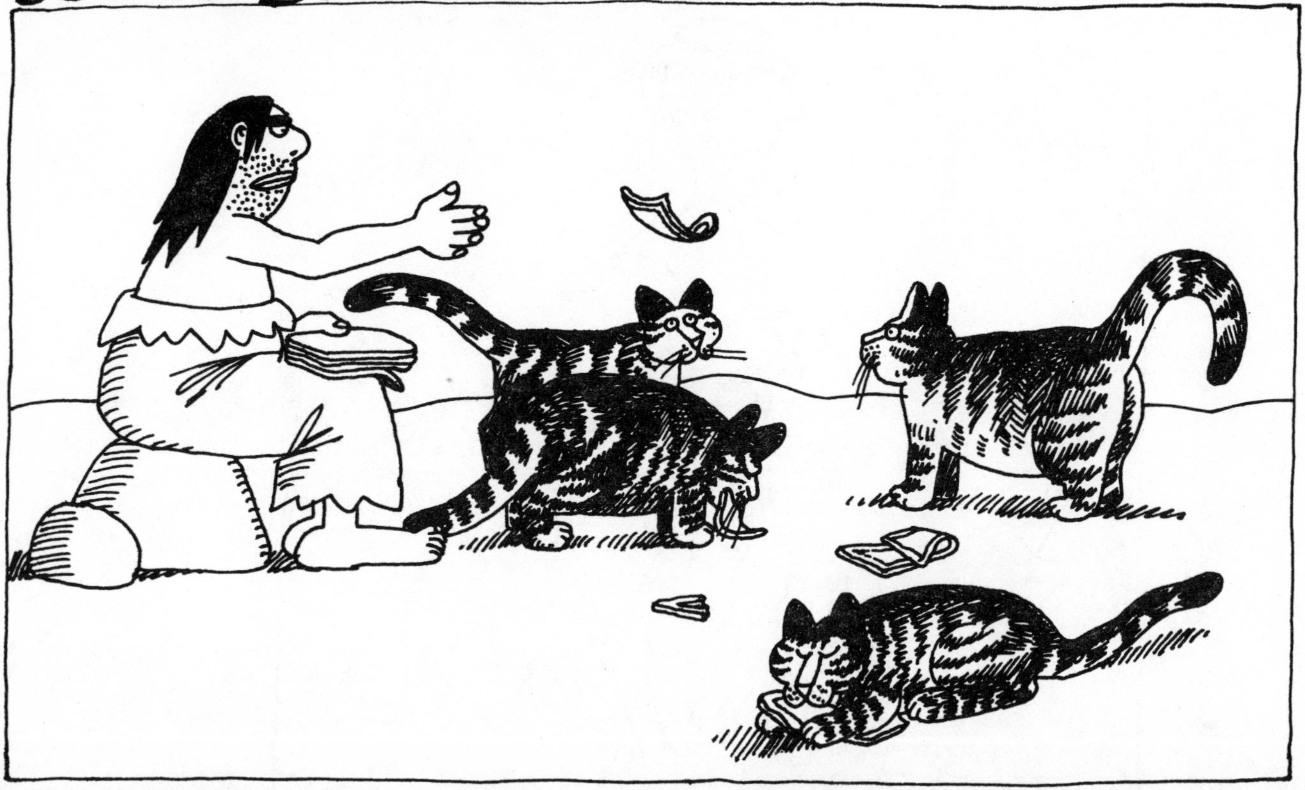

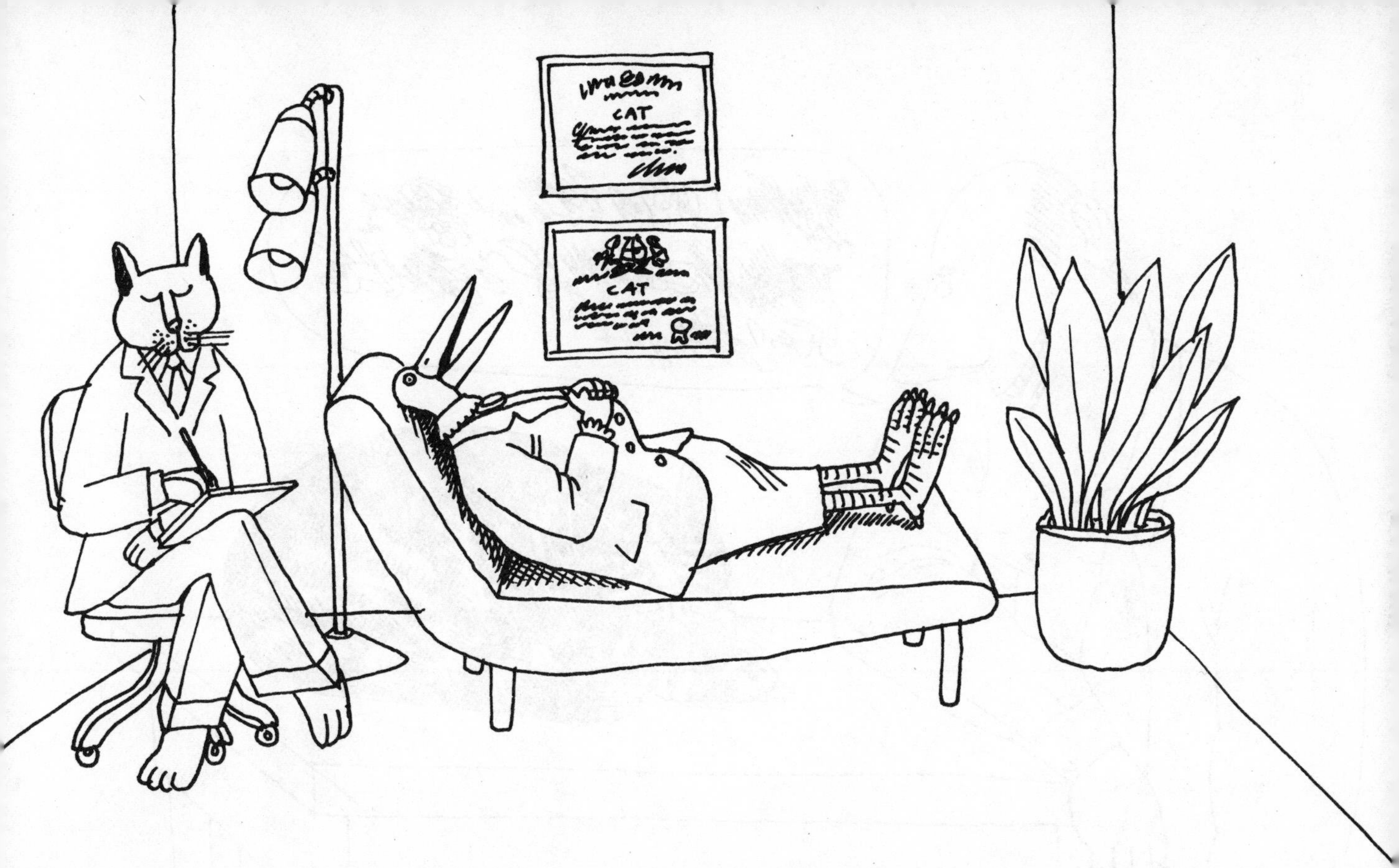
CAT
CAT

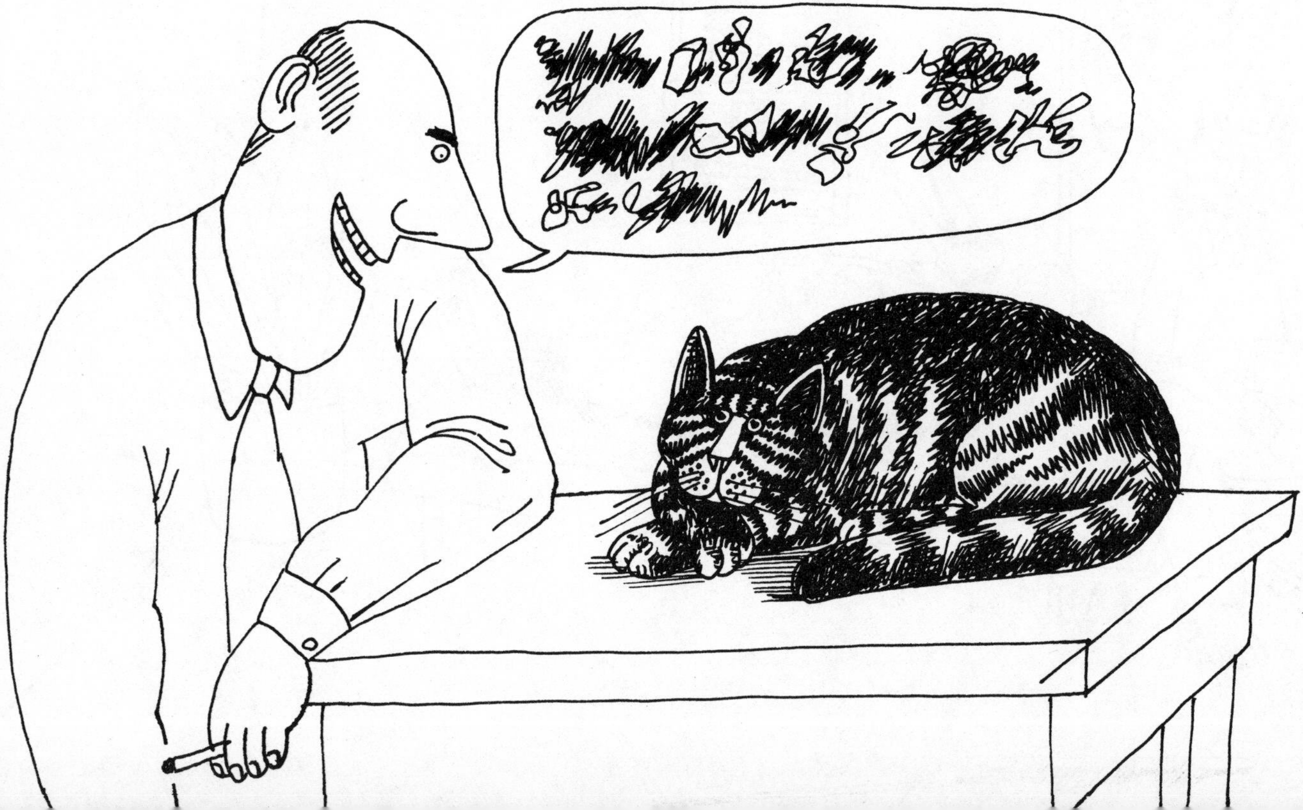

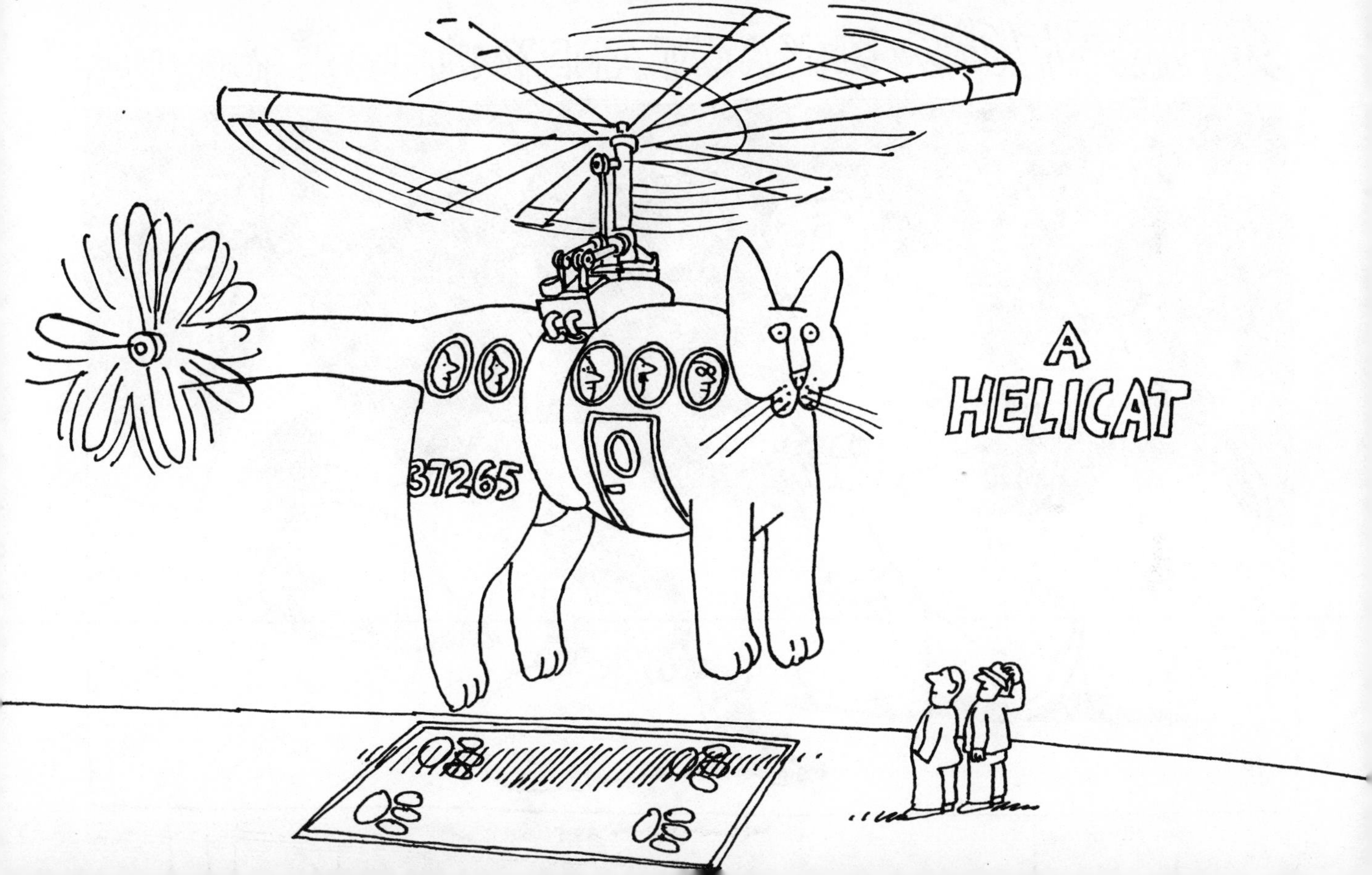
37265
0
A
HELICAT

SUPERSTITIONS • KICK A CAT AND YOU'LL LOSE YOUR HAT.

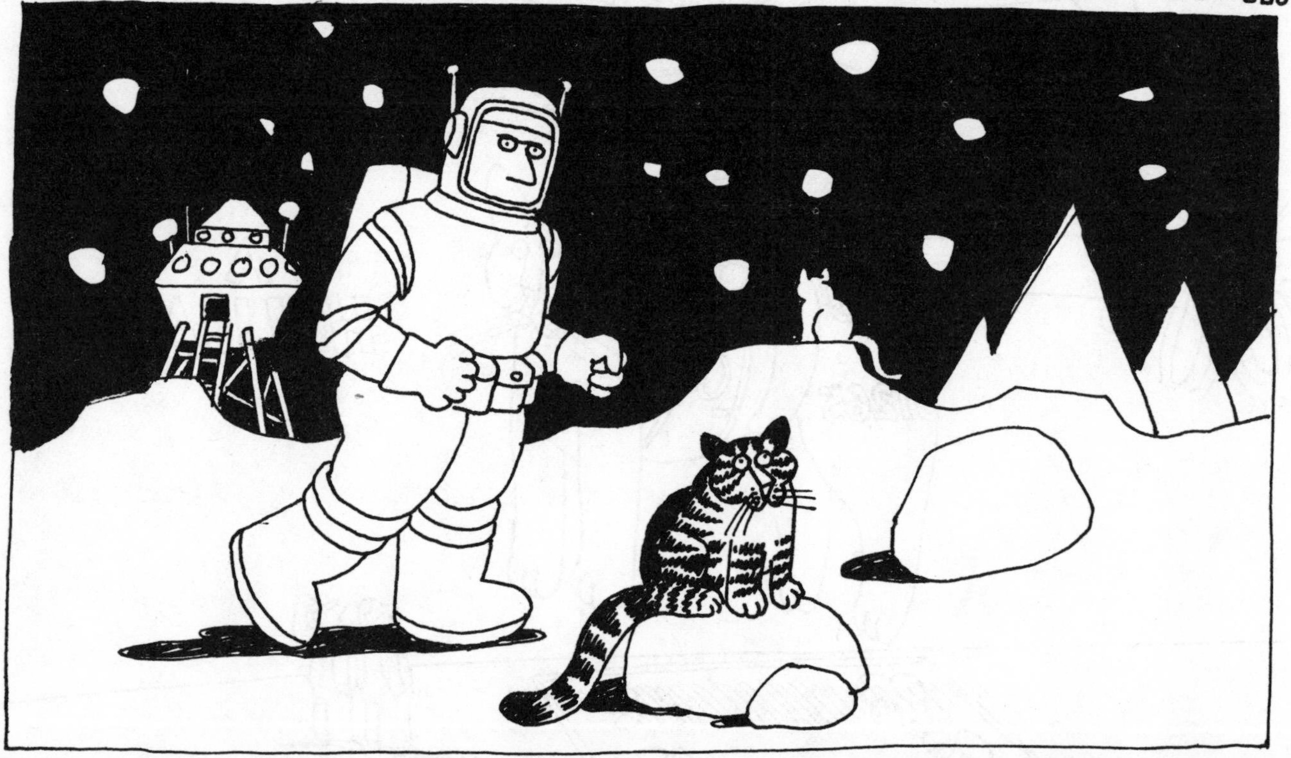

Mad

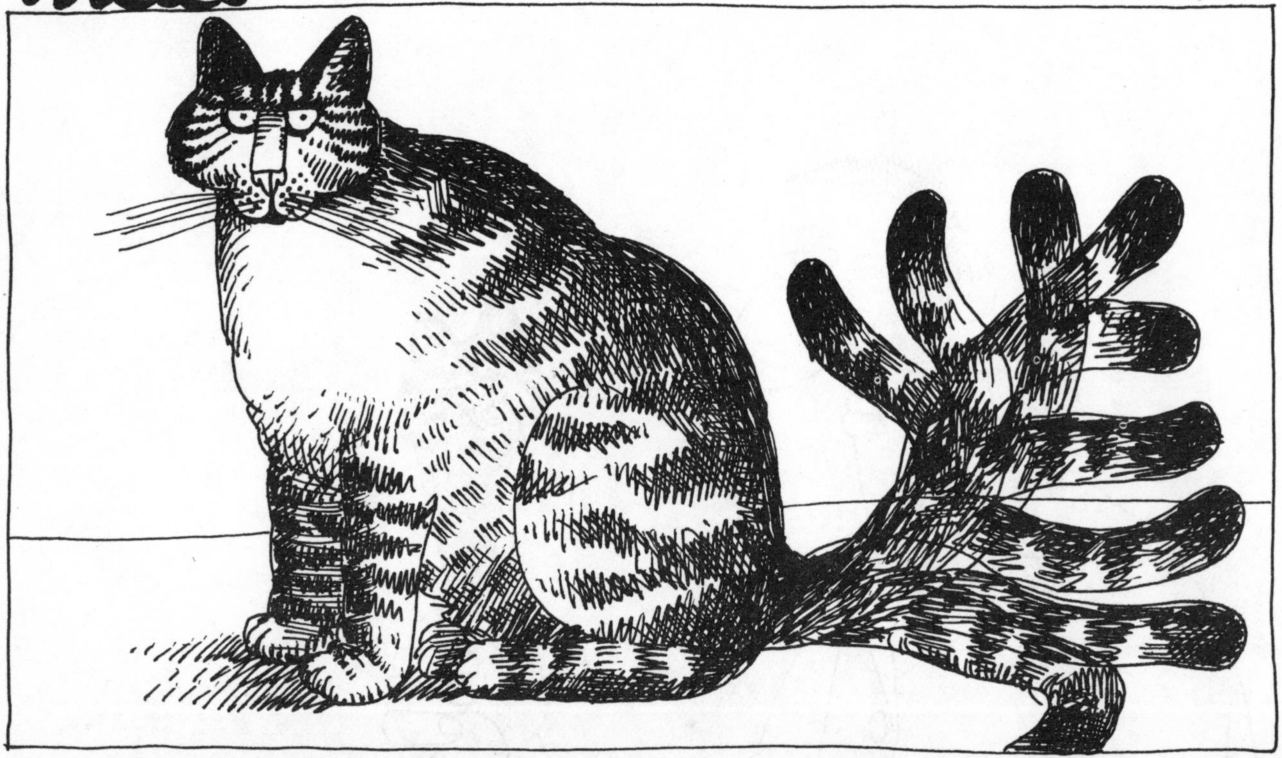

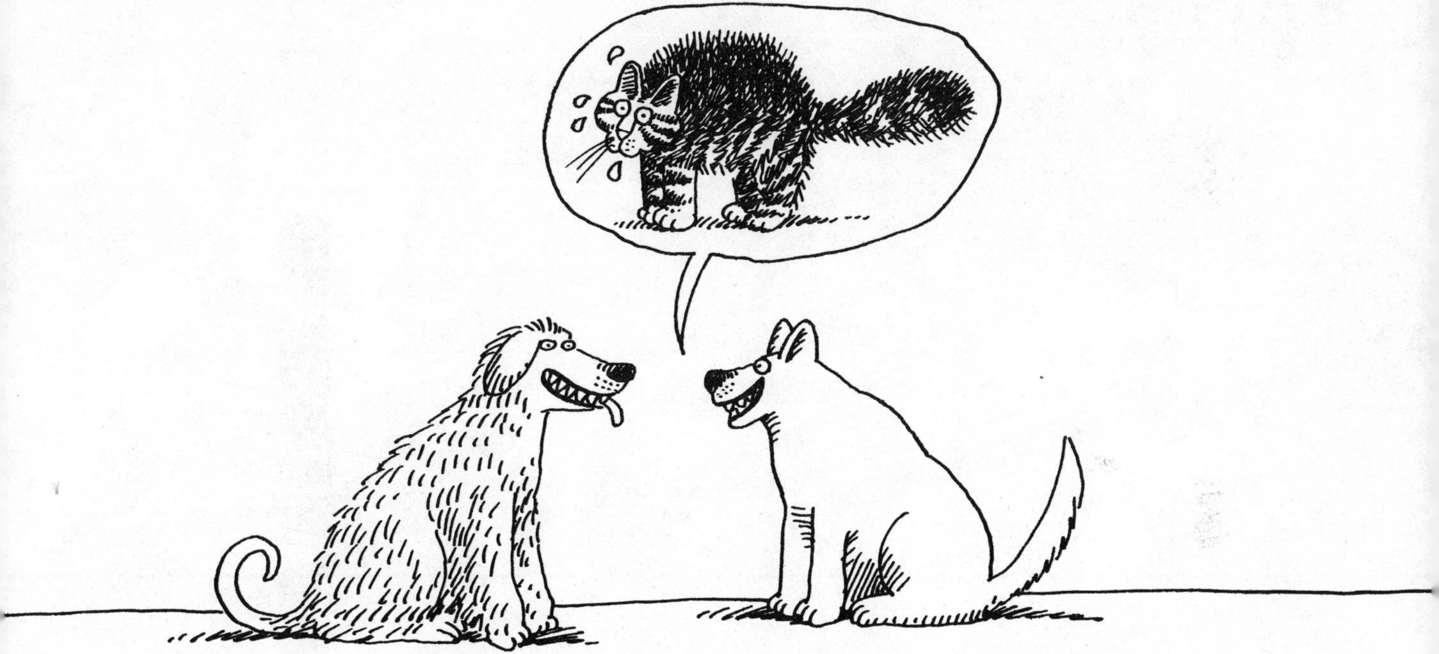

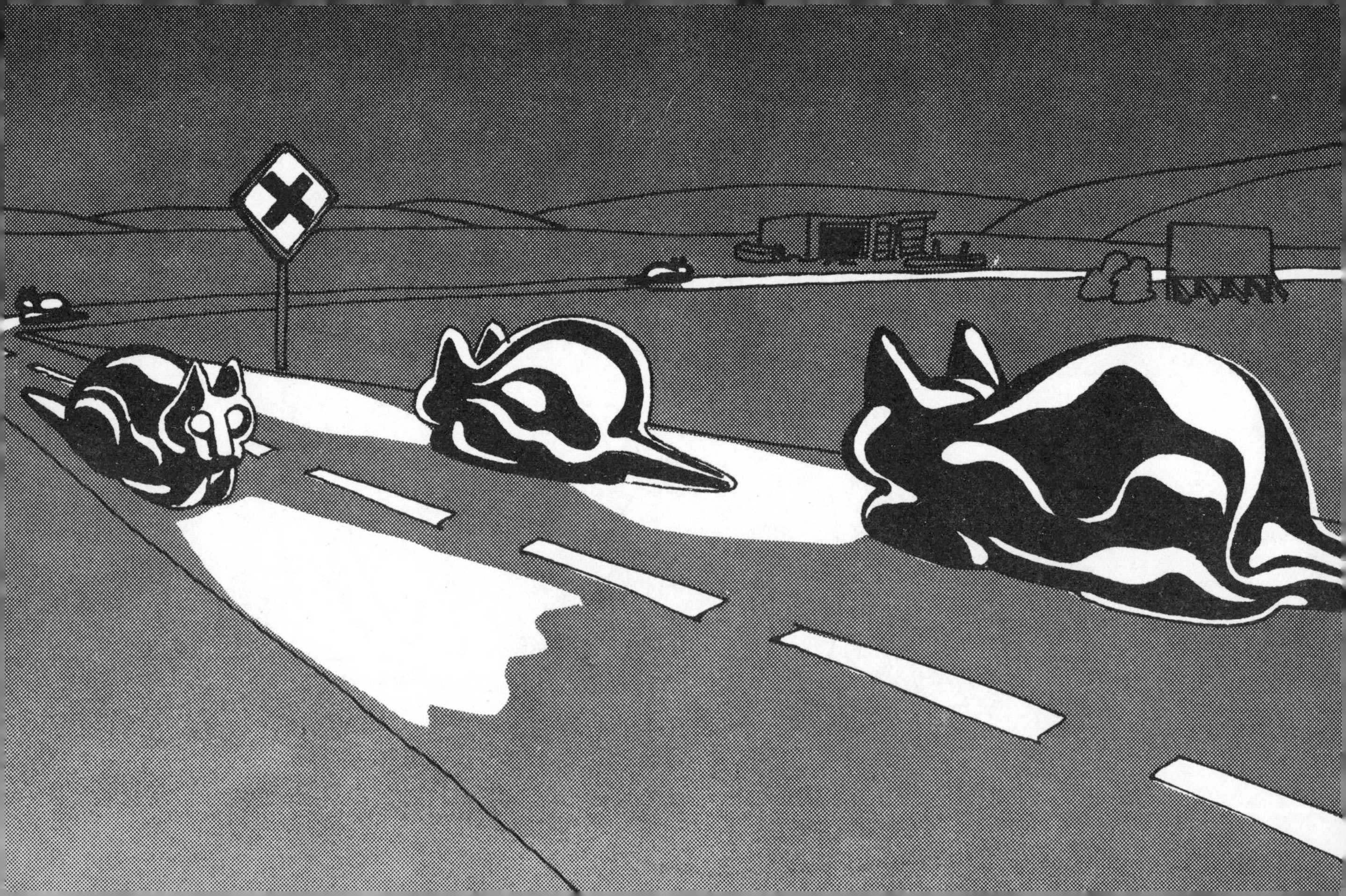

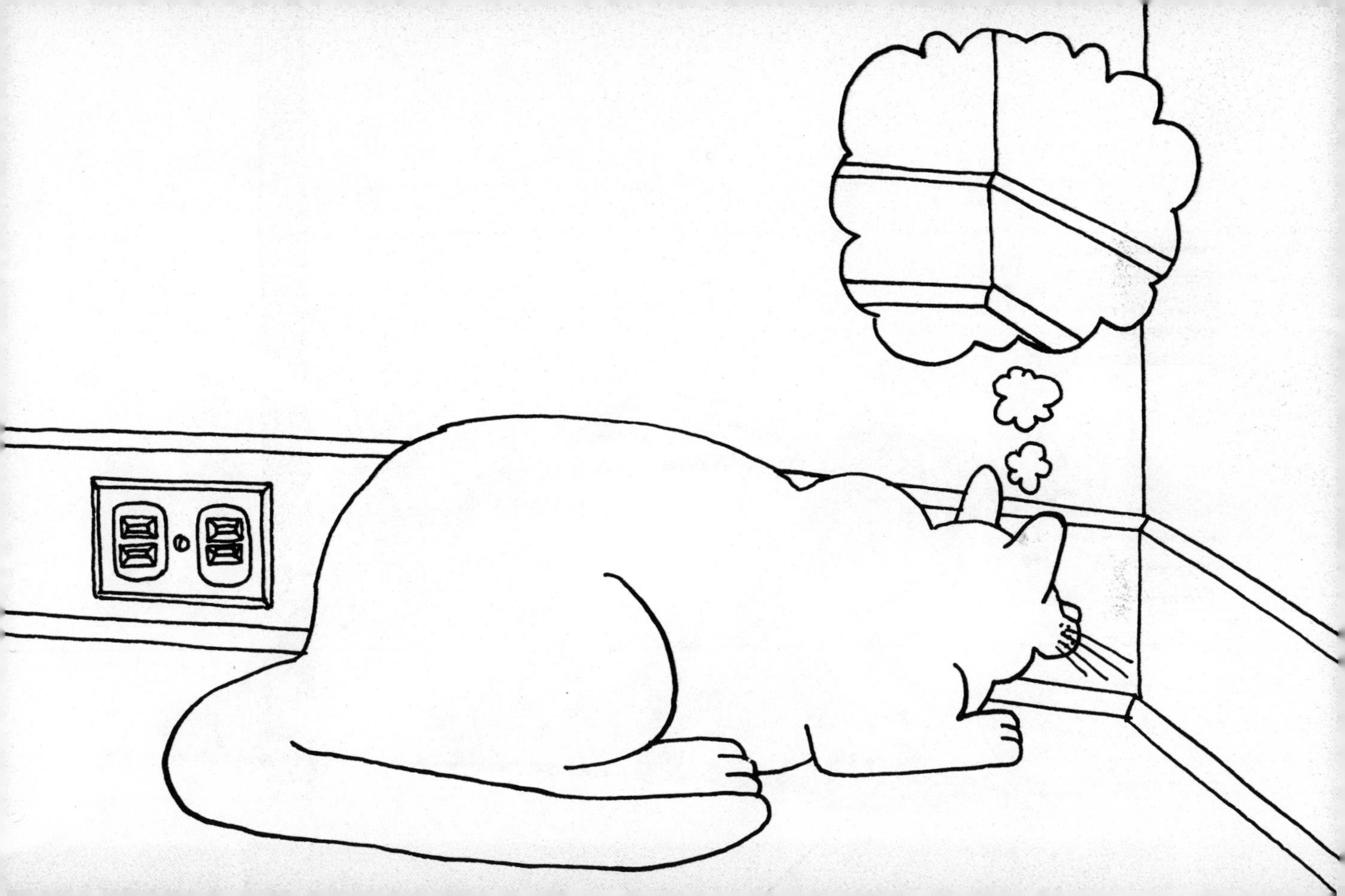

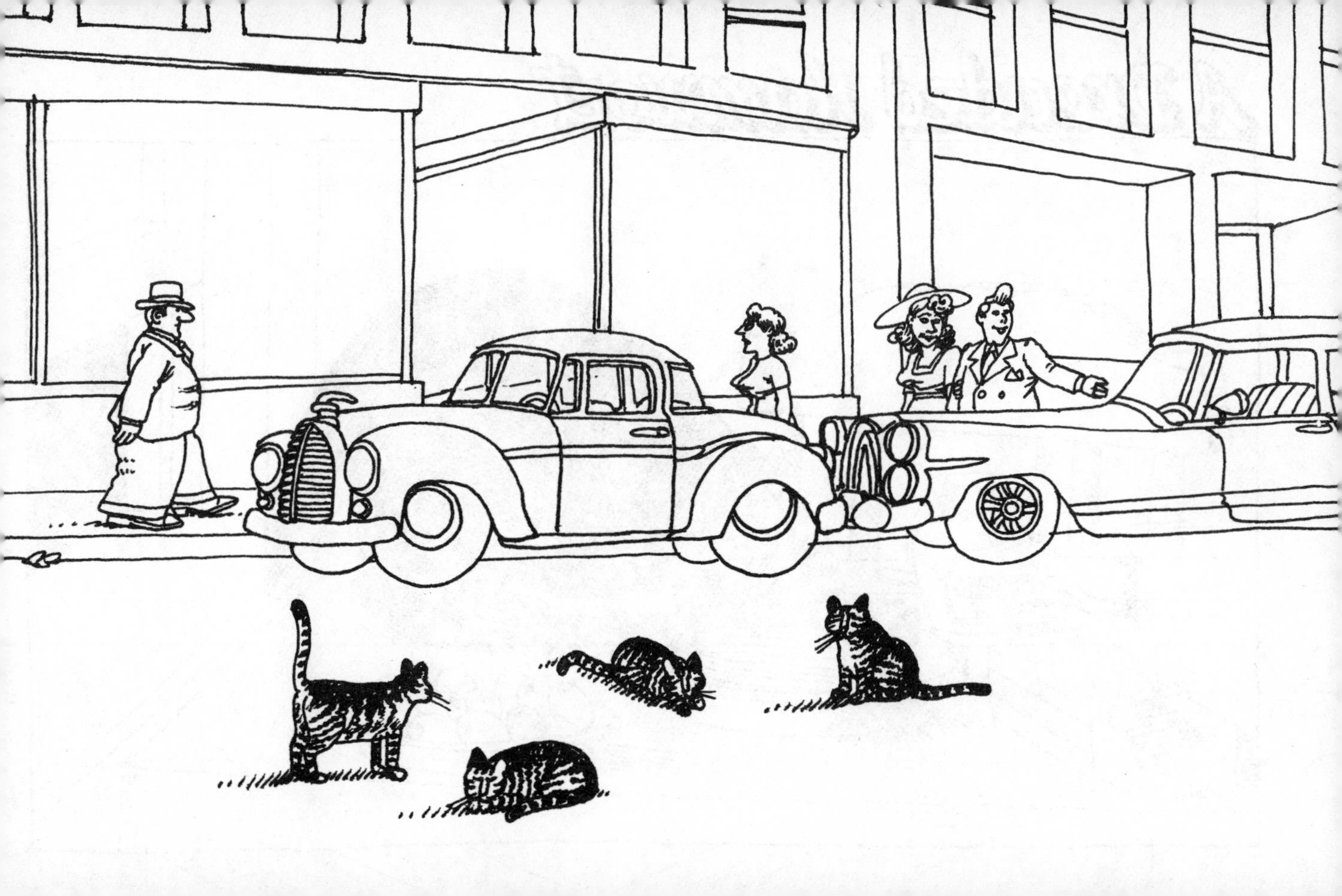

A Dreaded Hamwort

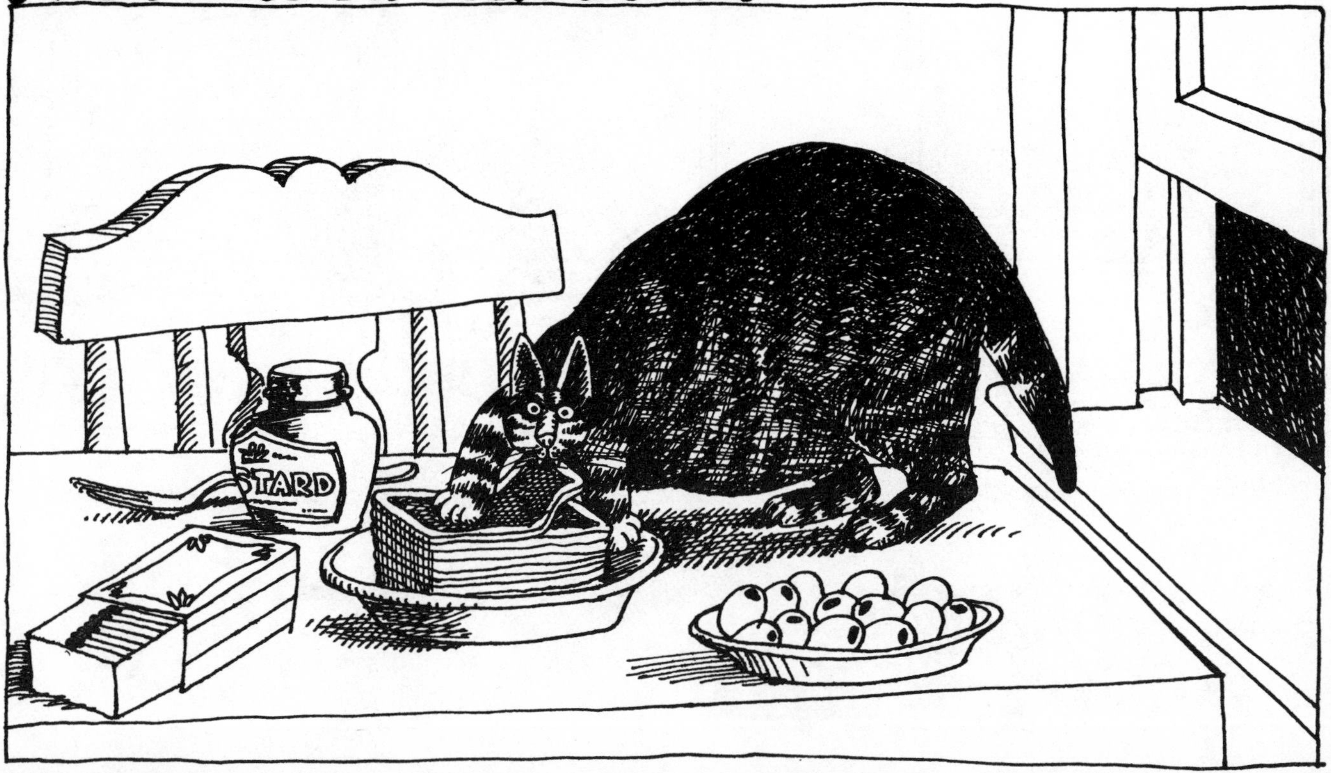
STARD

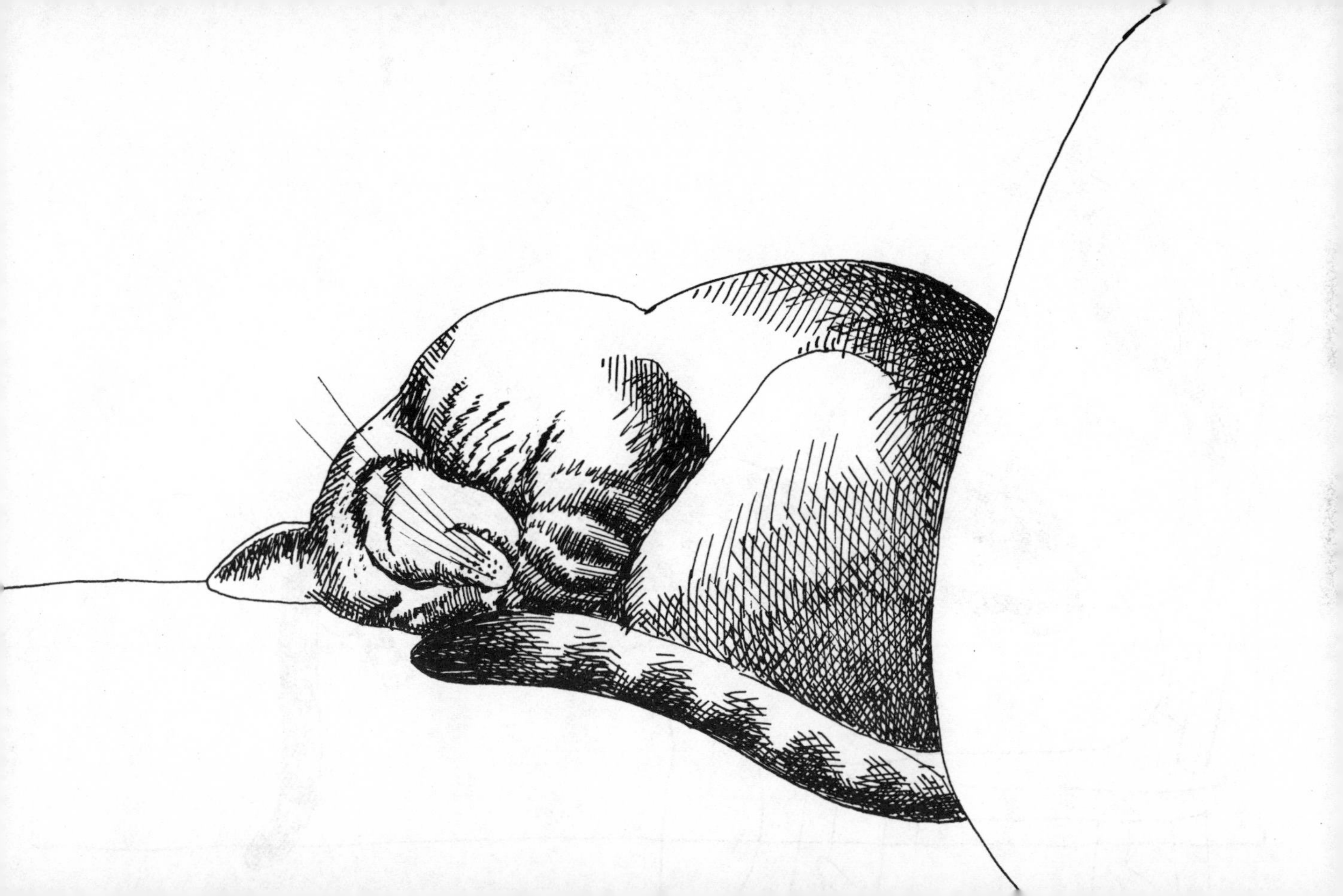

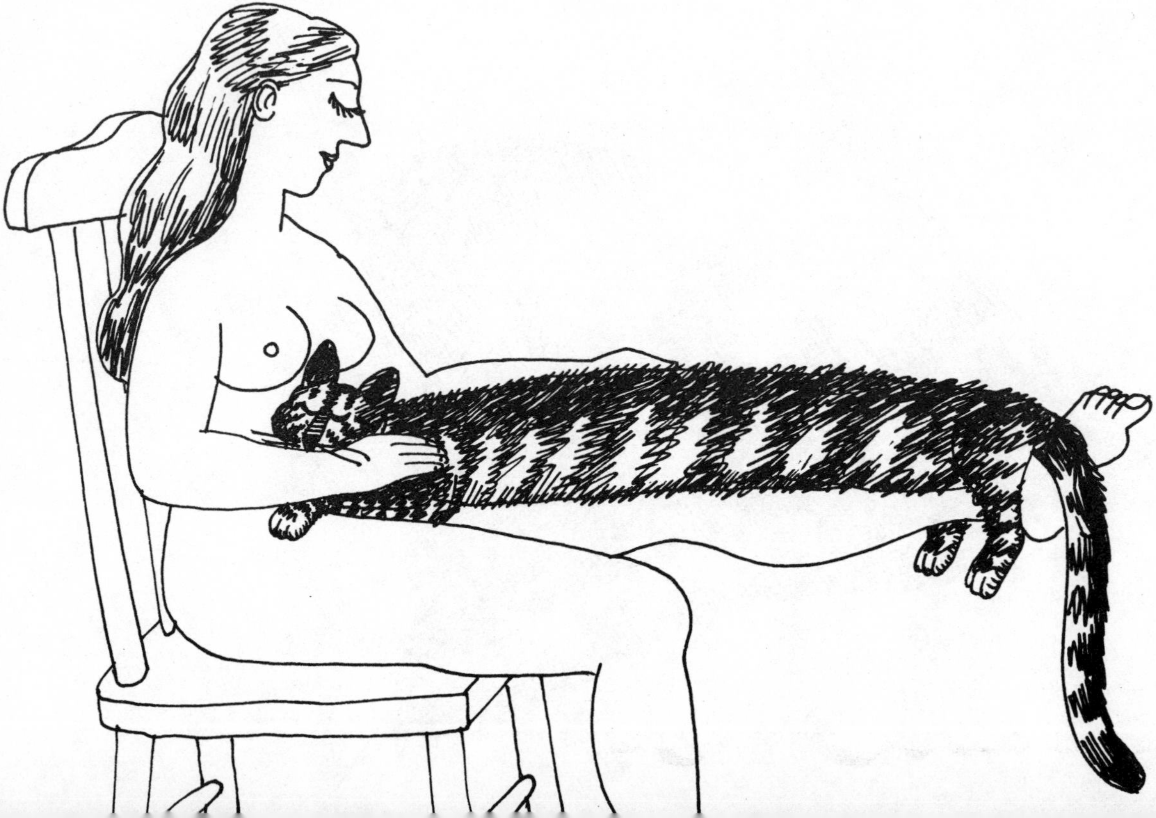

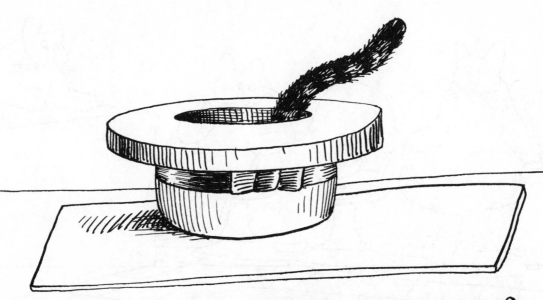

Cat in Fat Hat on Mat

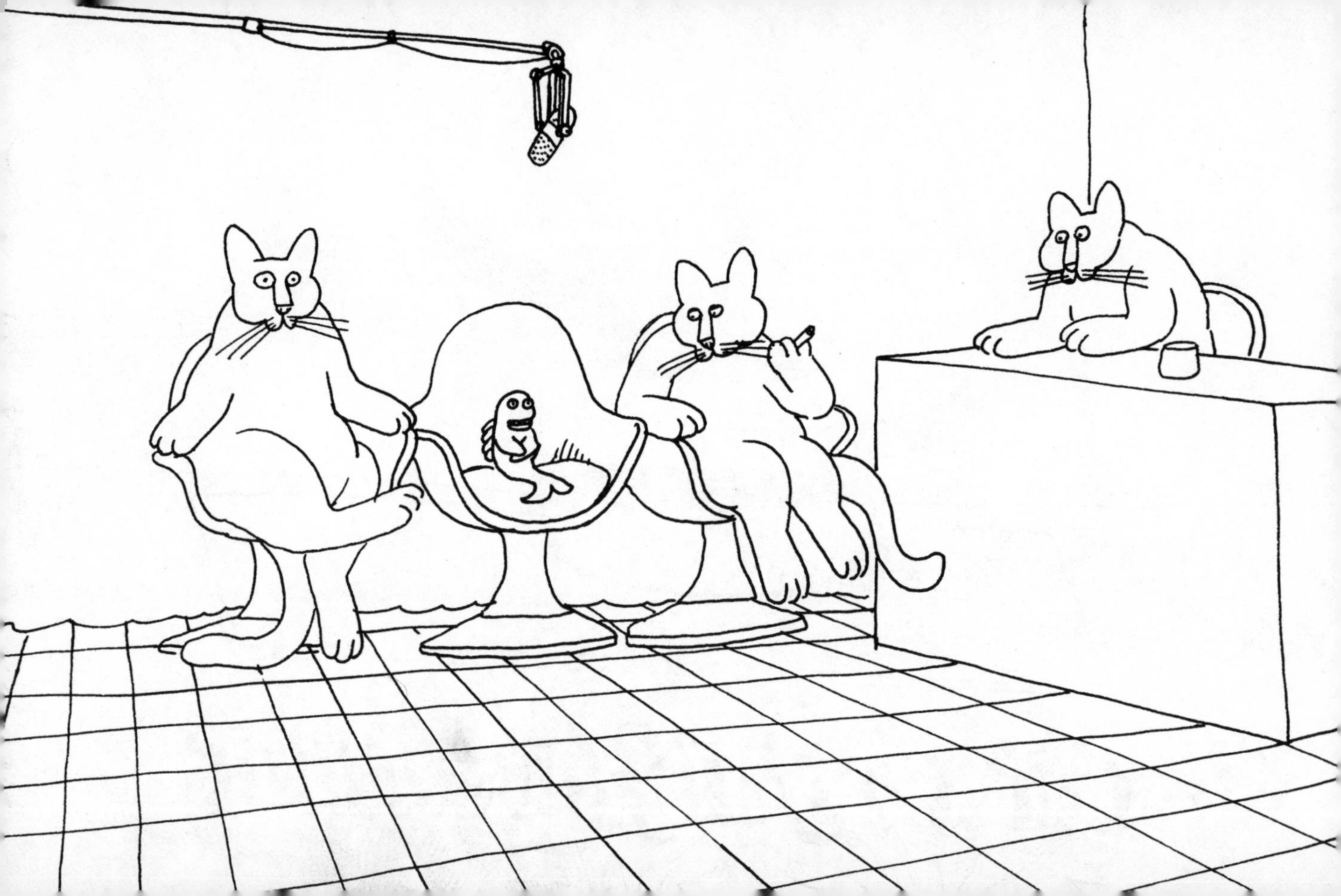

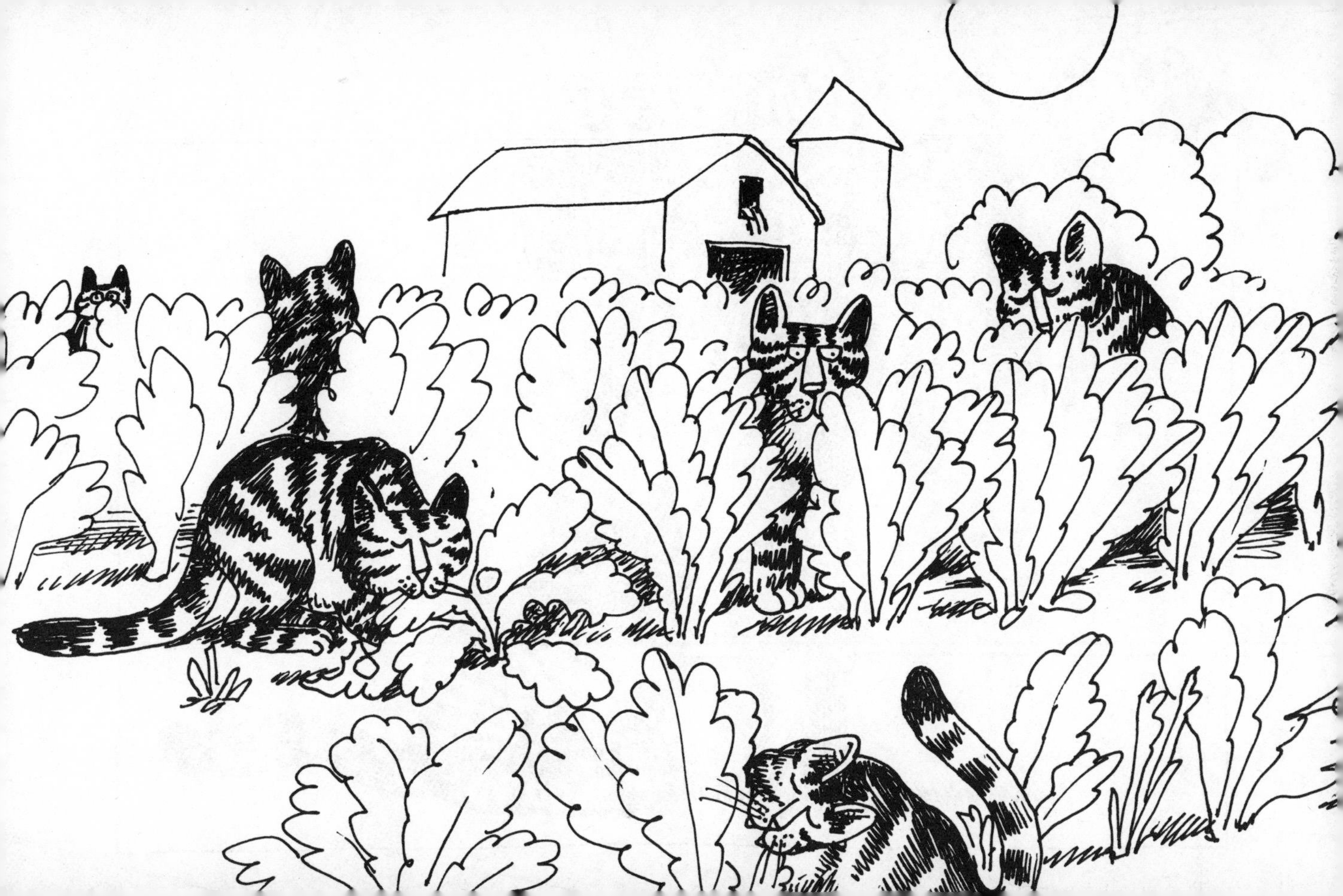

Nit & the Ham Tree

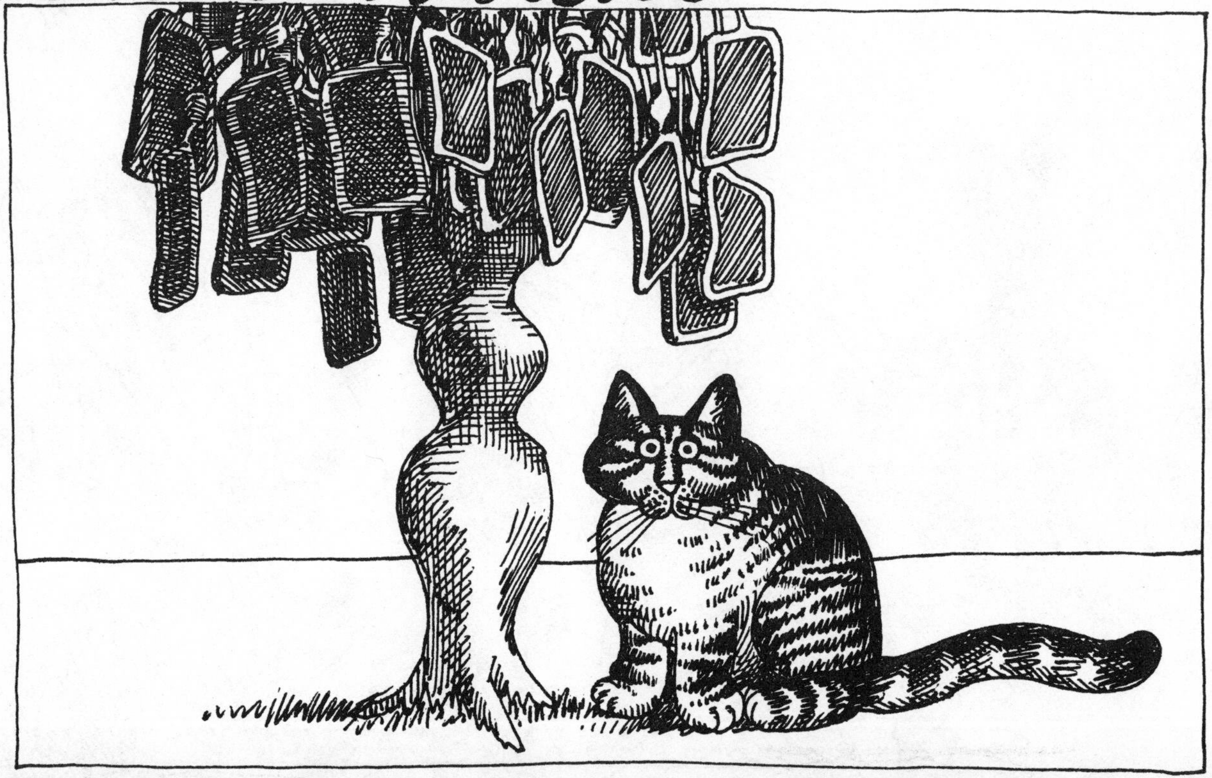

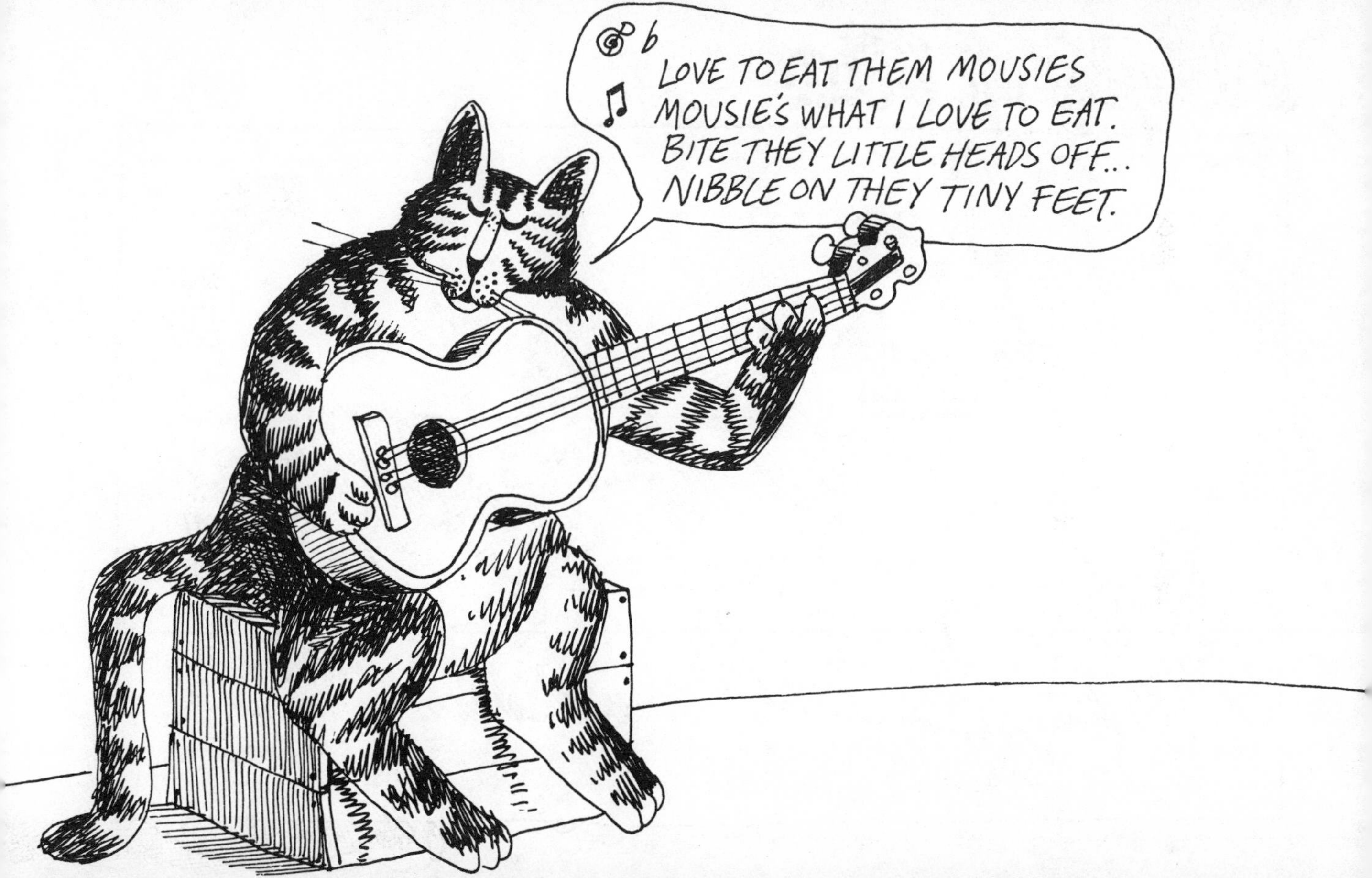
LOVE TO EAT THEM MOUSIES
MOUSIE'S WHAT I LOVE TO EAT.
BITE THEY LITTLE HEADS OFF...
NIBBLE ON THEY TINY FEET.

Sleight of Paw

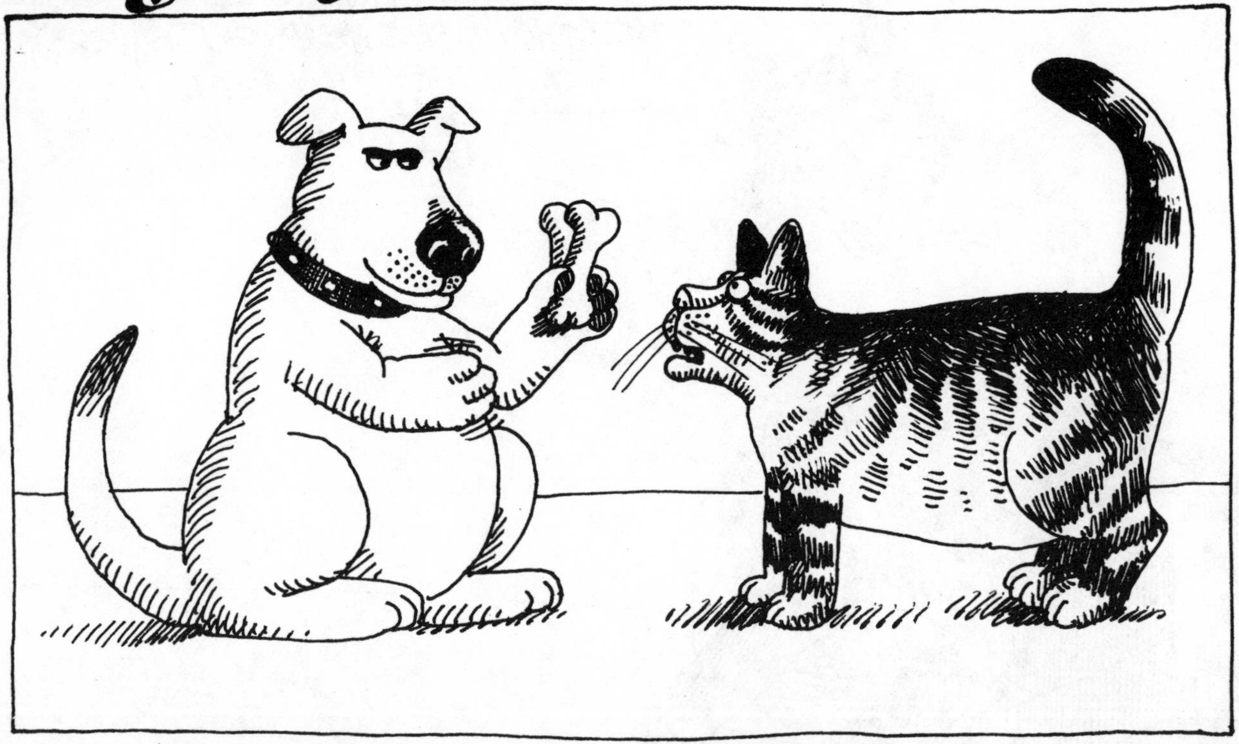

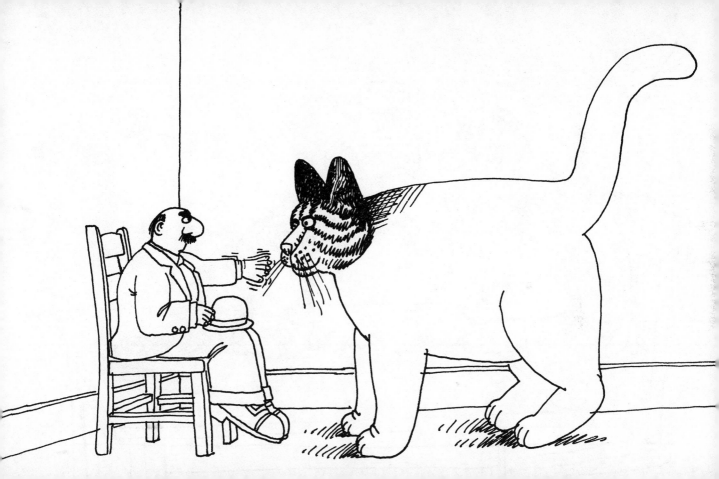

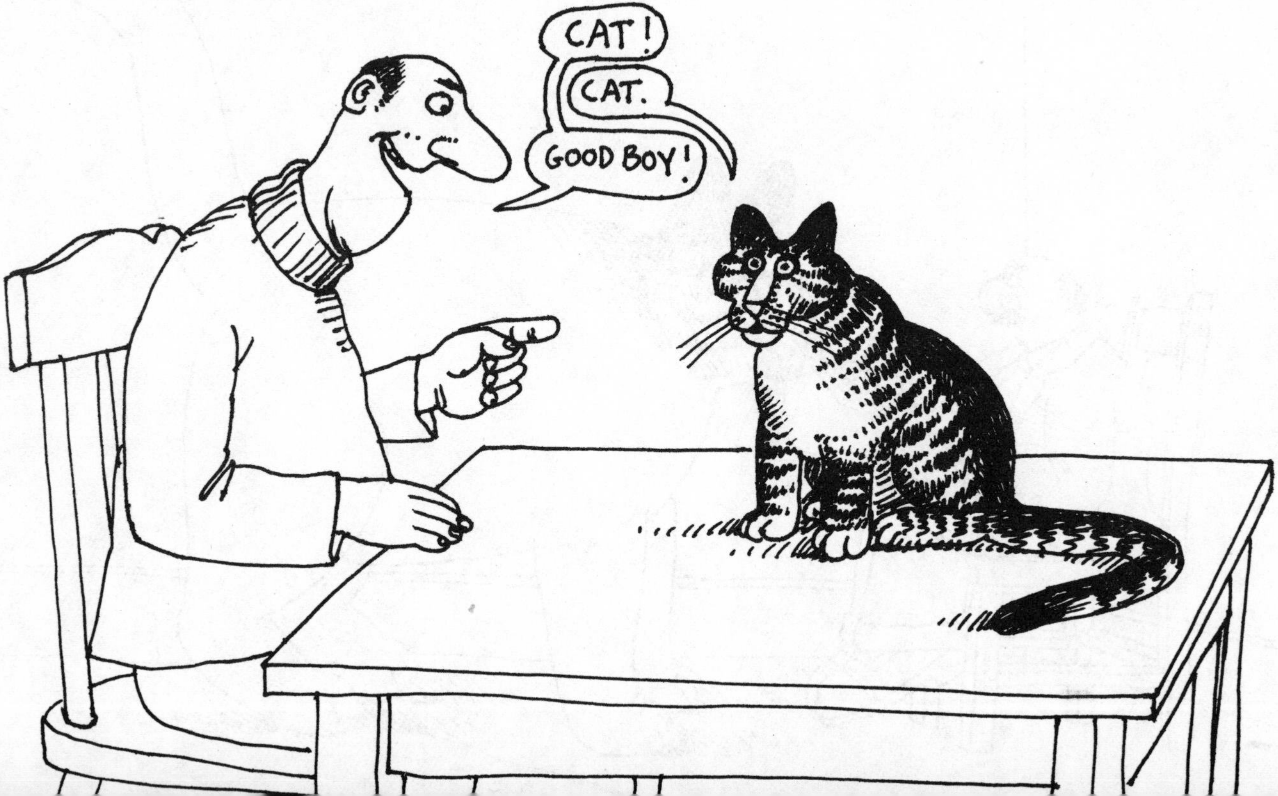
CAT!
CAT.
GOOD BOY!

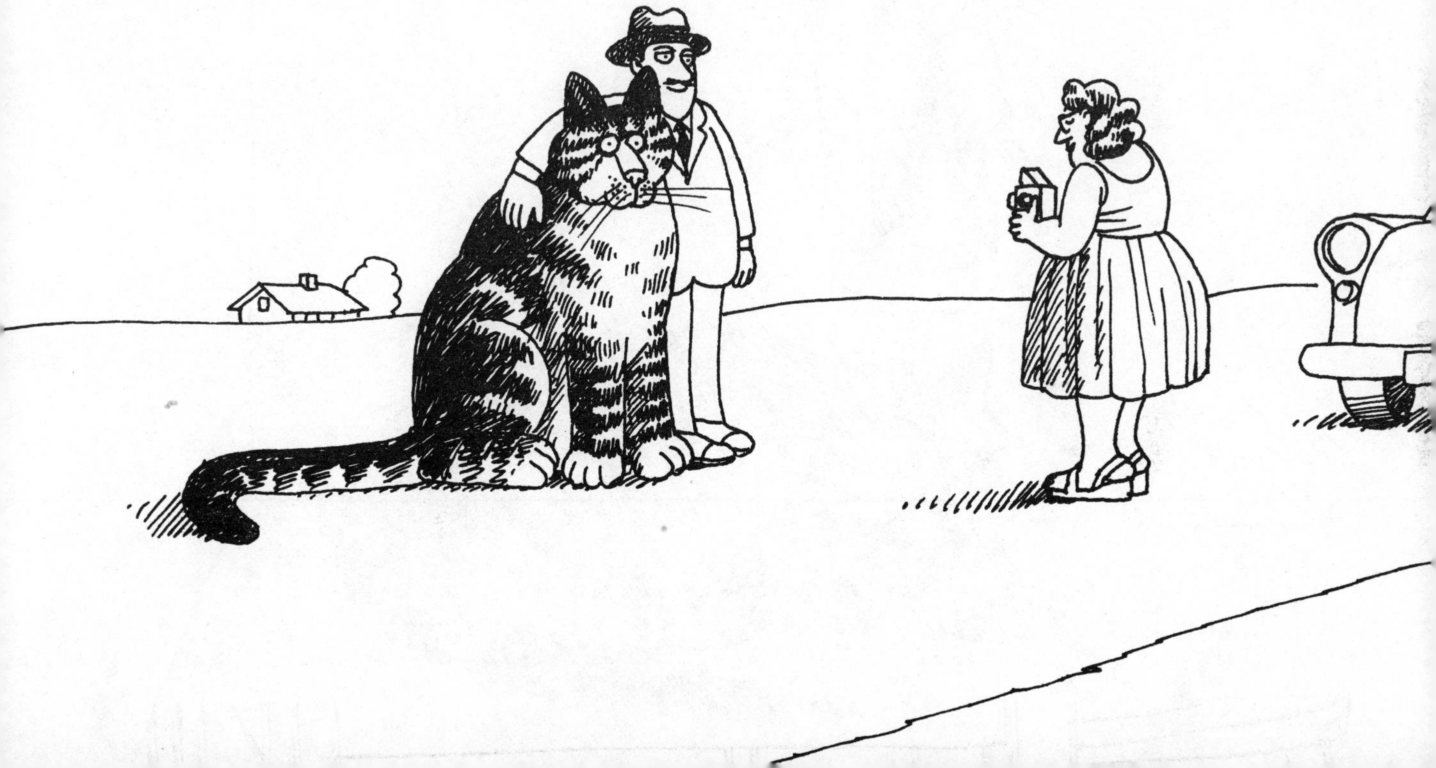

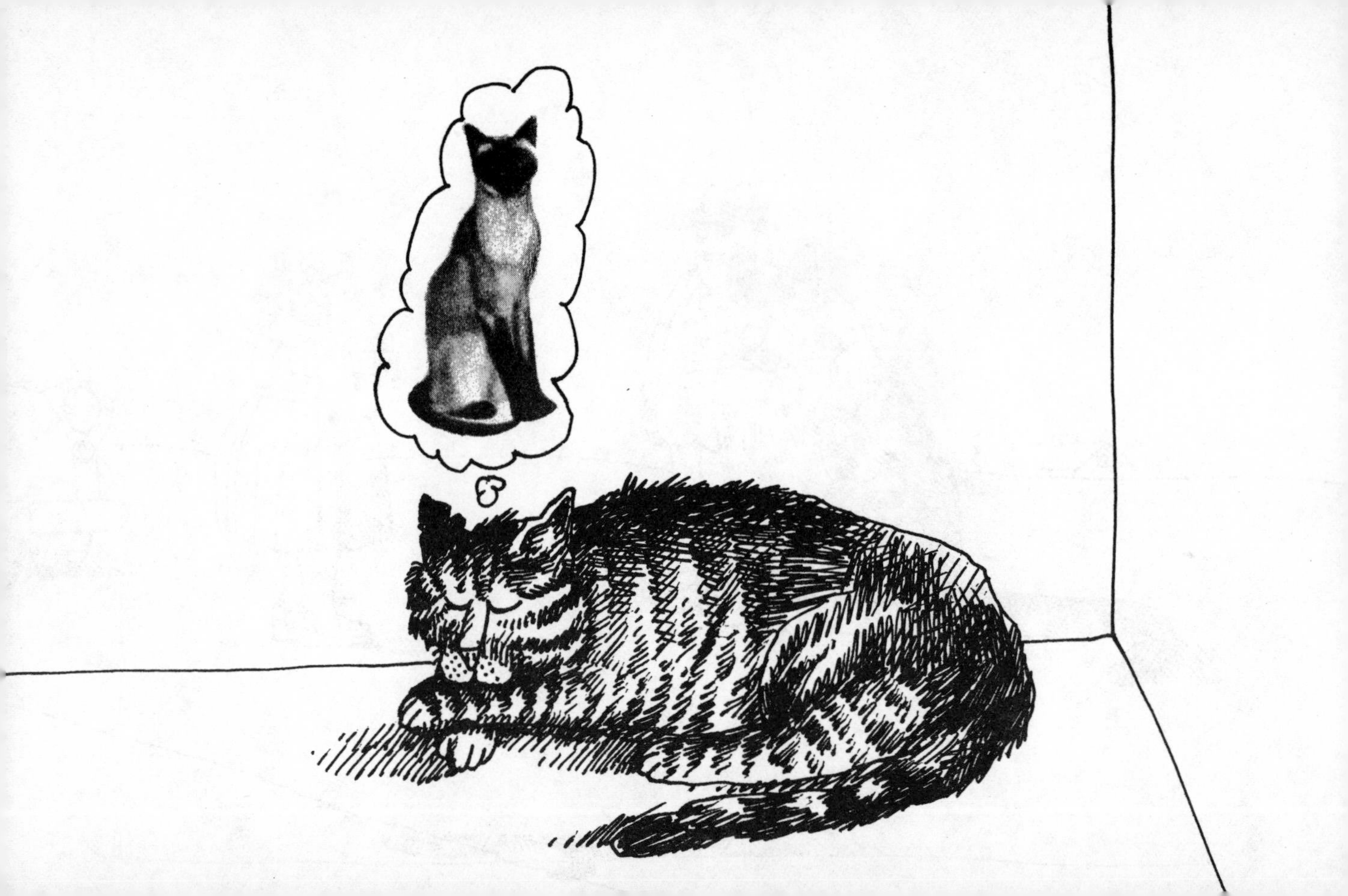

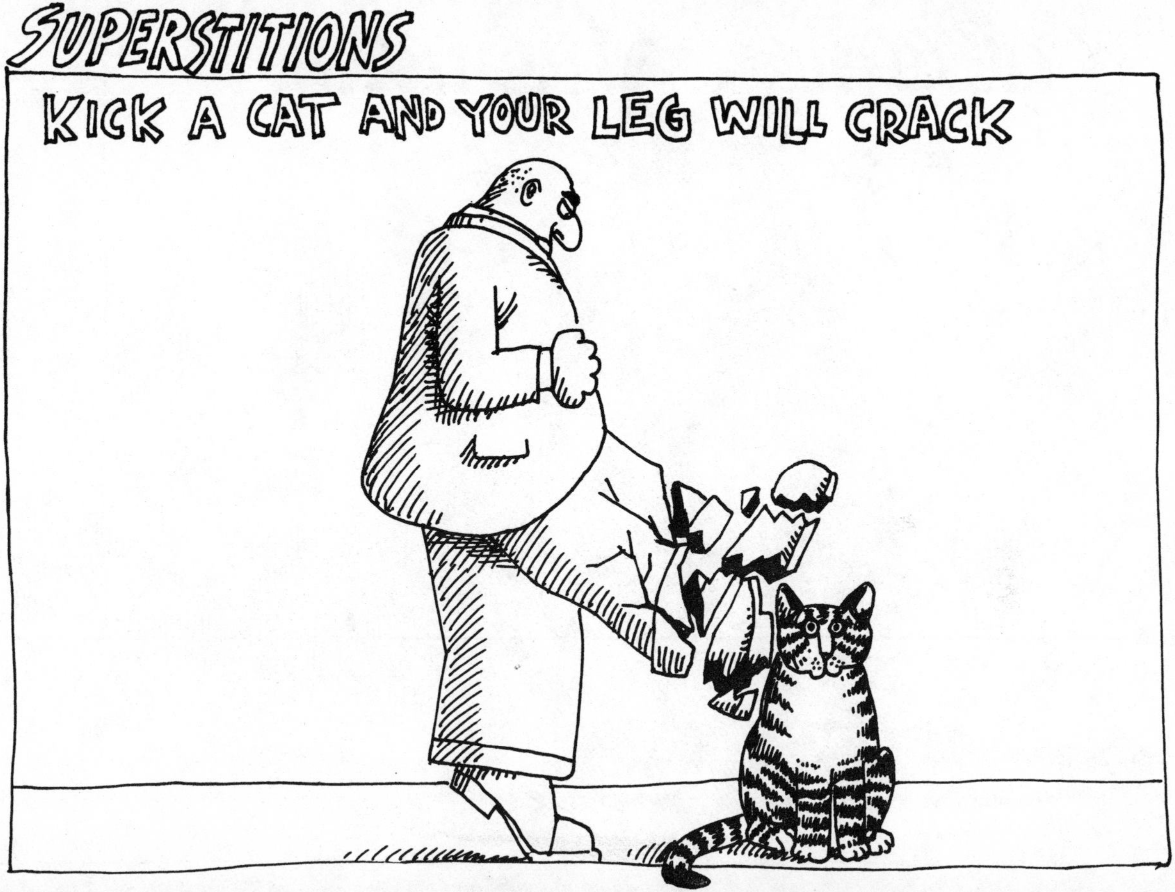
SUPERSTITIONS
KICK A CAT AND YOUR LEG WILL CRACK

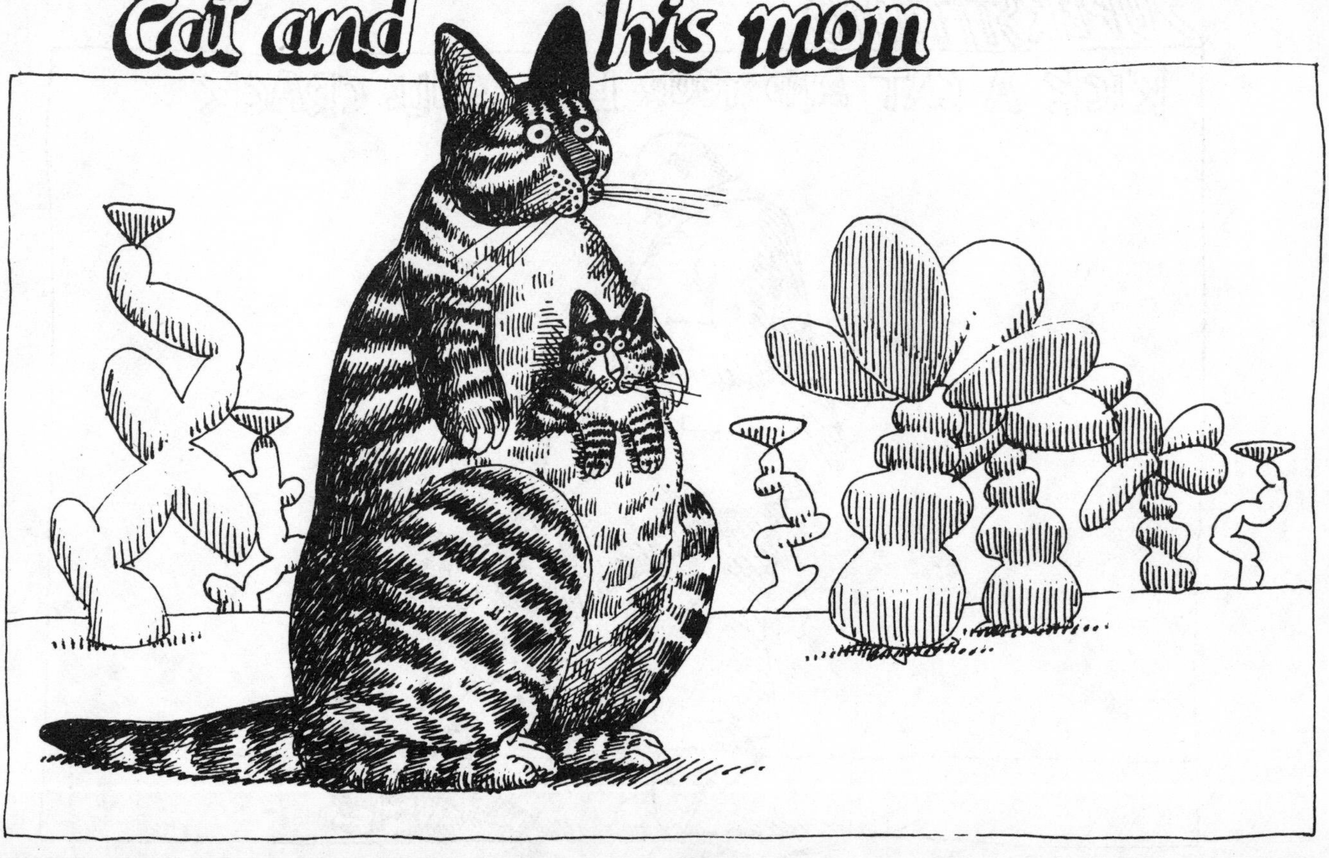
Cat and his mom

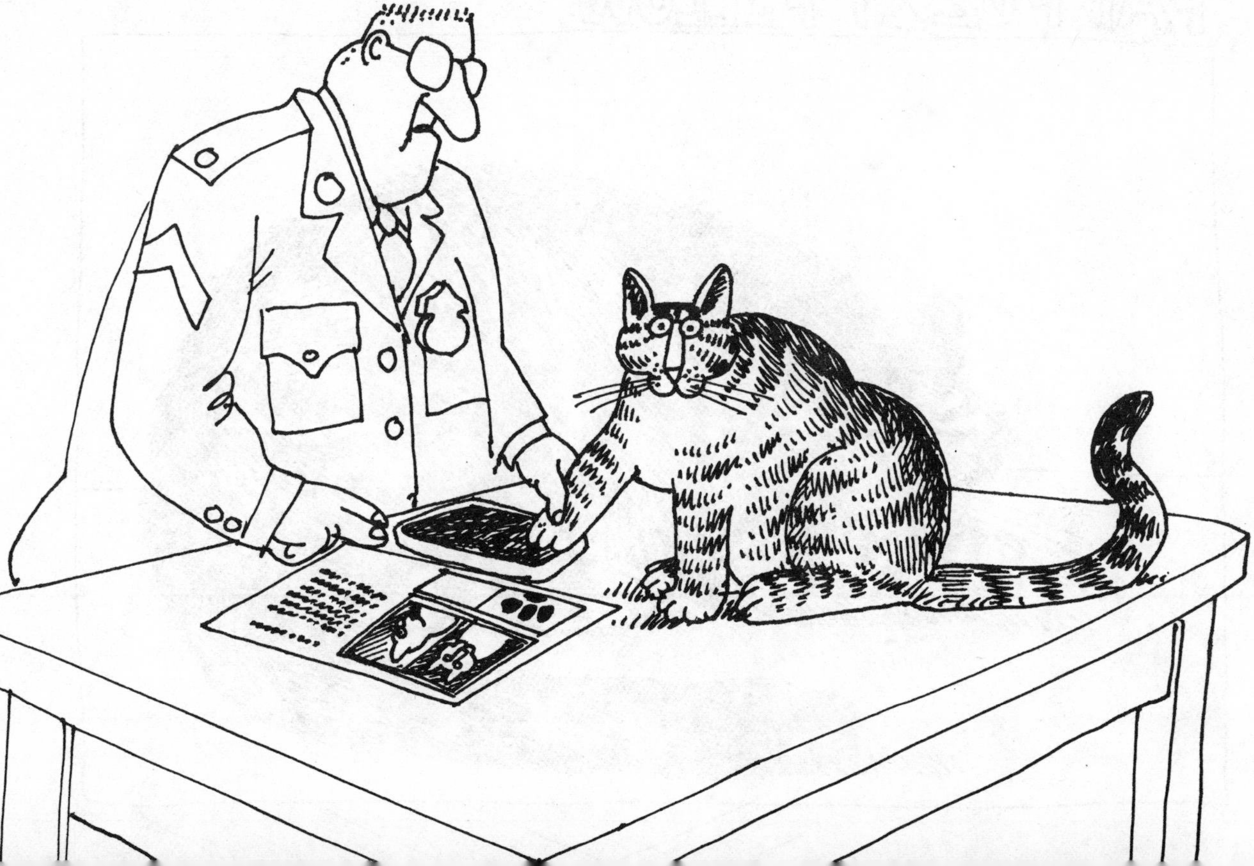

FAT FUZZY FELLOW

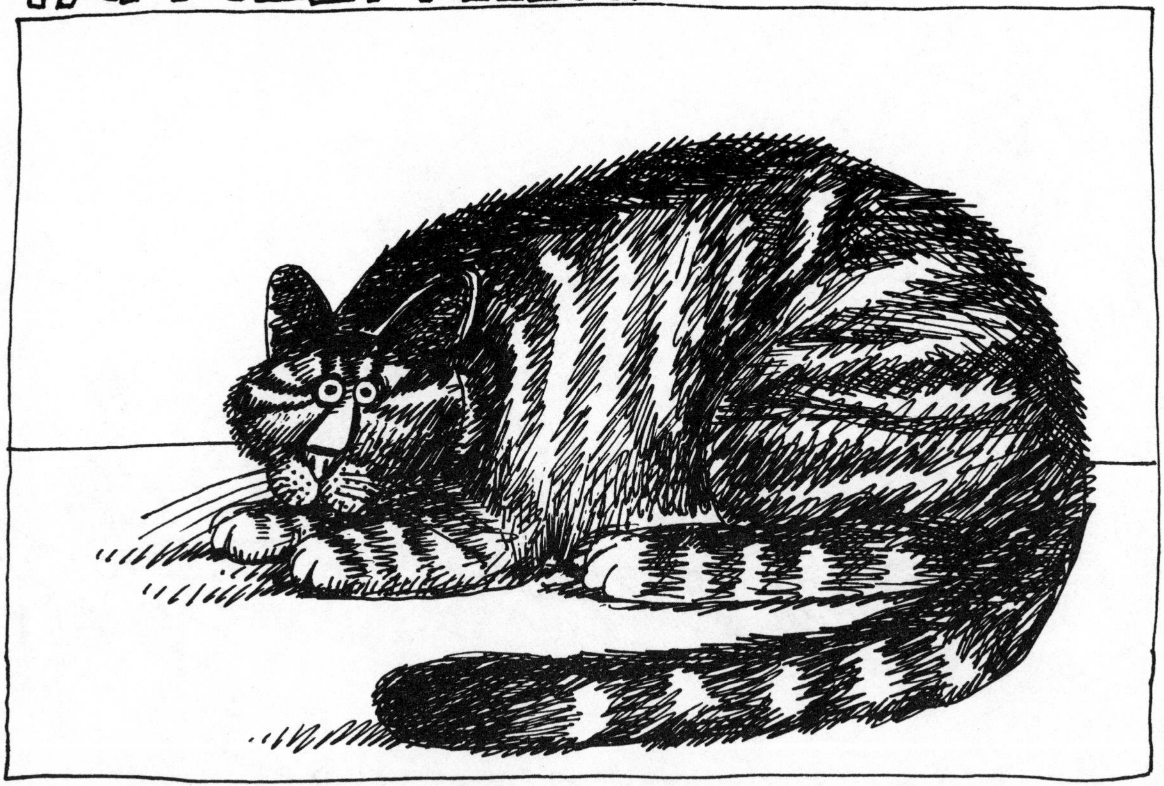

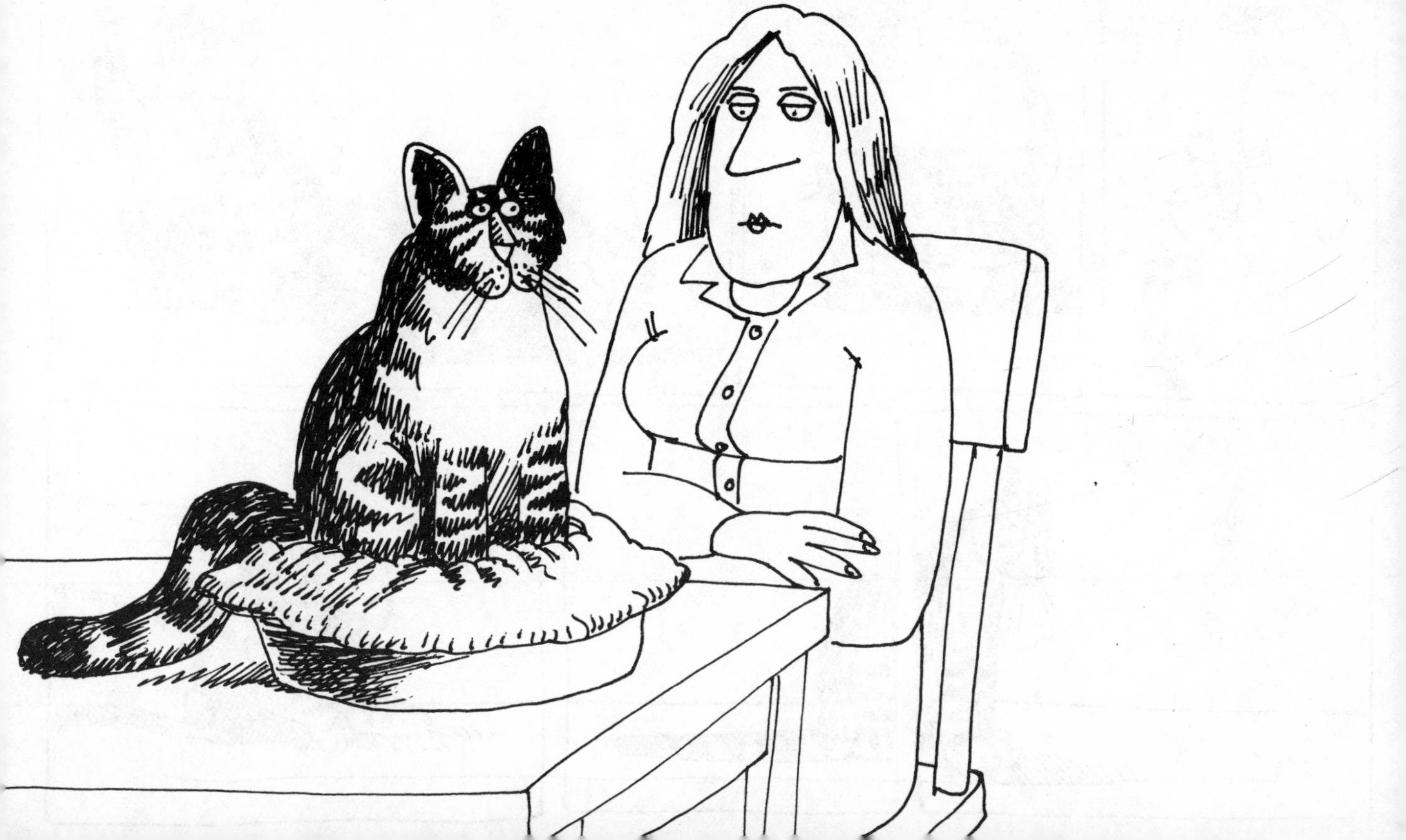

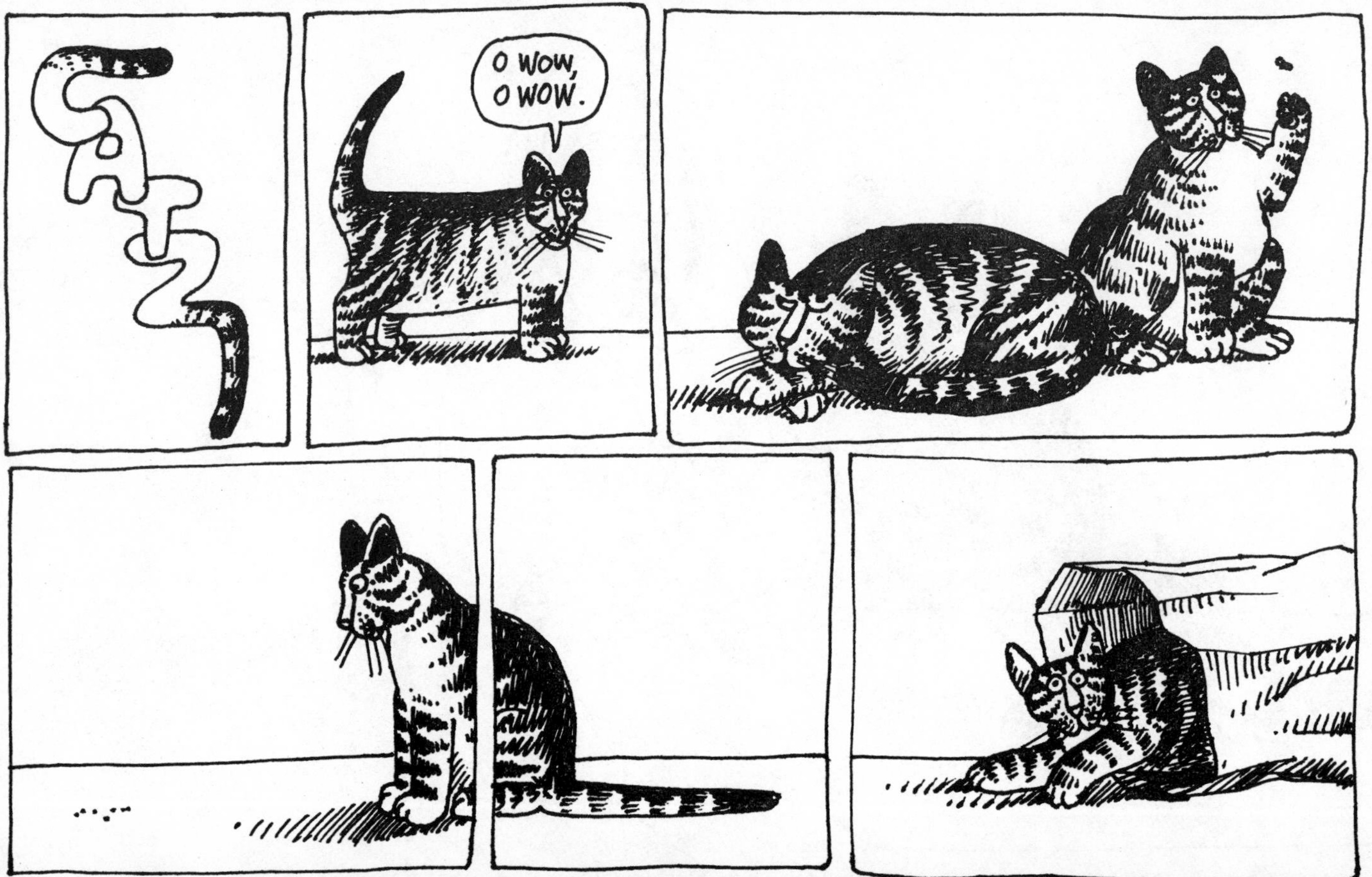
CATZ
O WOW,
O WOW.

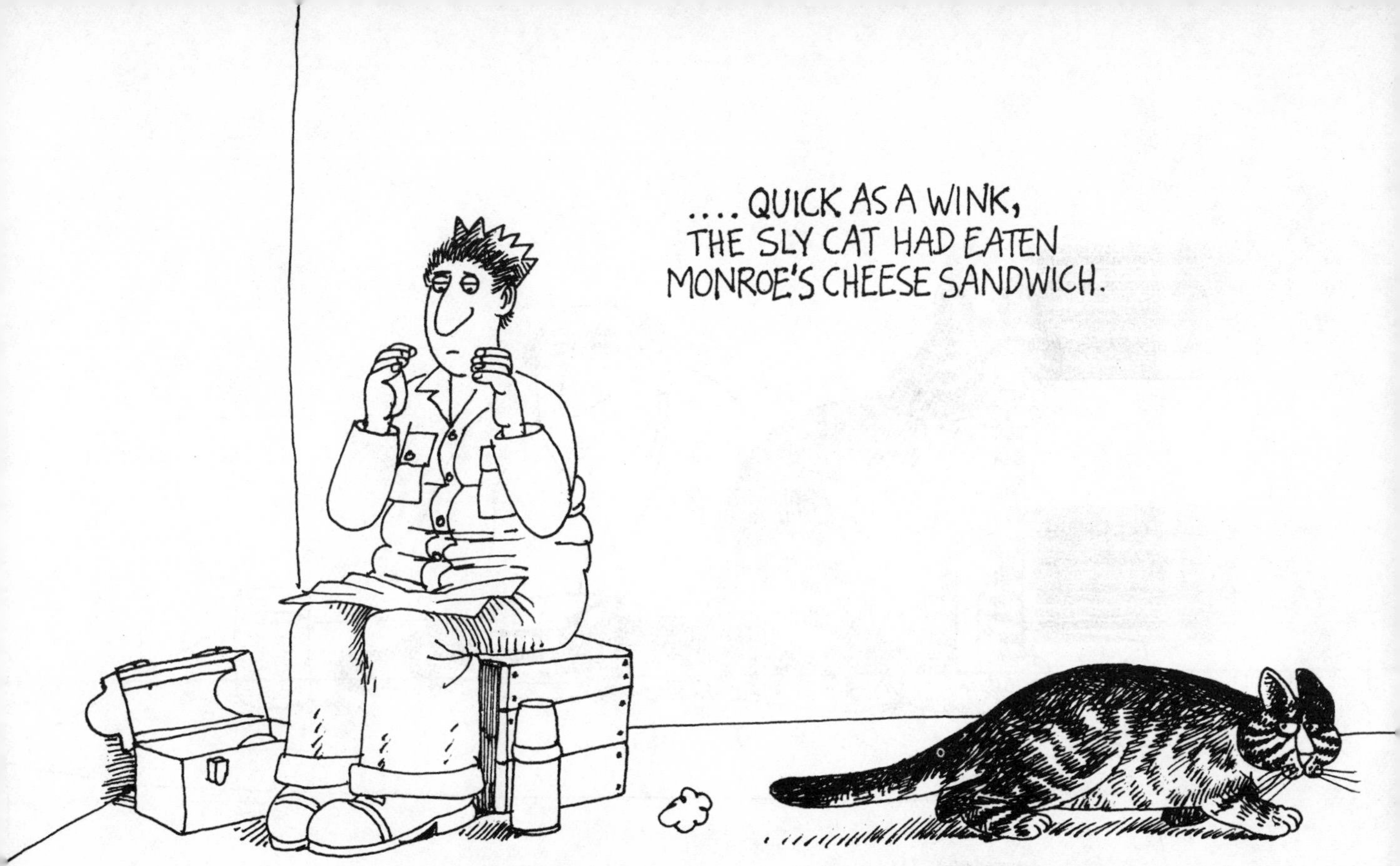
....QUICK AS A WINK,
THE SLY CAT HAD EATEN
MONROE'S CHEESE SANDWICH.

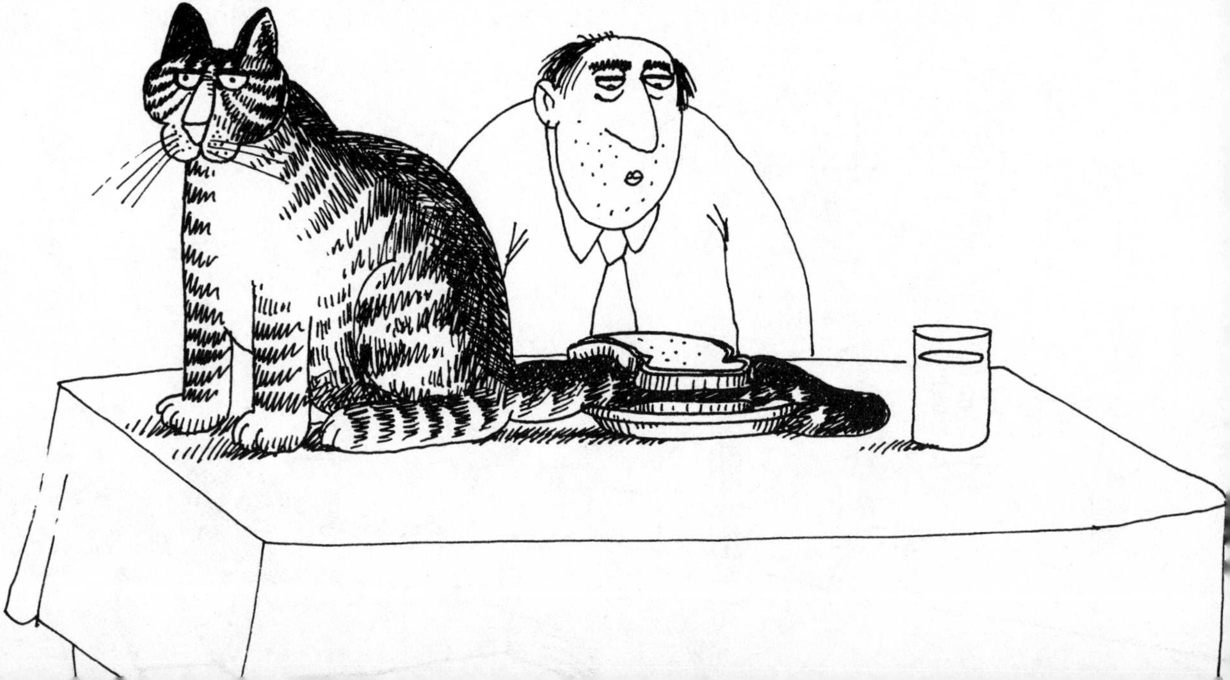

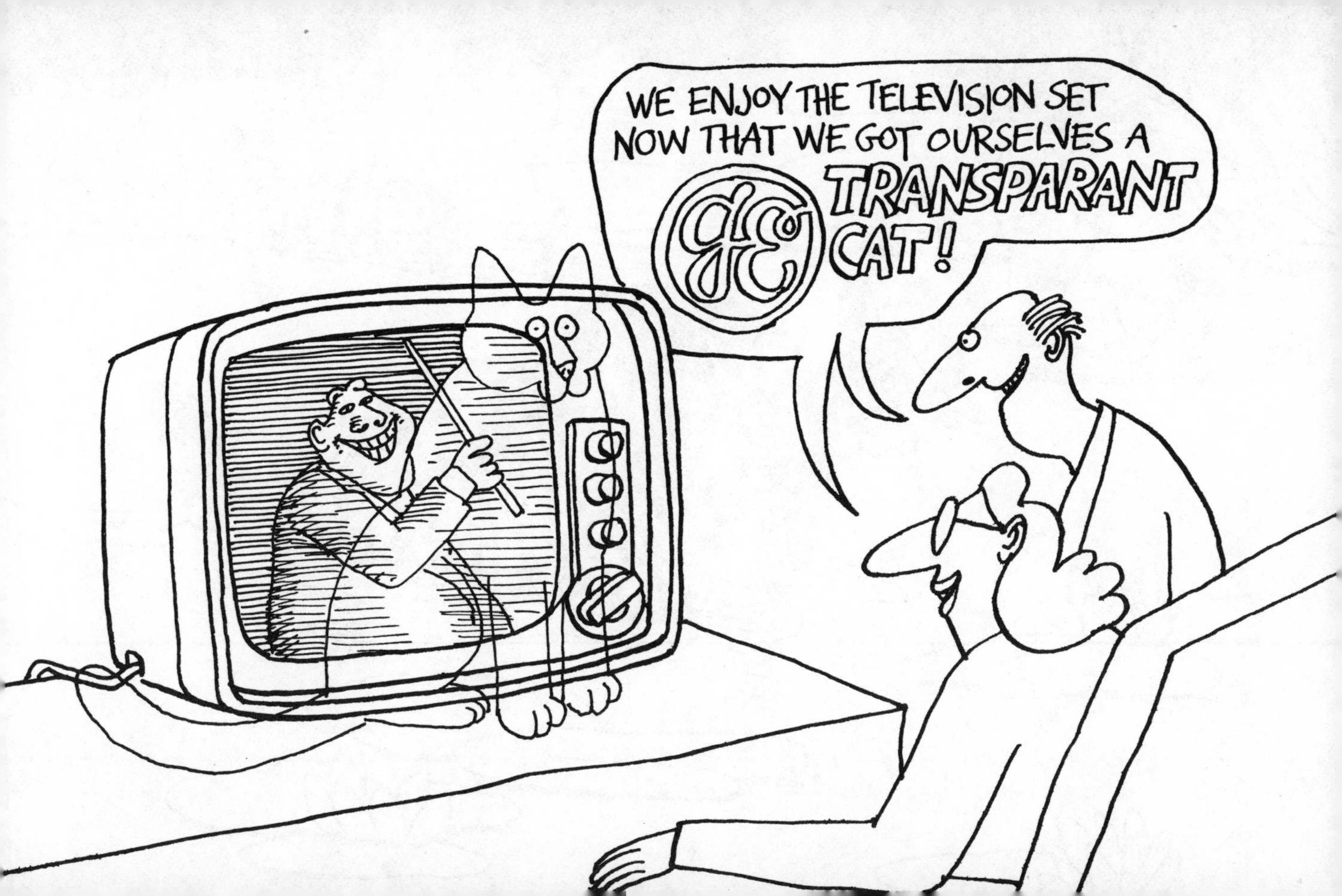
WE ENJOY THE TELEVISION SET NOW THAT WE GOT OURSELVES A TRANSPARANT CAT!

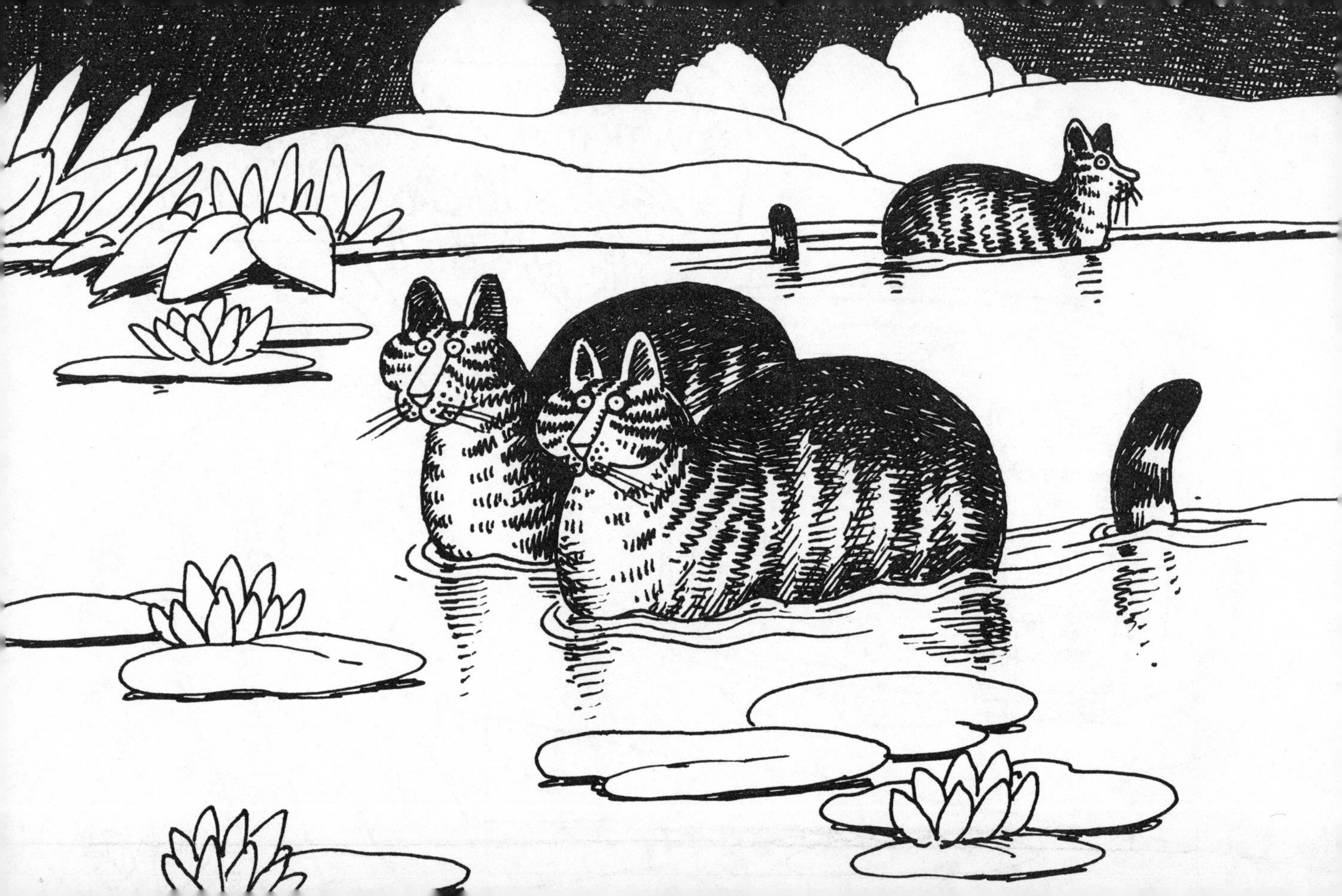

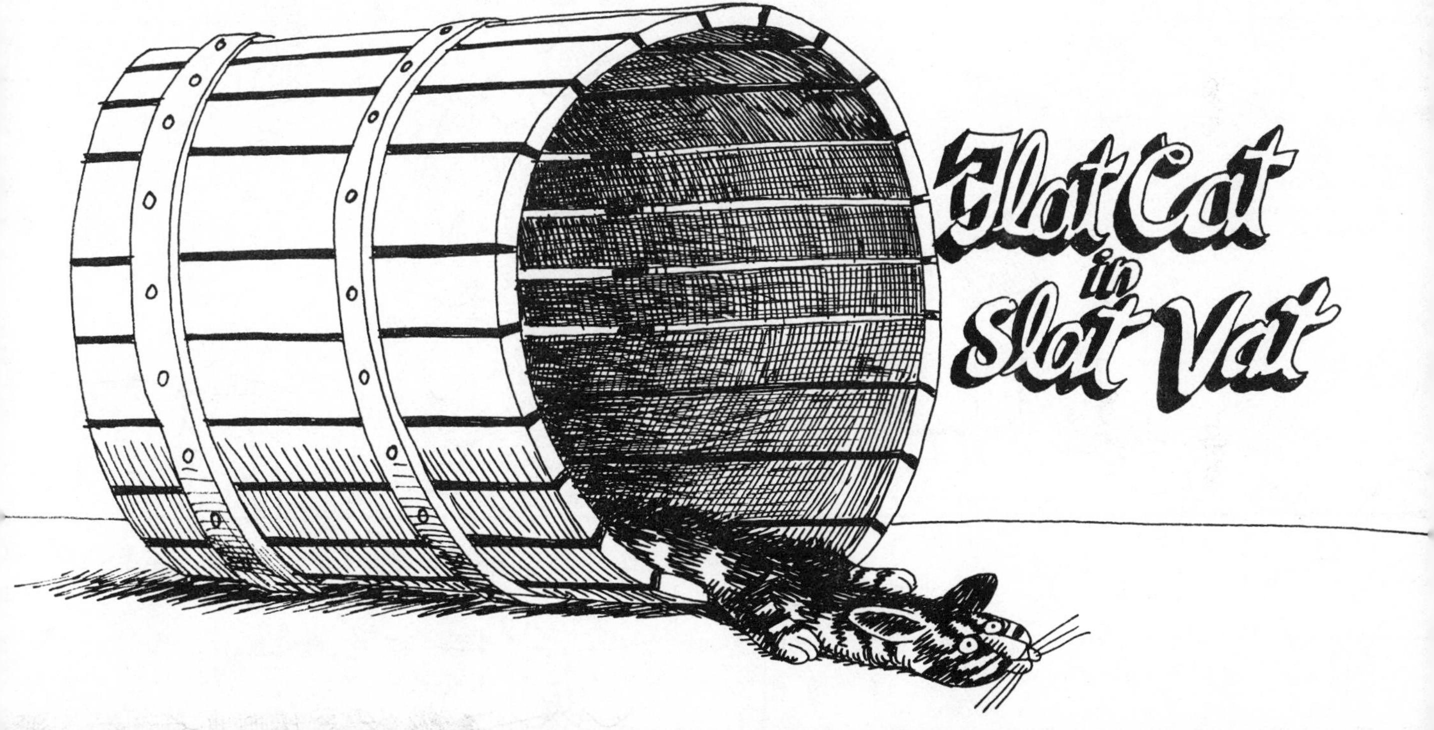
Flat Cat
in
Slat Vat

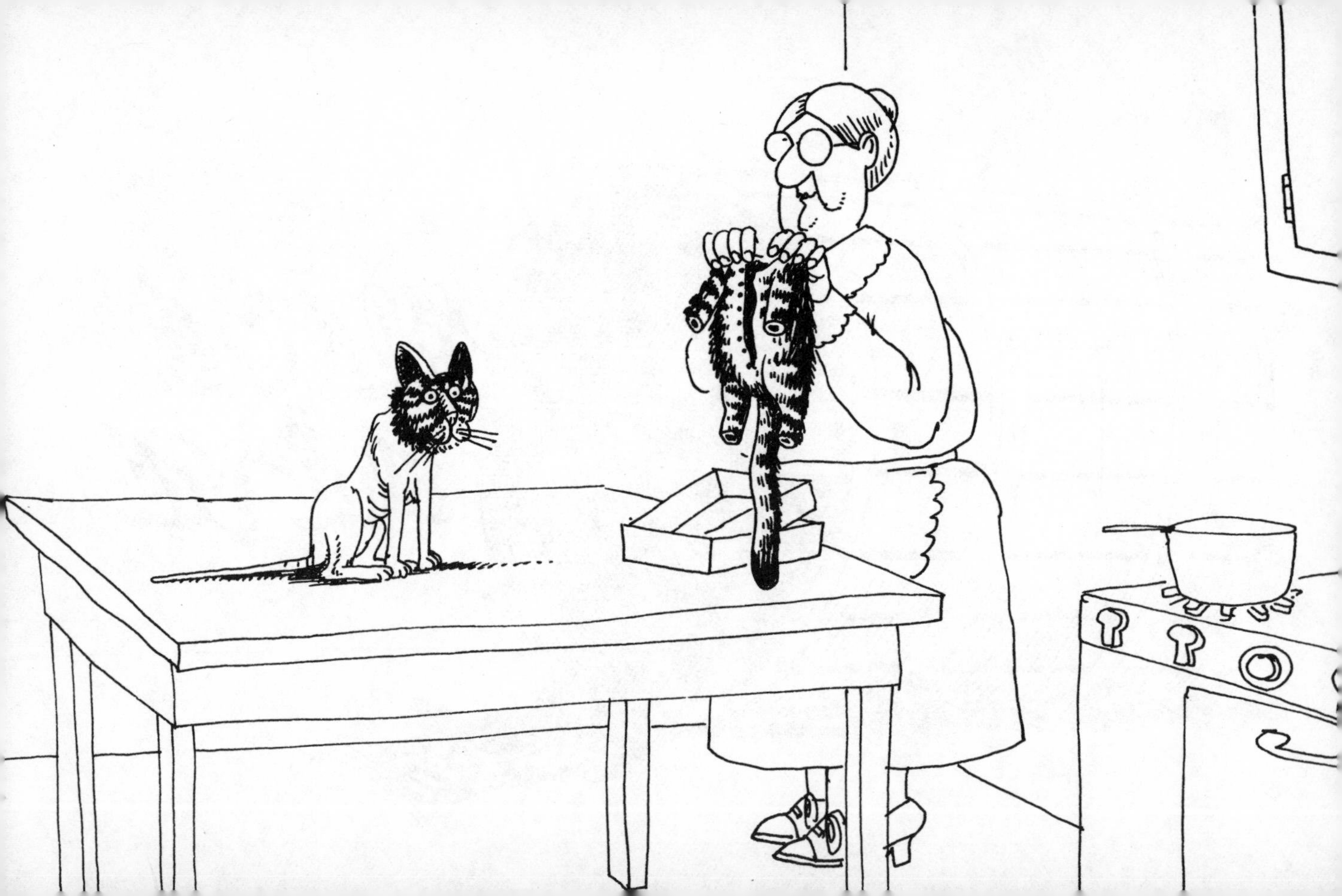

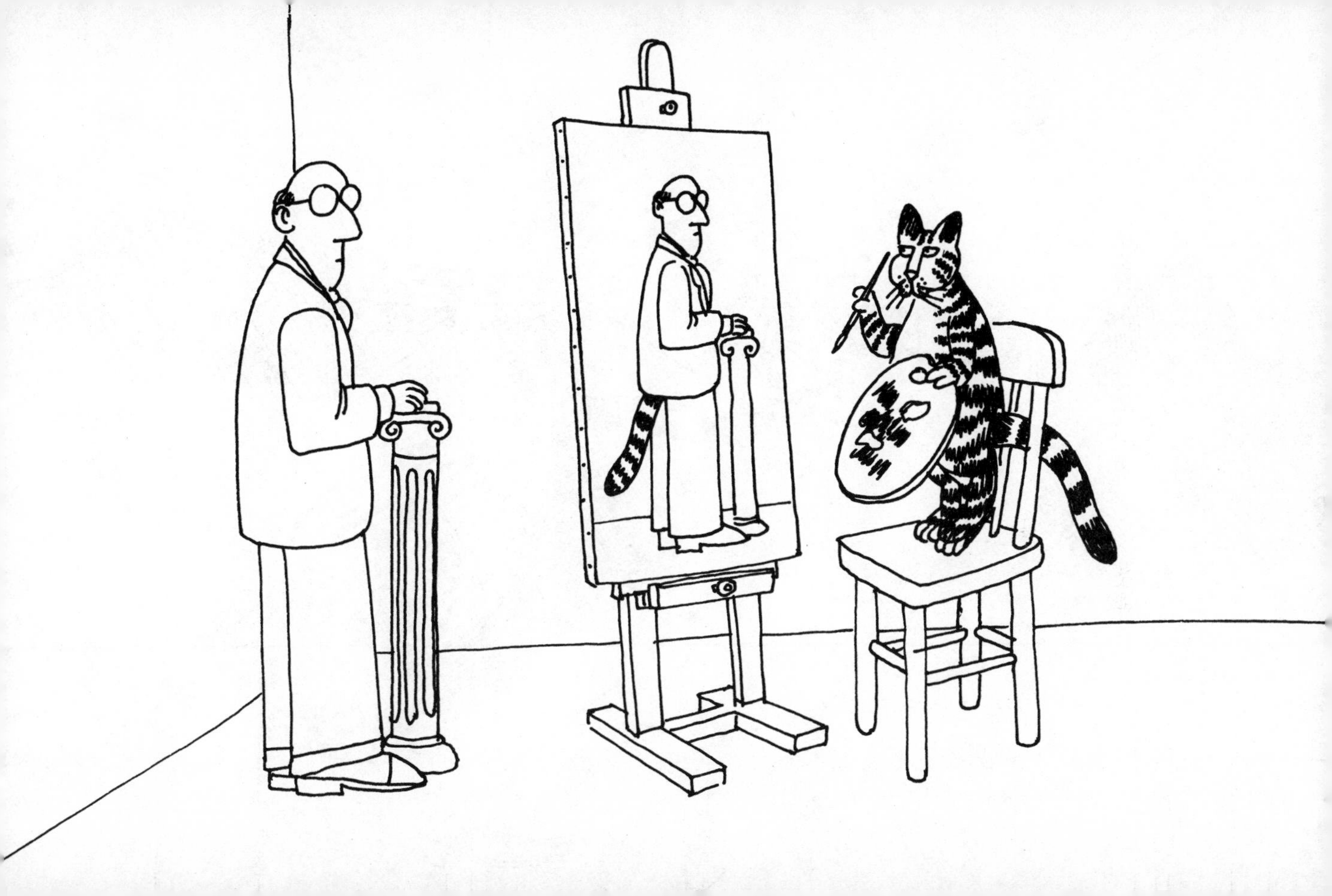

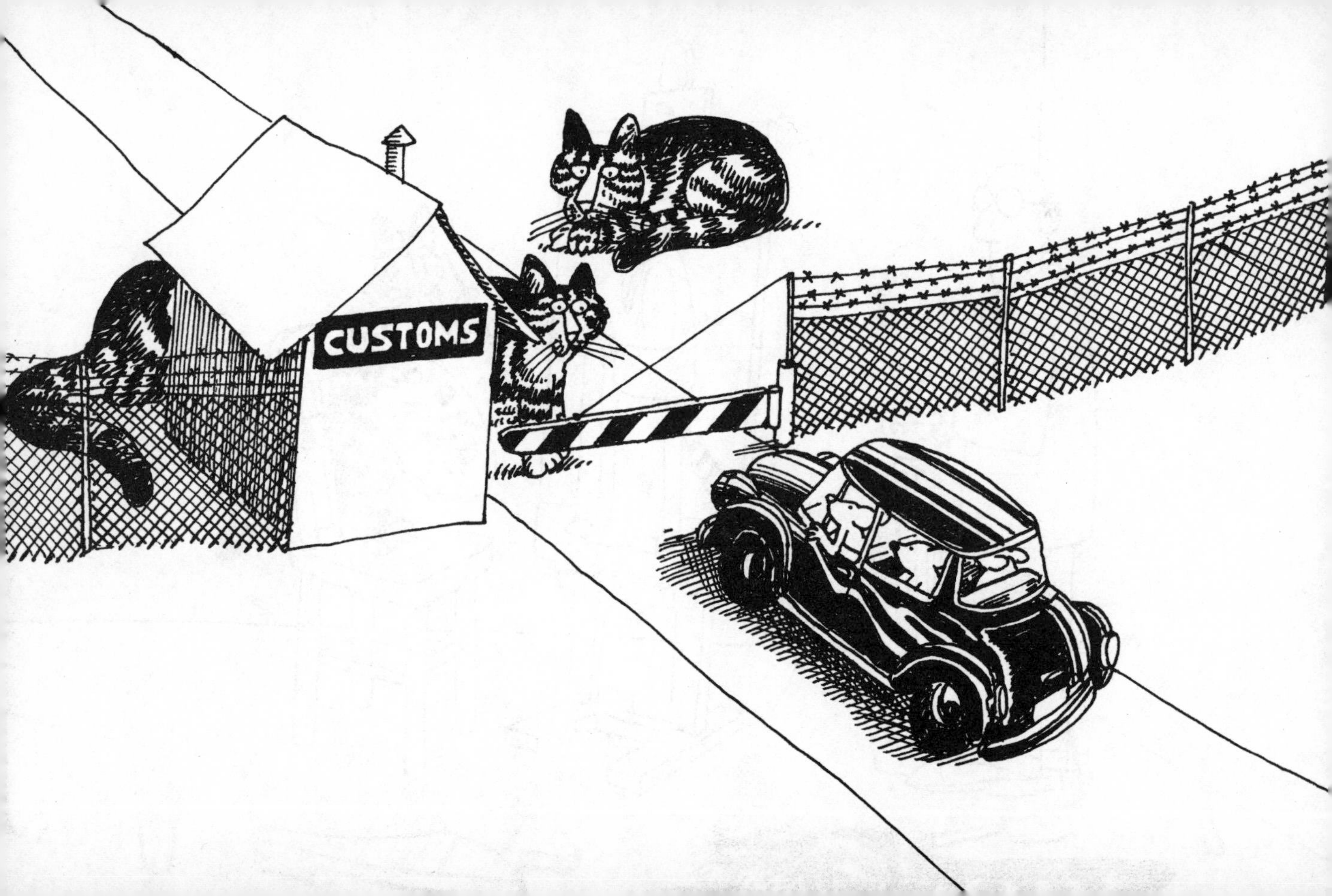
CUSTOMS

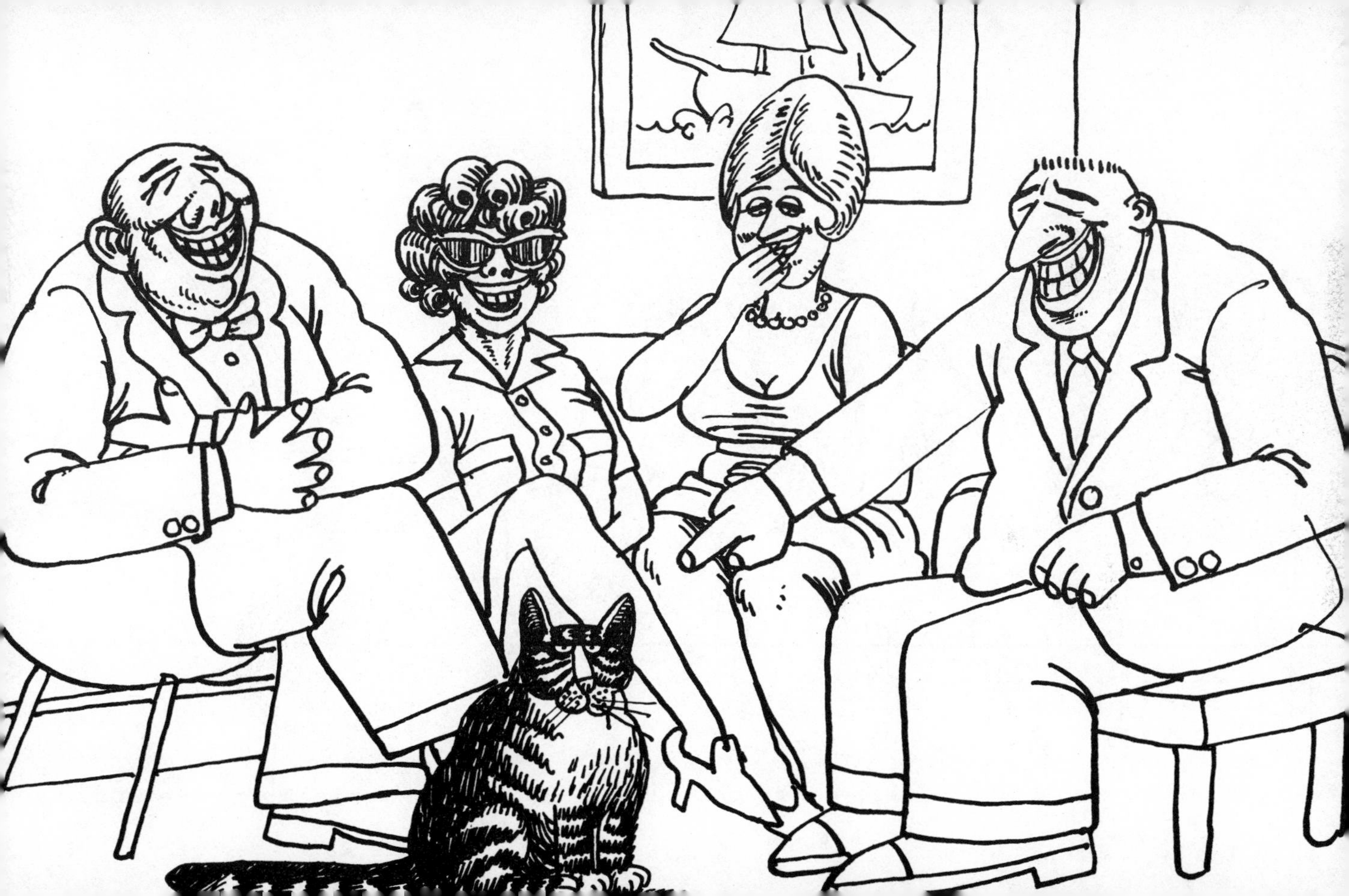

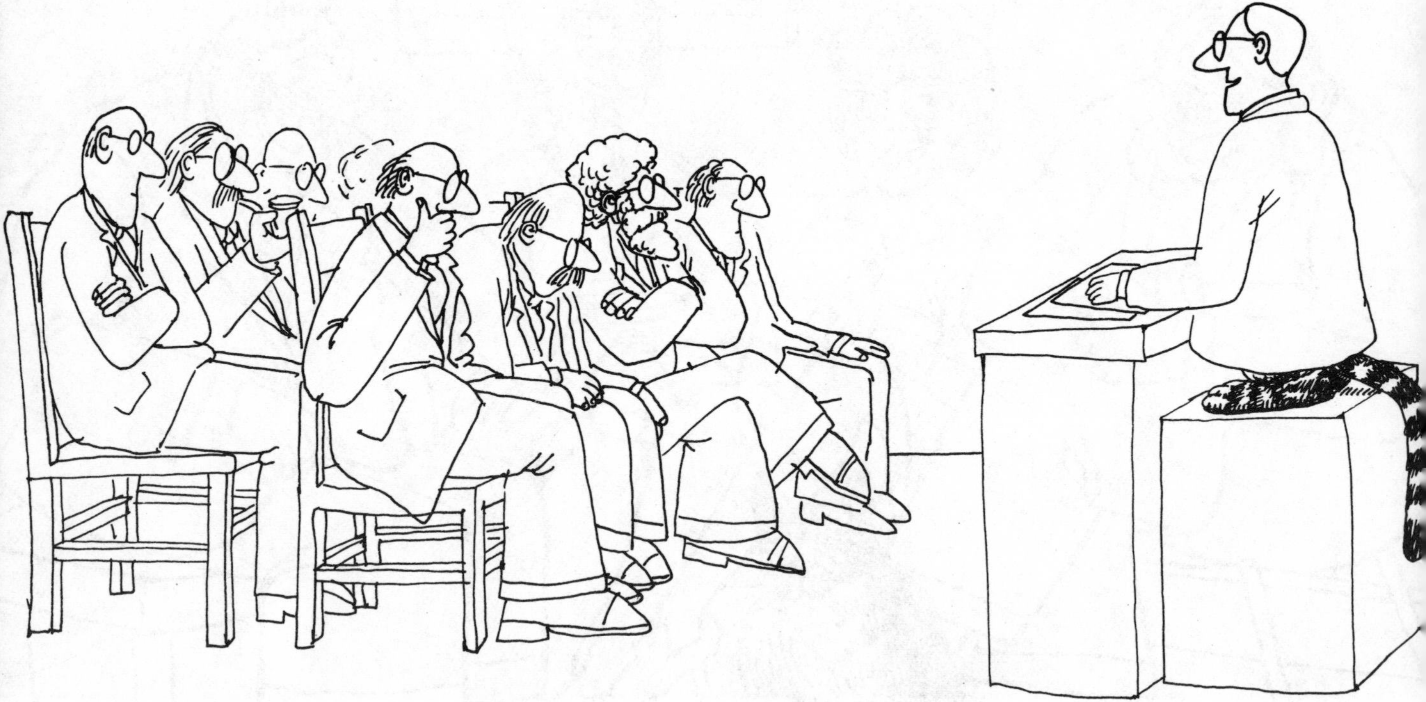

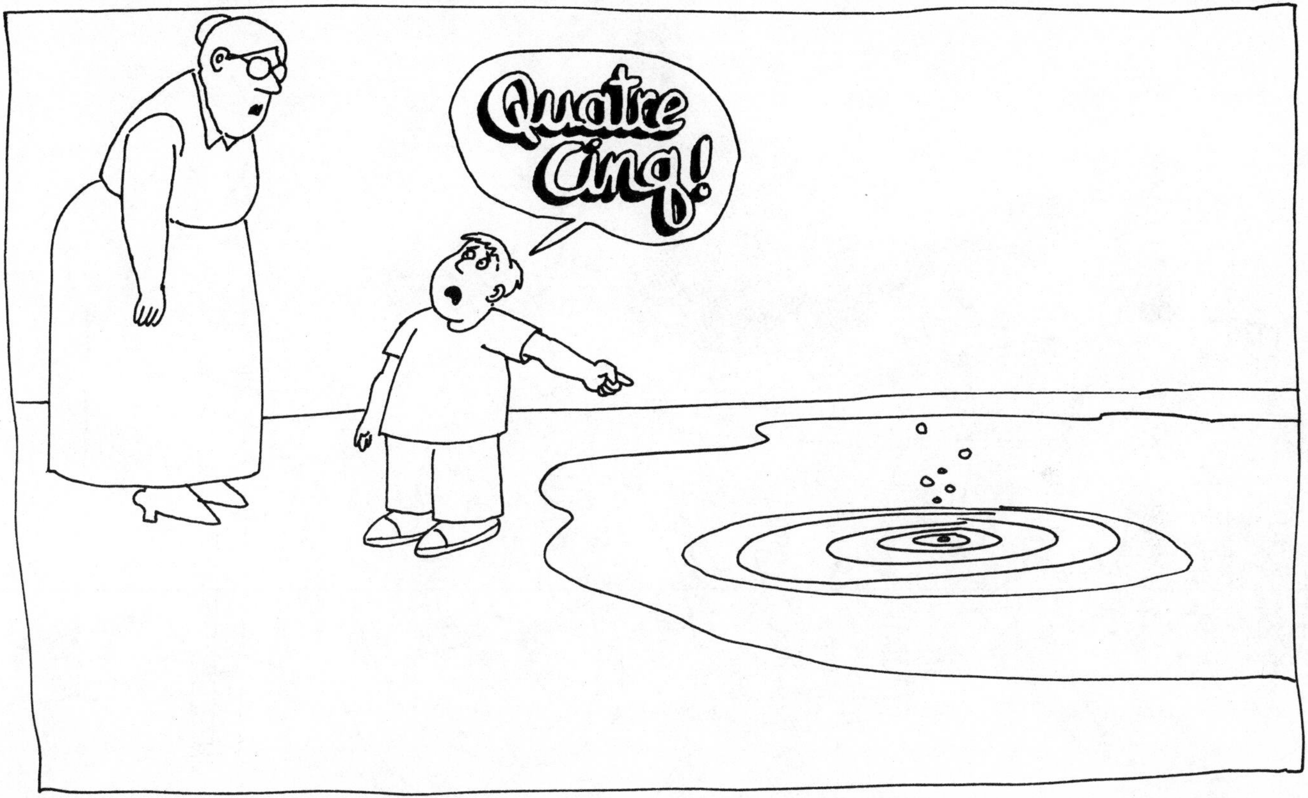
Quatre Cinq!

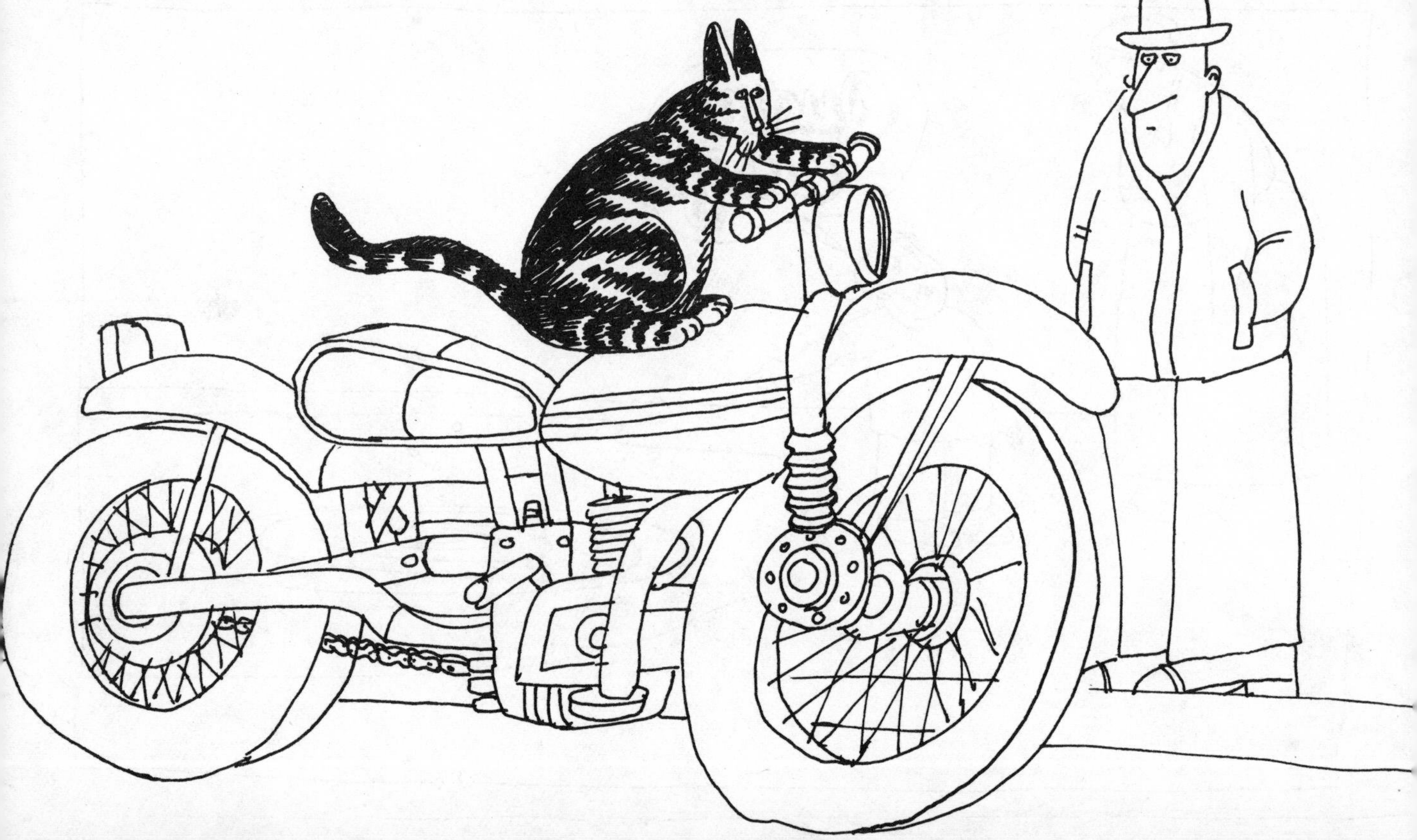

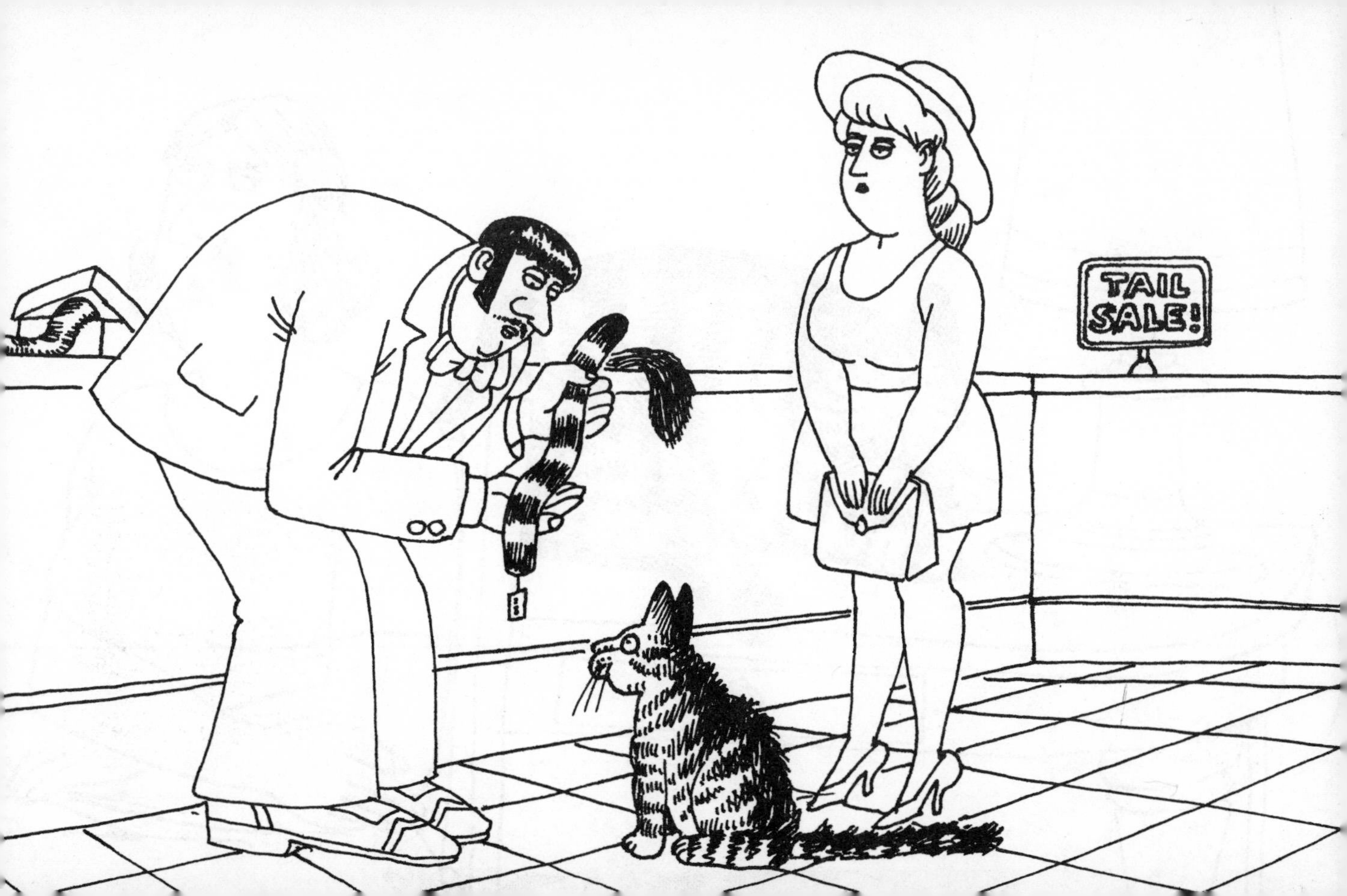
TAIL
SALE!

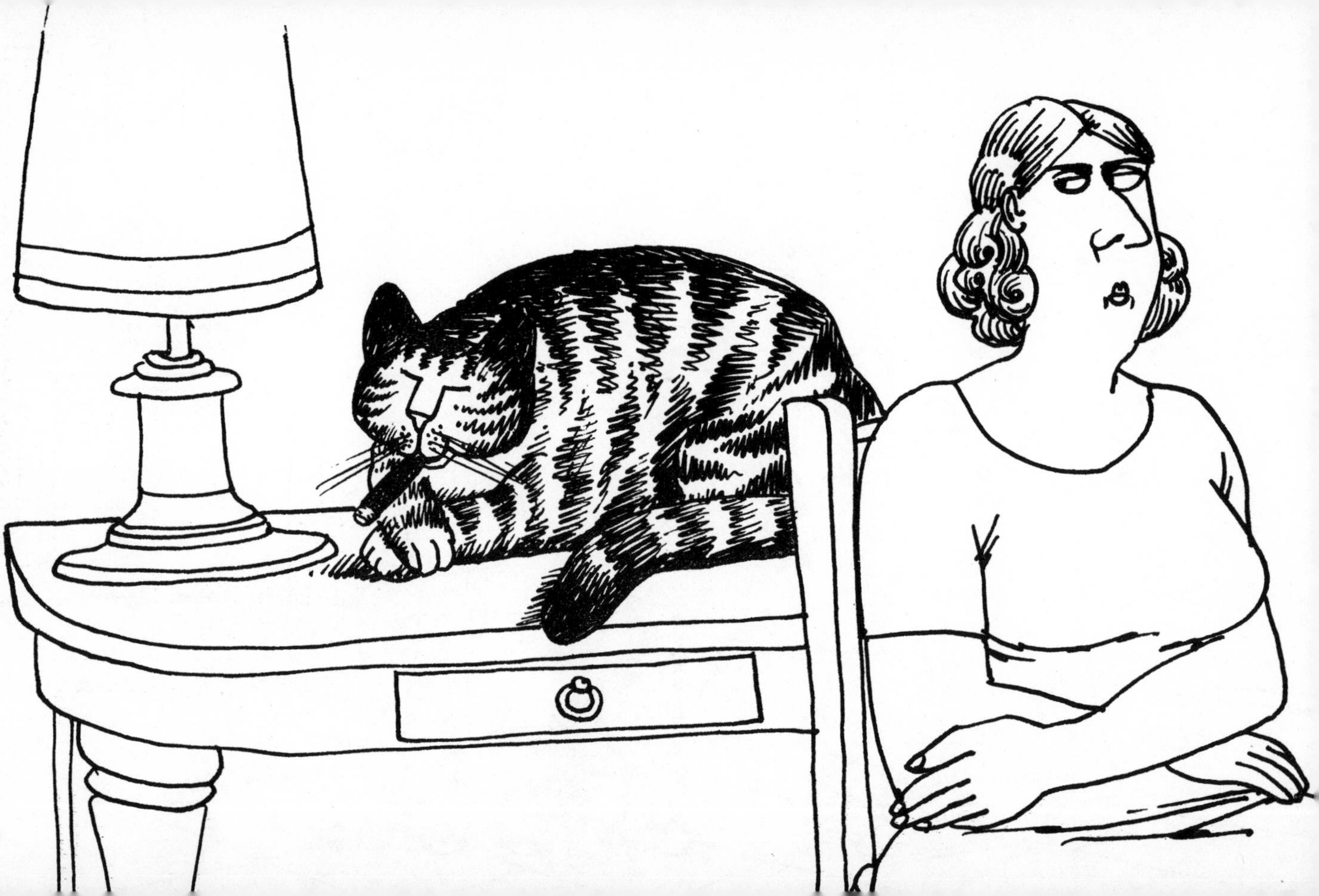

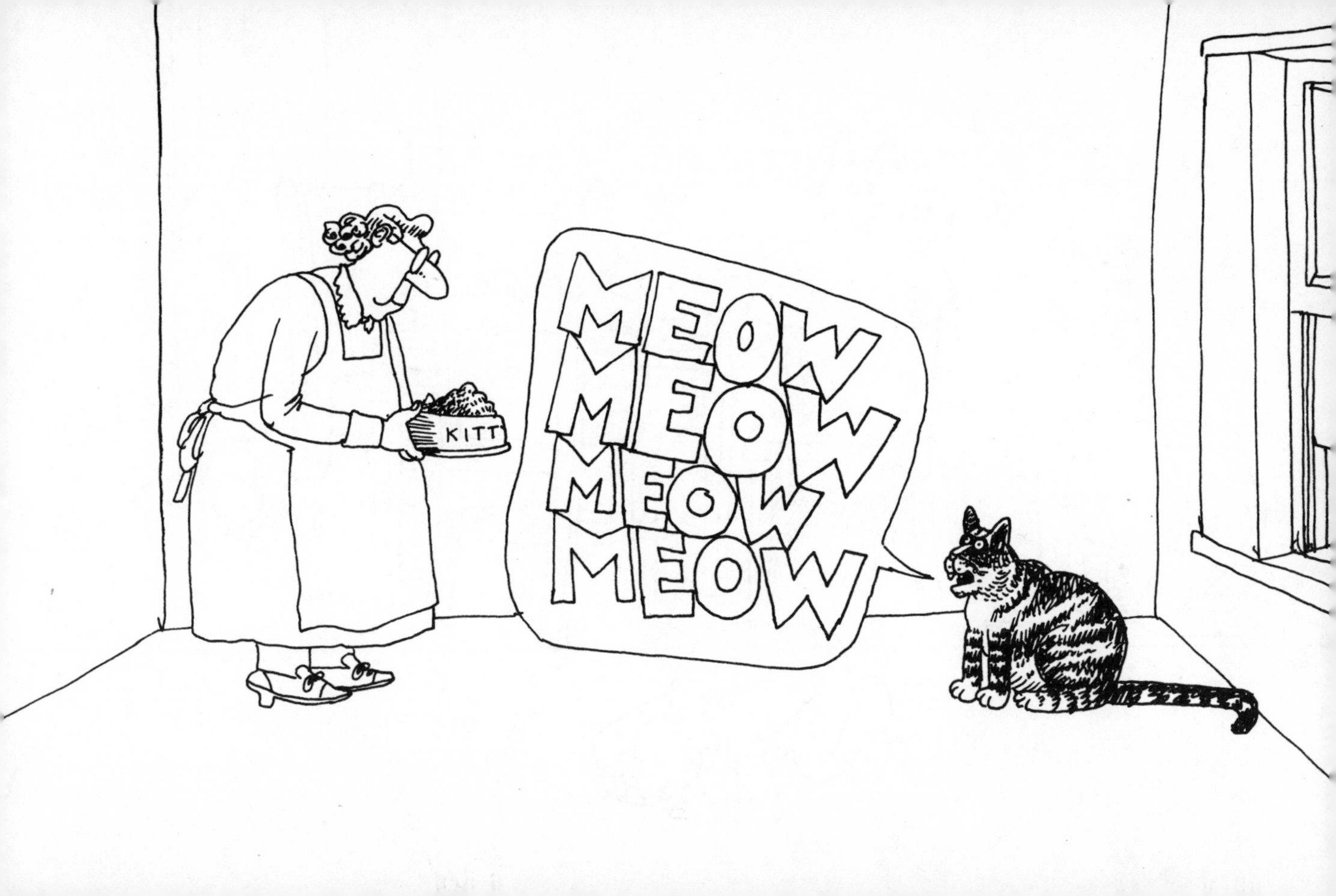
KITT
MEOW MEOW MEOW MEOW

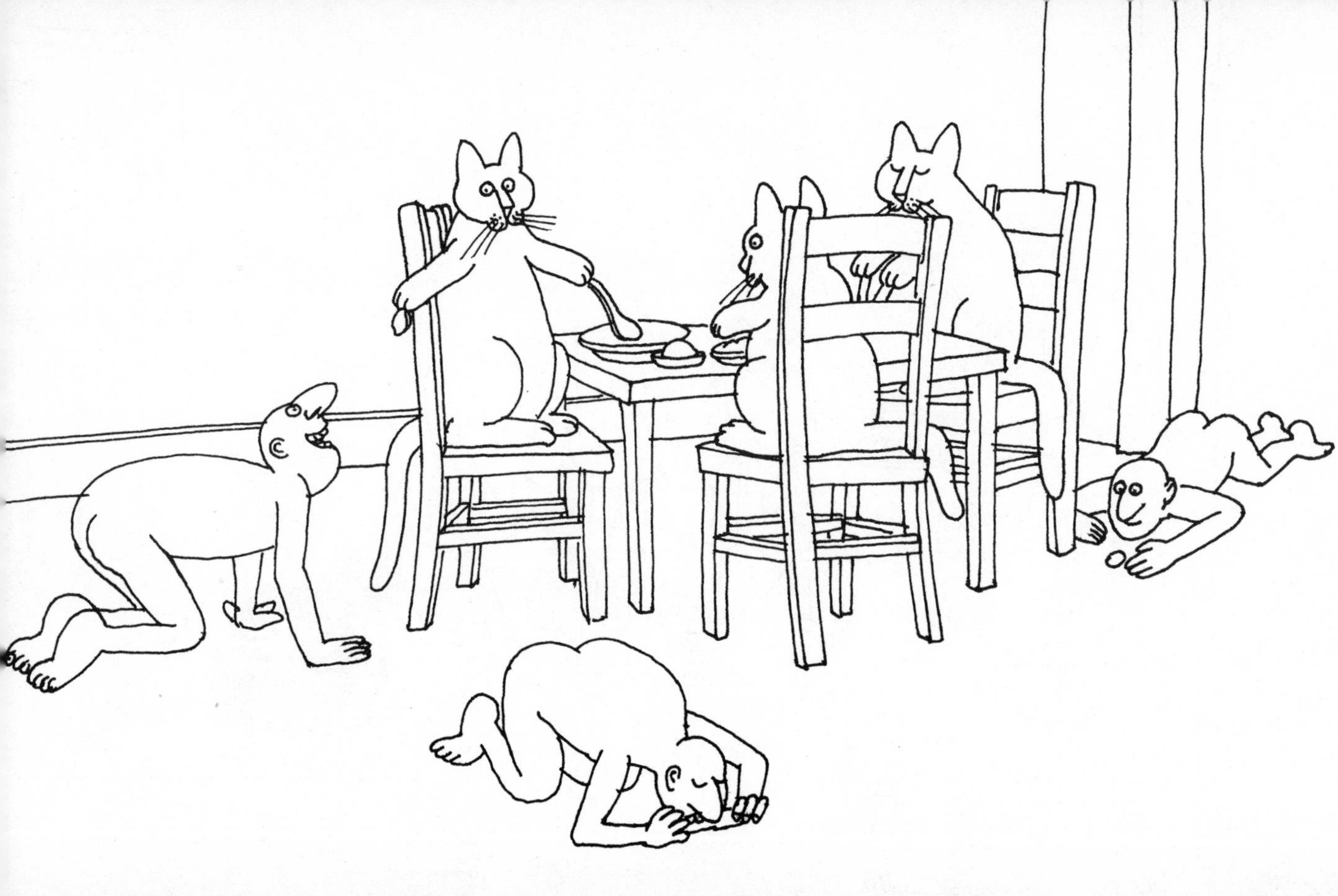

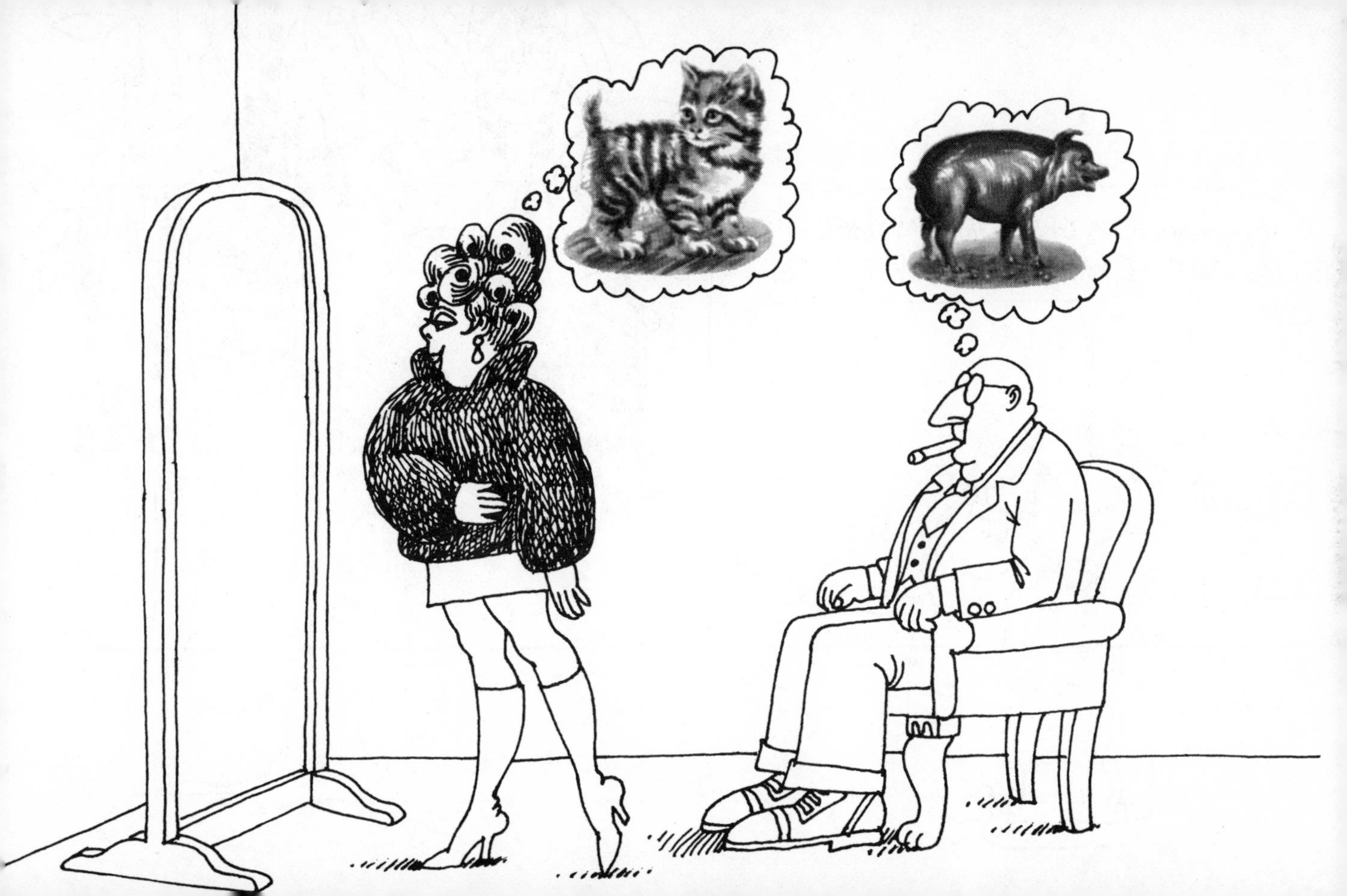

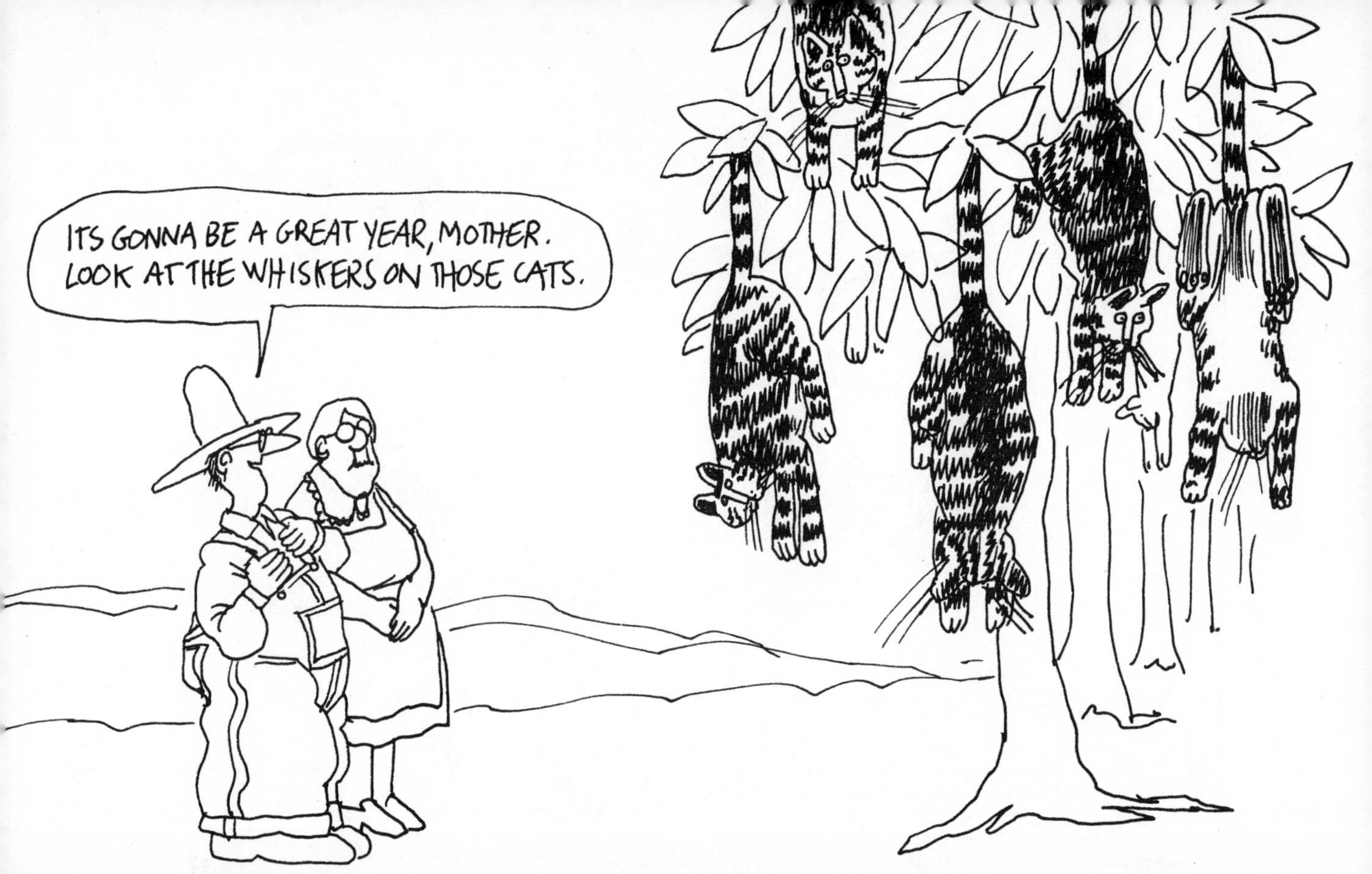
ITS GONNA BE A GREAT YEAR, MOTHER.
LOOK AT THE WHISKERS ON THOSE CATS.

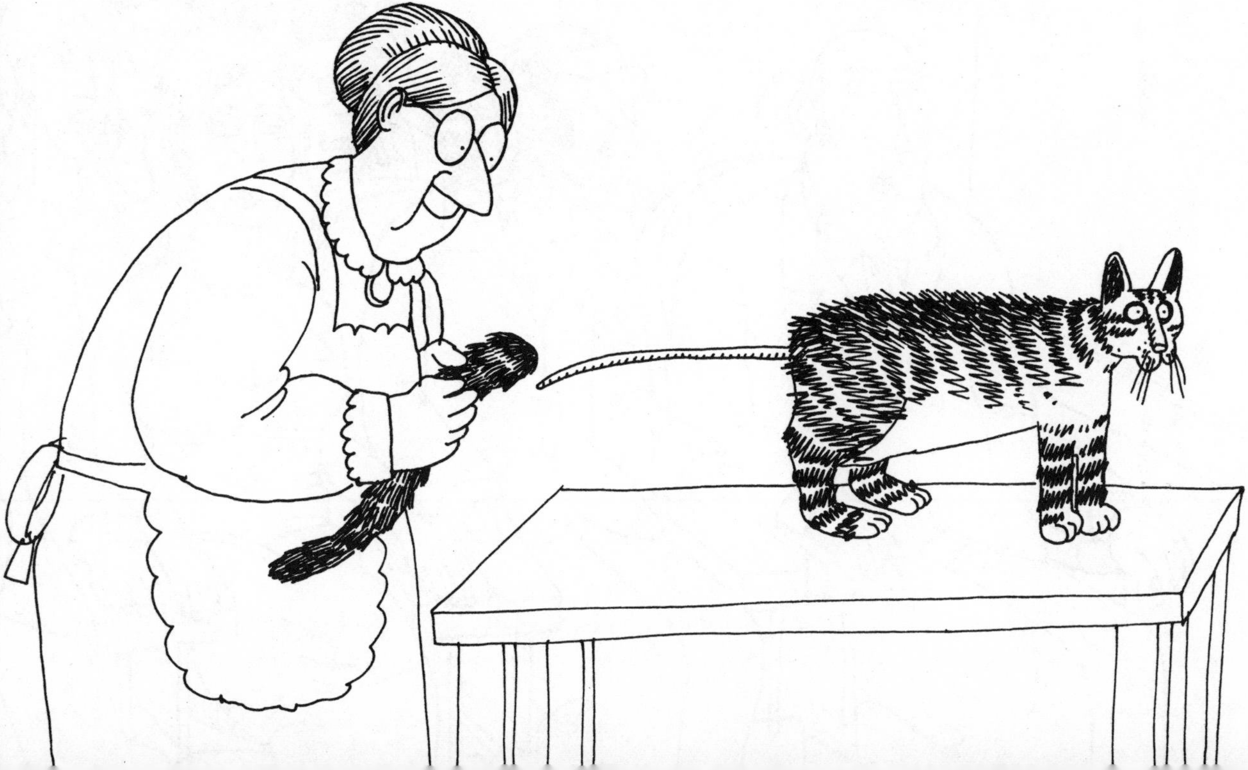

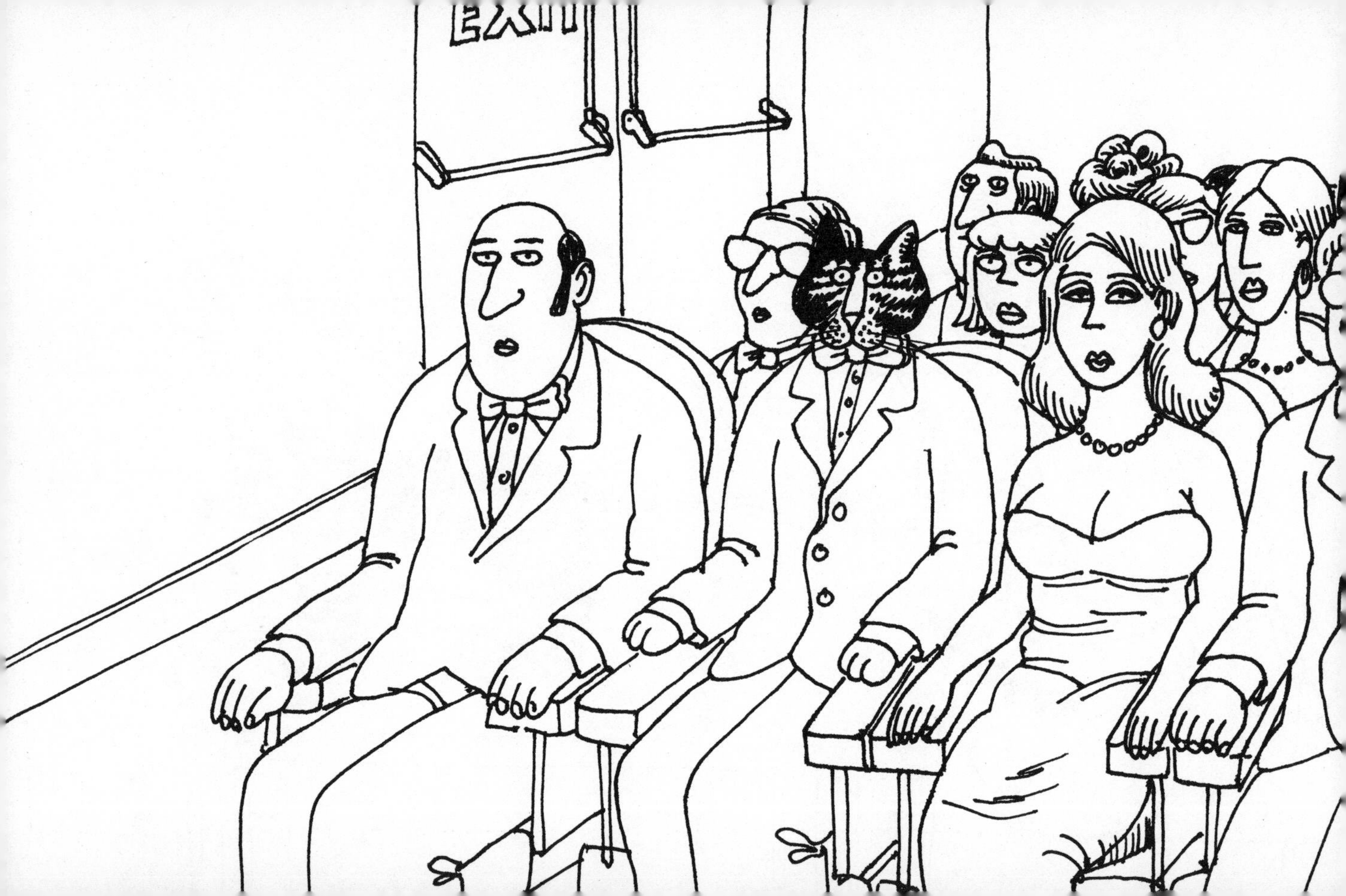
EXIT

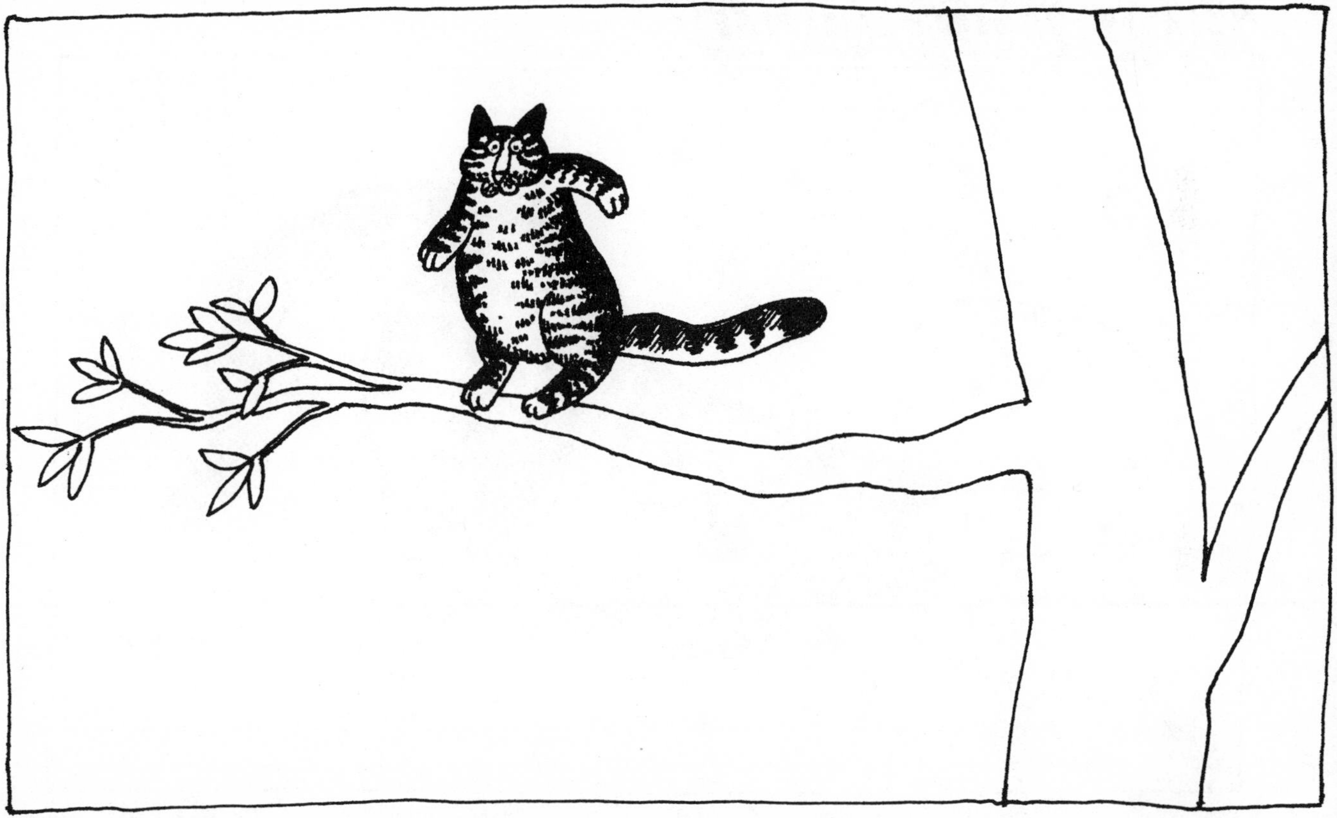

How they do it

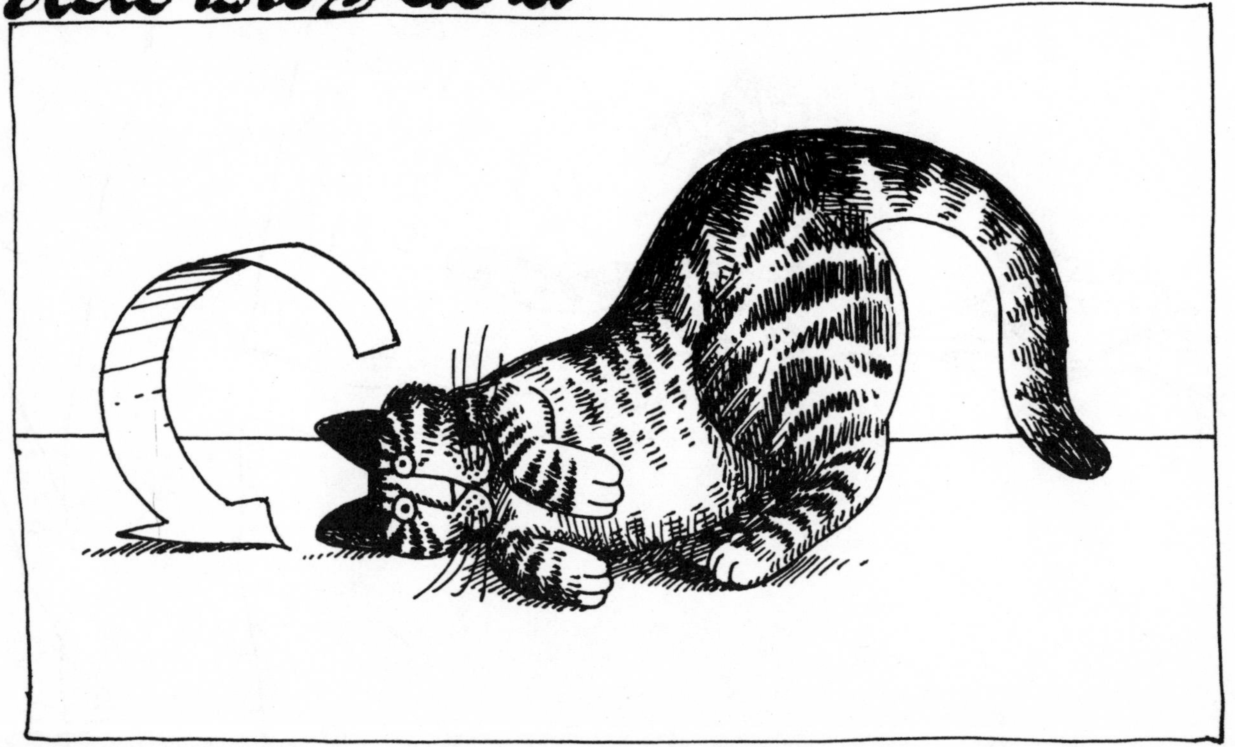

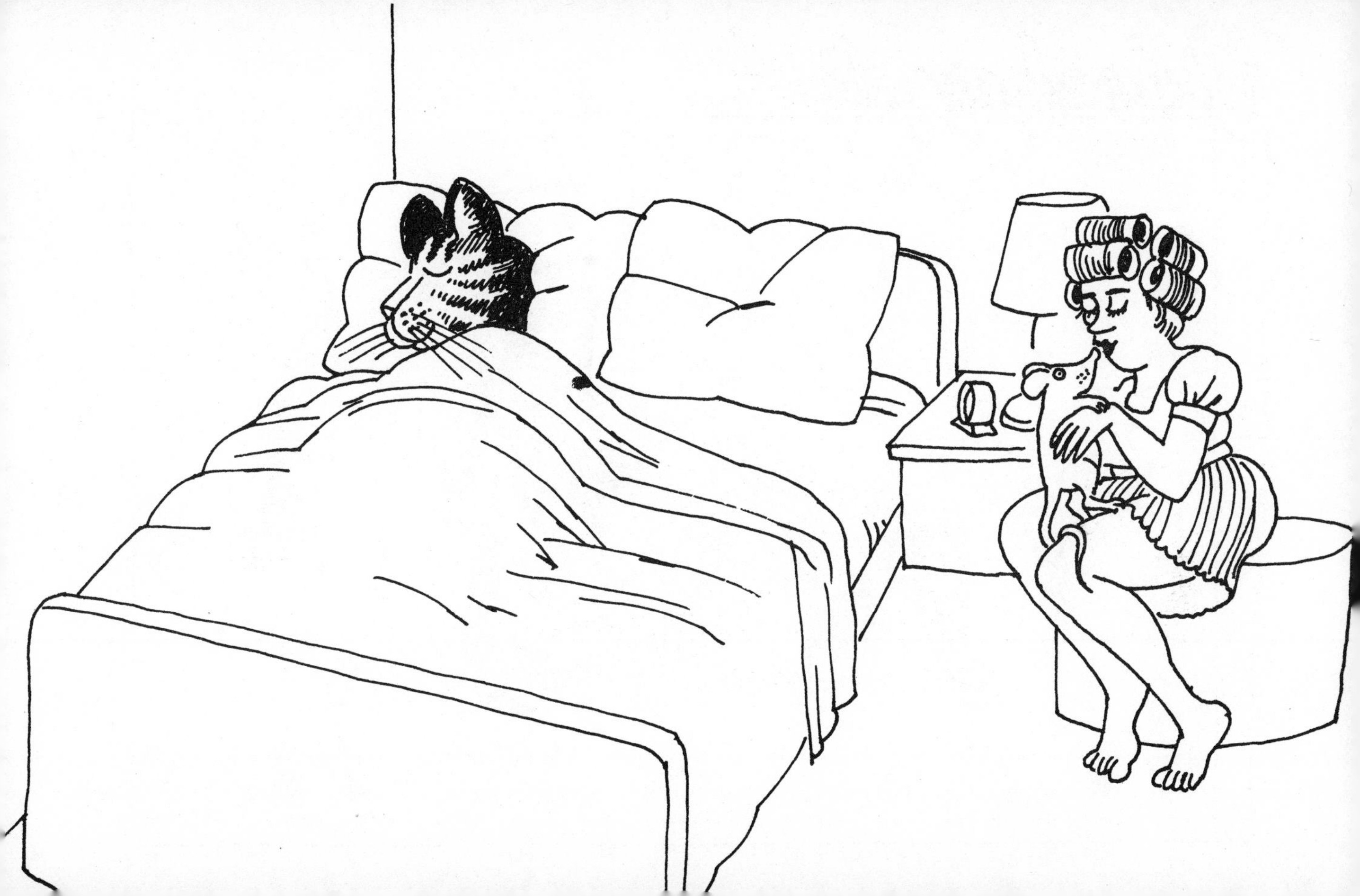

Nosechair Cat

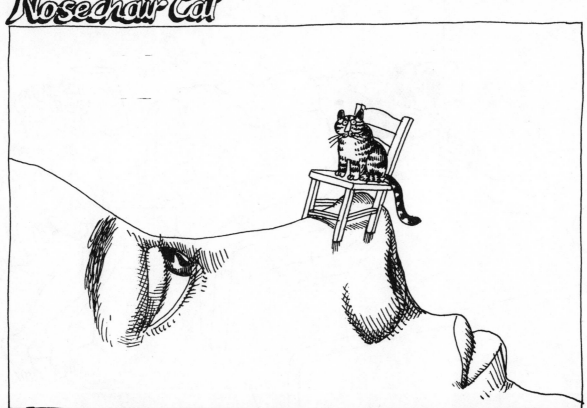

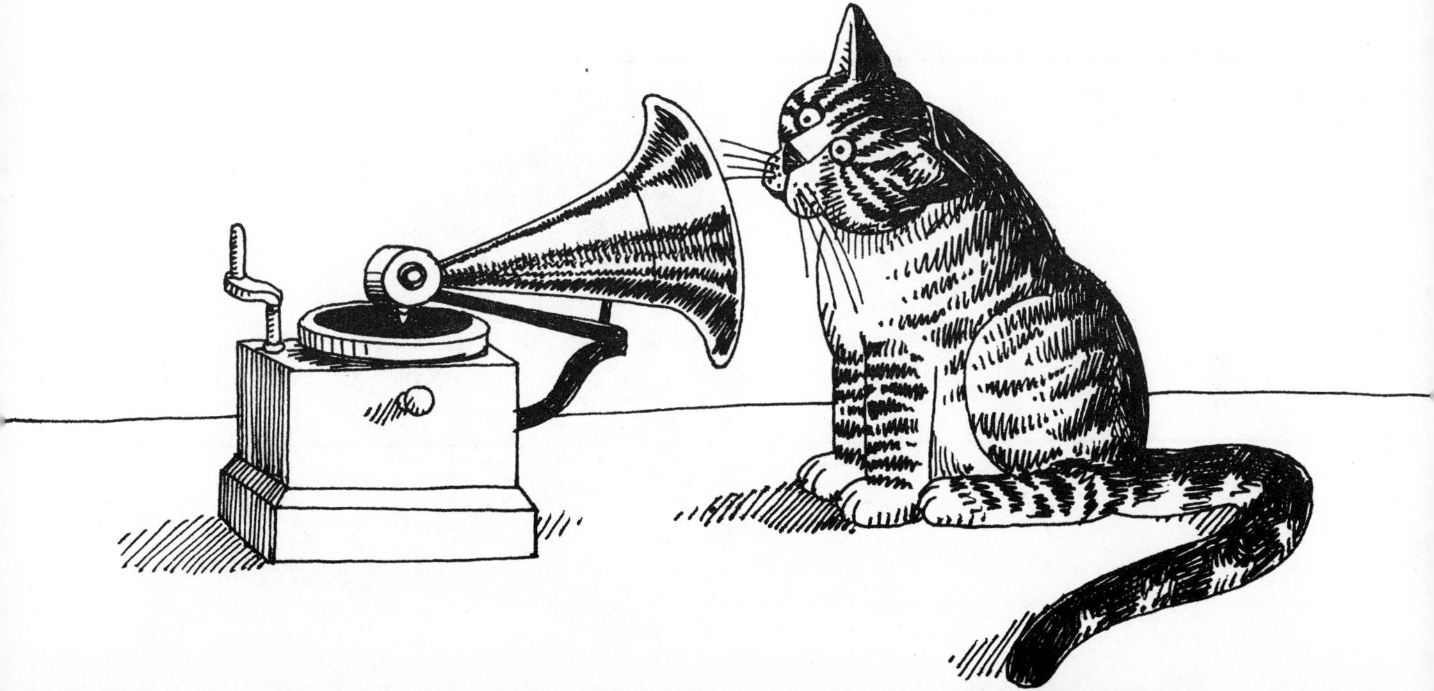

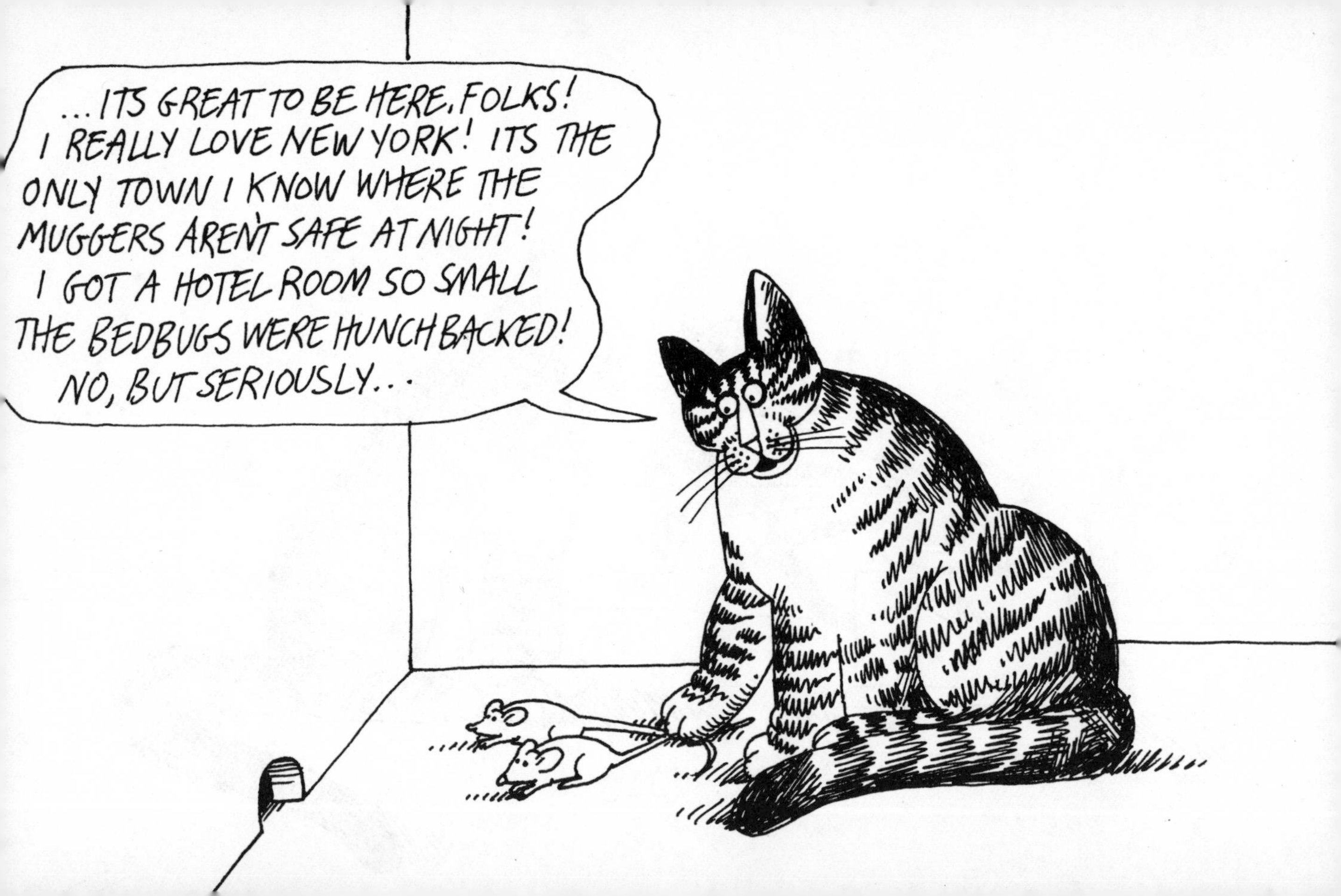
...ITS GREAT TO BE HERE, FOLKS! I REALLY LOVE NEW YORK! ITS THE ONLY TOWN I KNOW WHERE THE MUGGERS AREN'T SAFE AT NIGHT! I GOT A HOTEL ROOM SO SMALL THE BEDBUGS WERE HUNCHBACKED! NO, BUT SERIOUSLY...

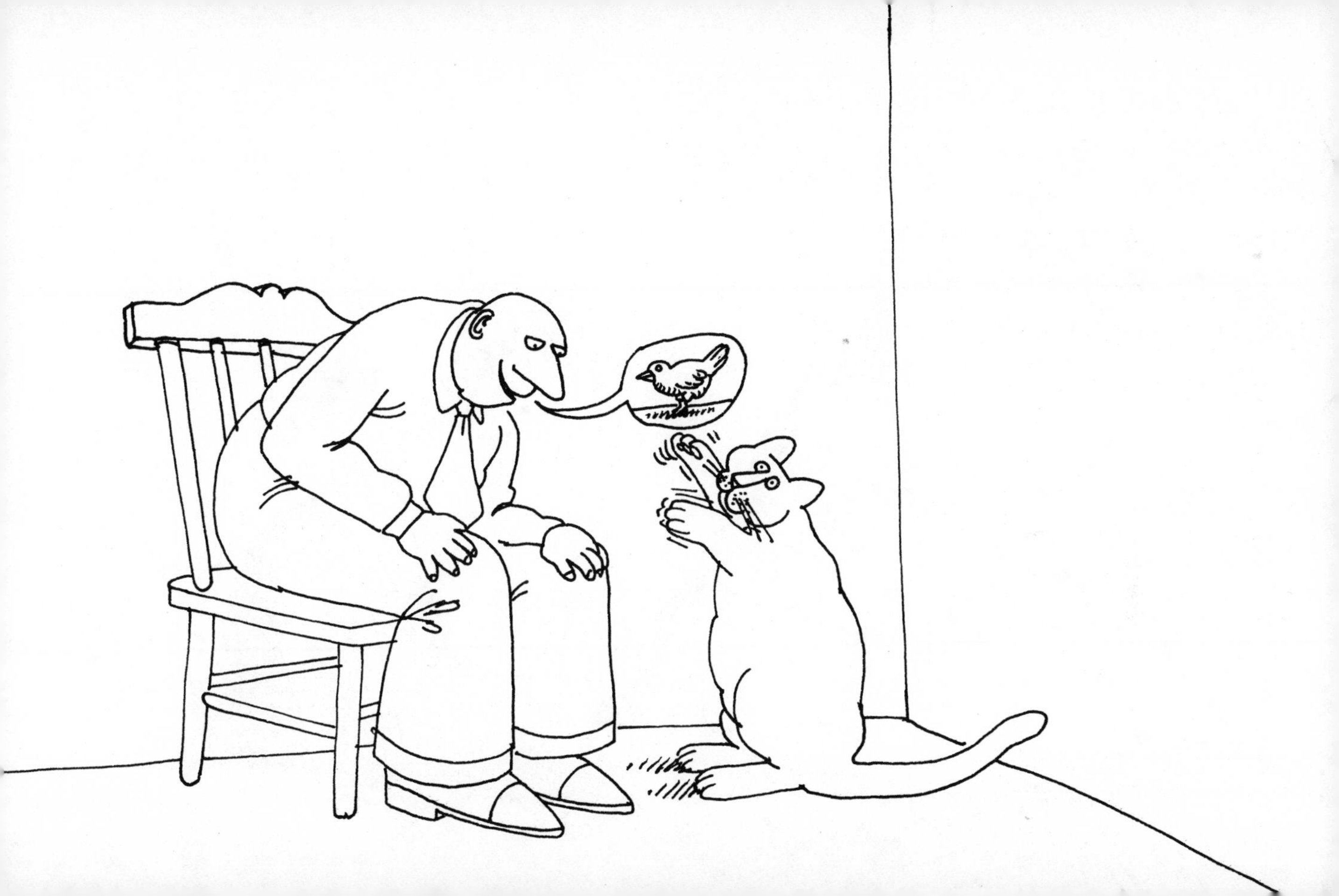

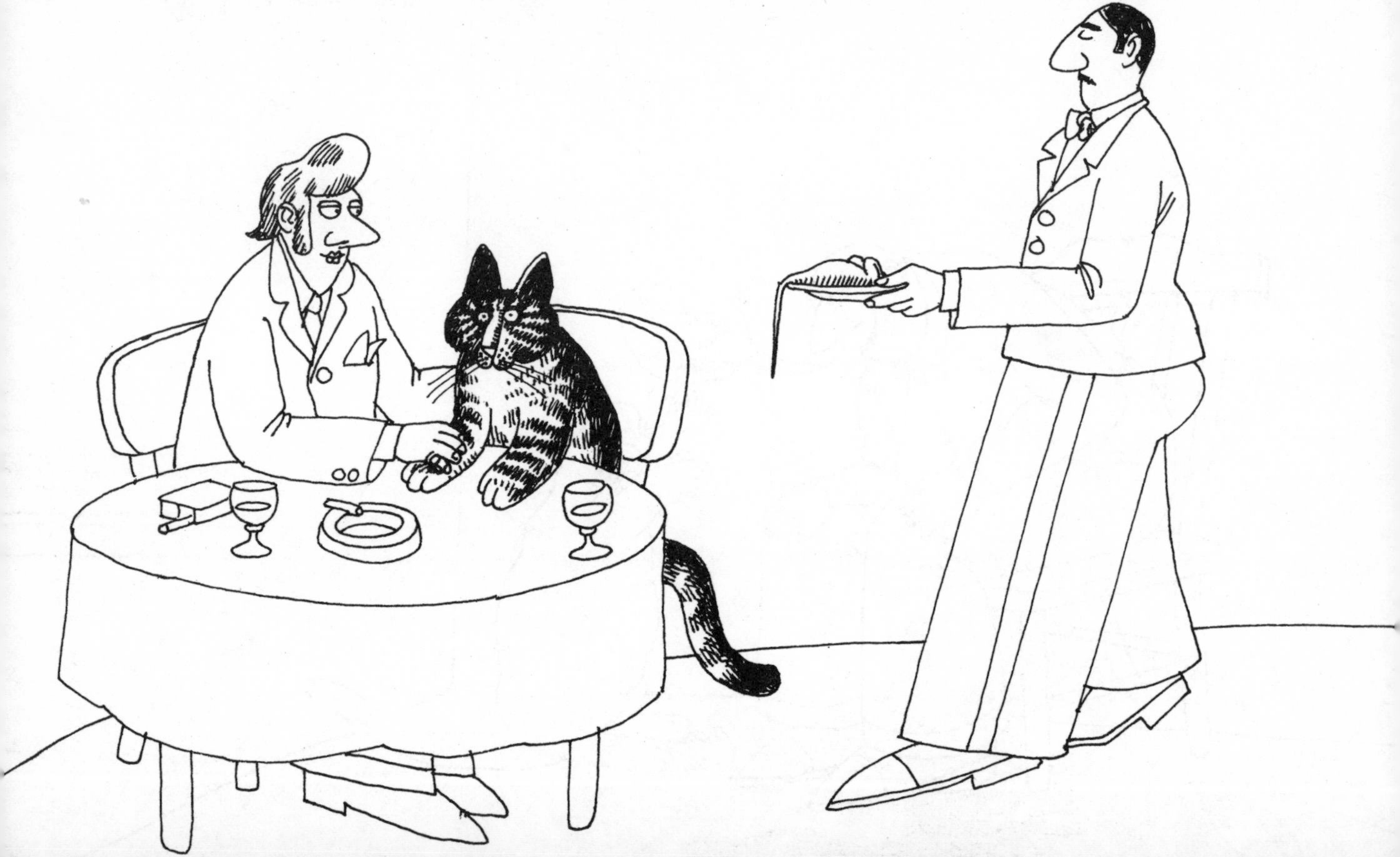

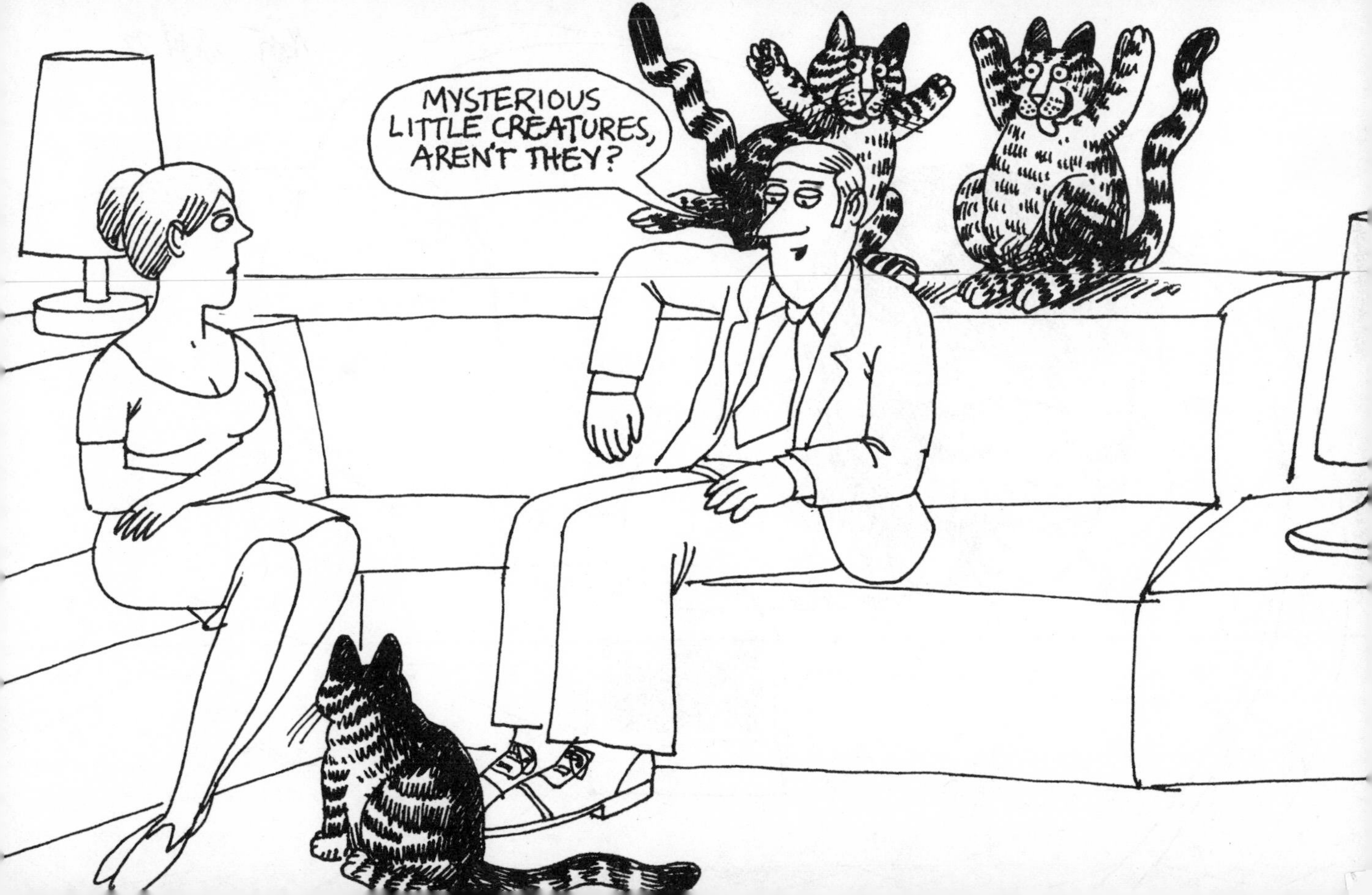
MYSTERIOUS LITTLE CREATURES, AREN'T THEY?

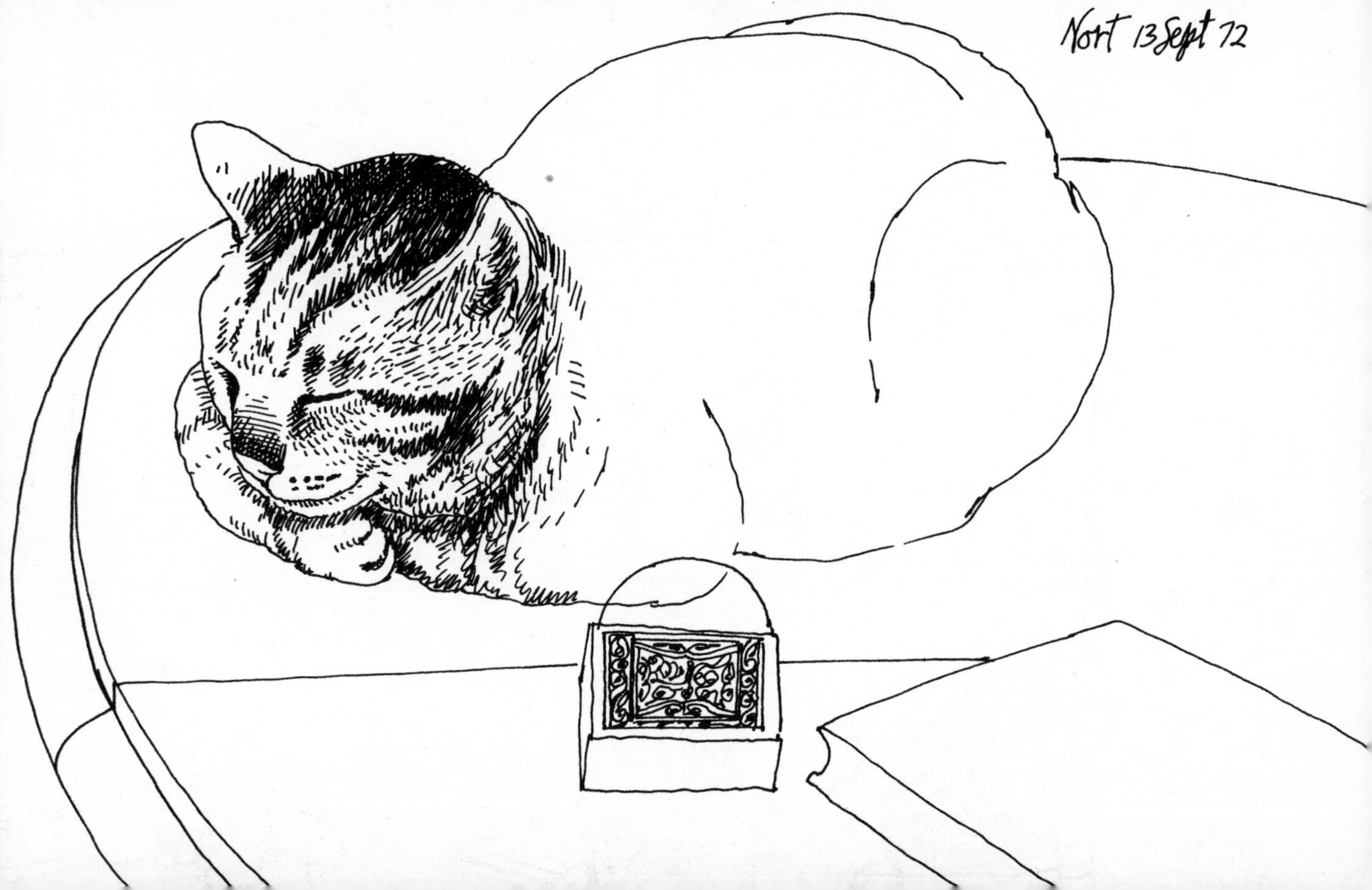
Nort 13 Sept 72

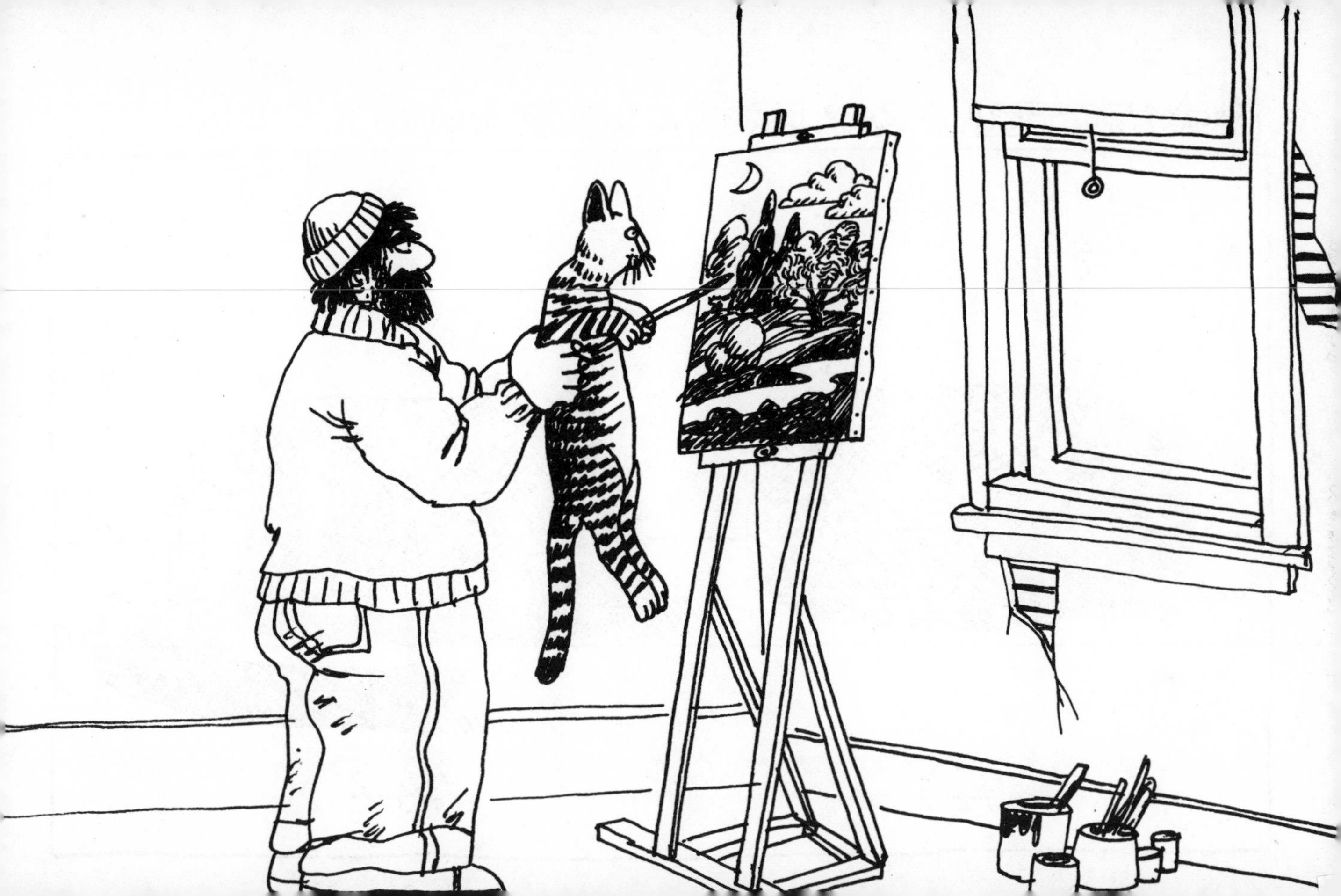

HOW TO TELL A CAT FROM A MEAT LOAF

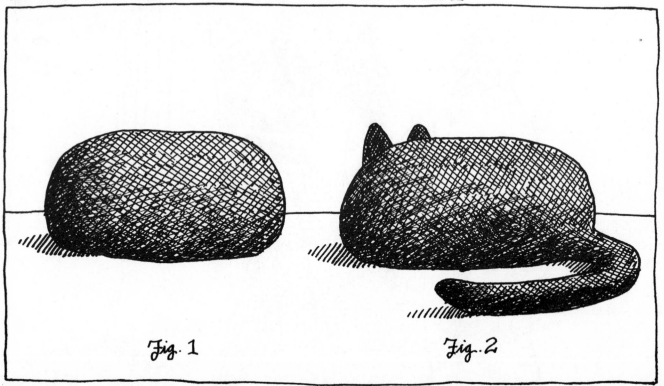

Fig. 1

Fig. 2

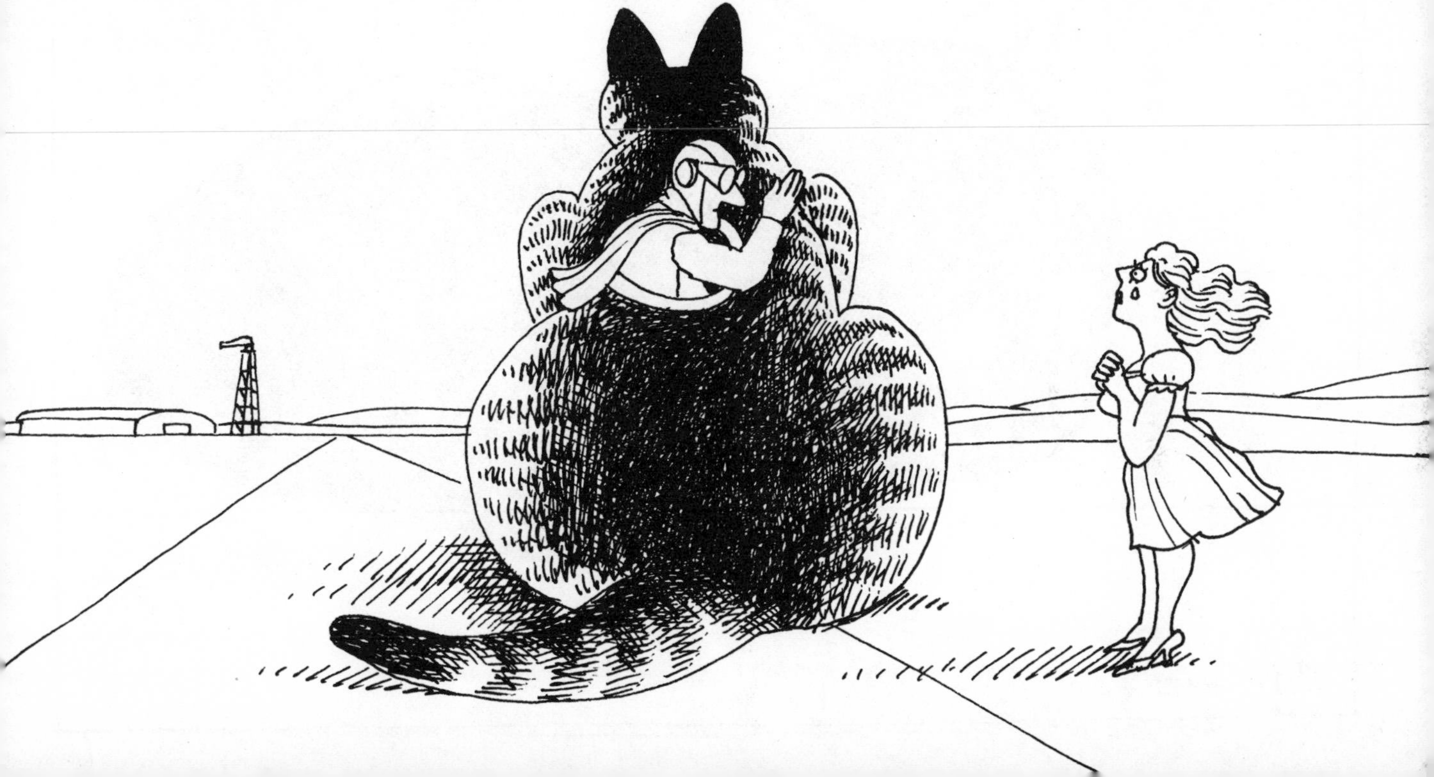

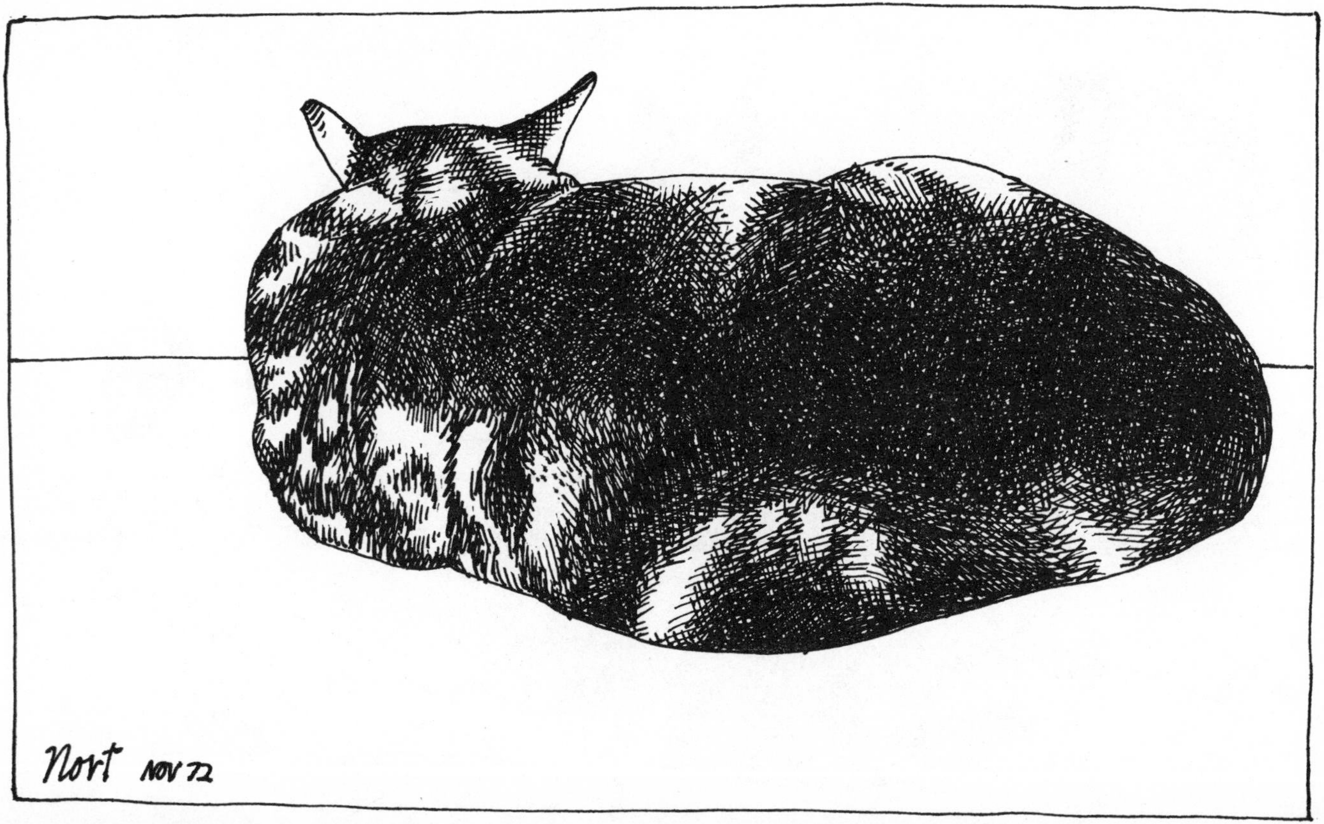
Nort NOV 72

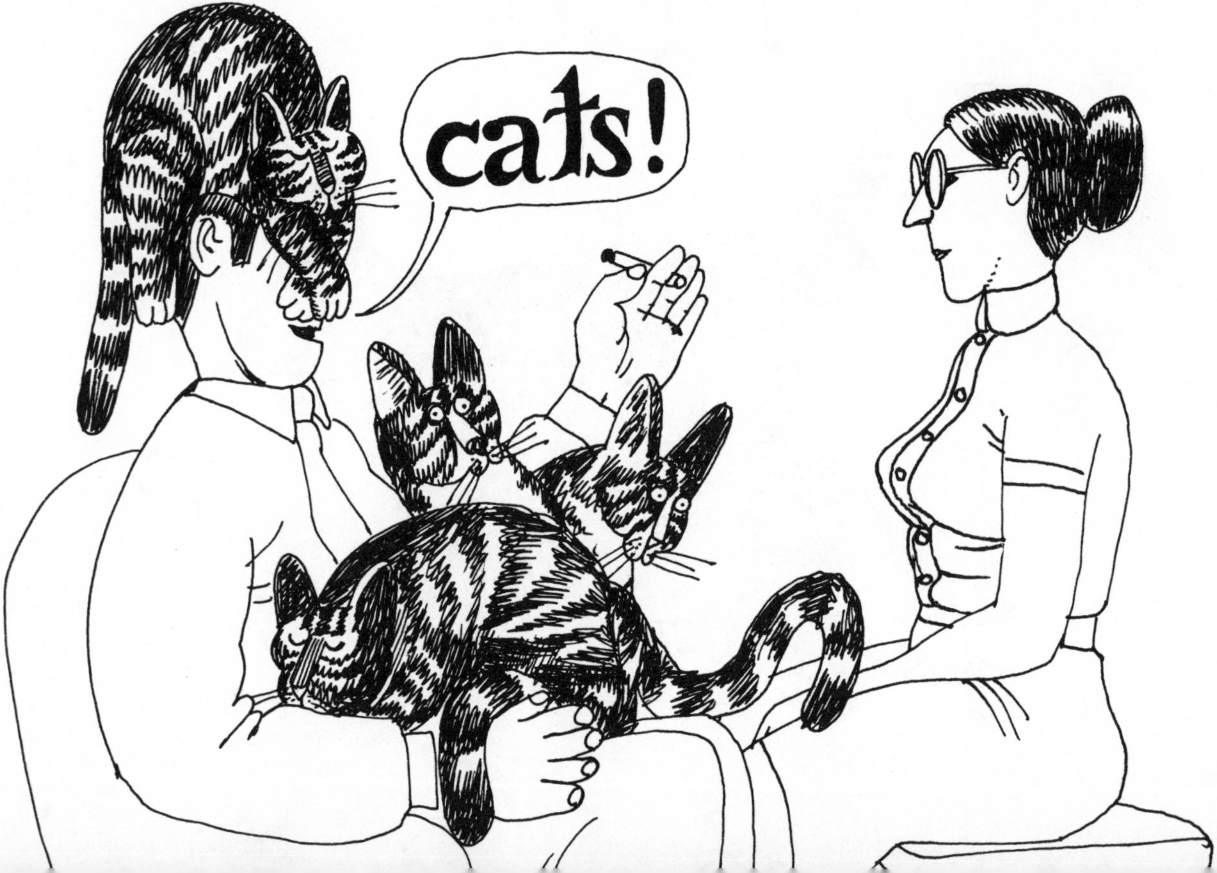
cats!

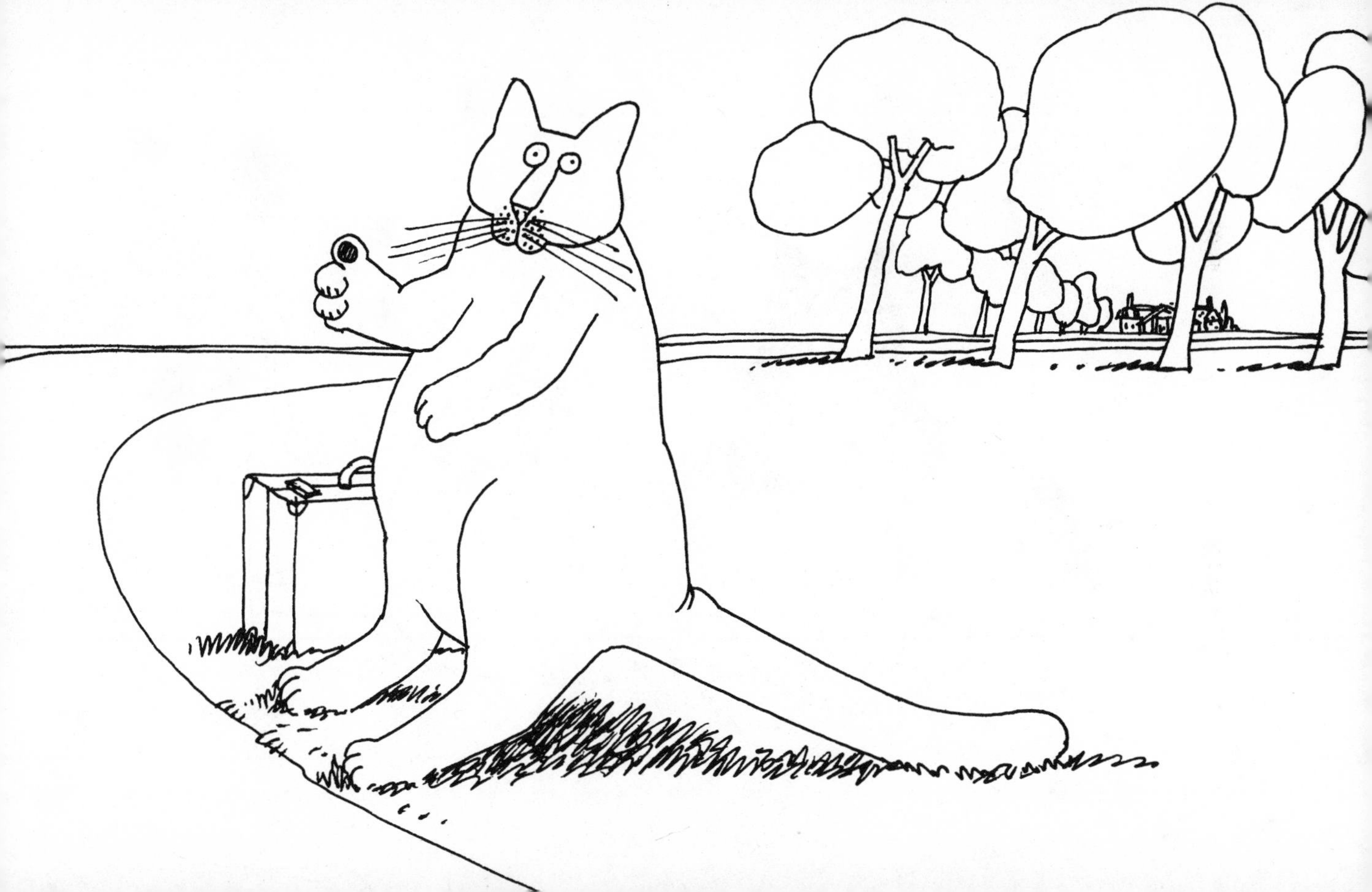

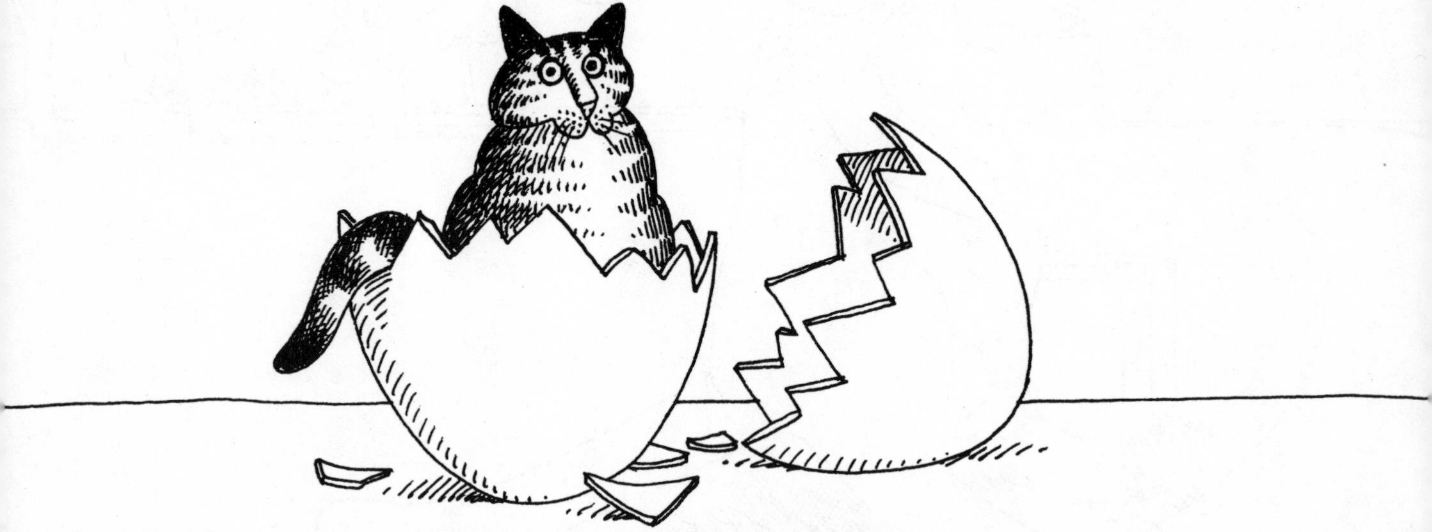

... ANOTHER THING I LIKE ABOUT YOU GUYS IS THAT YOU MAKE GREAT PETS, TOO.

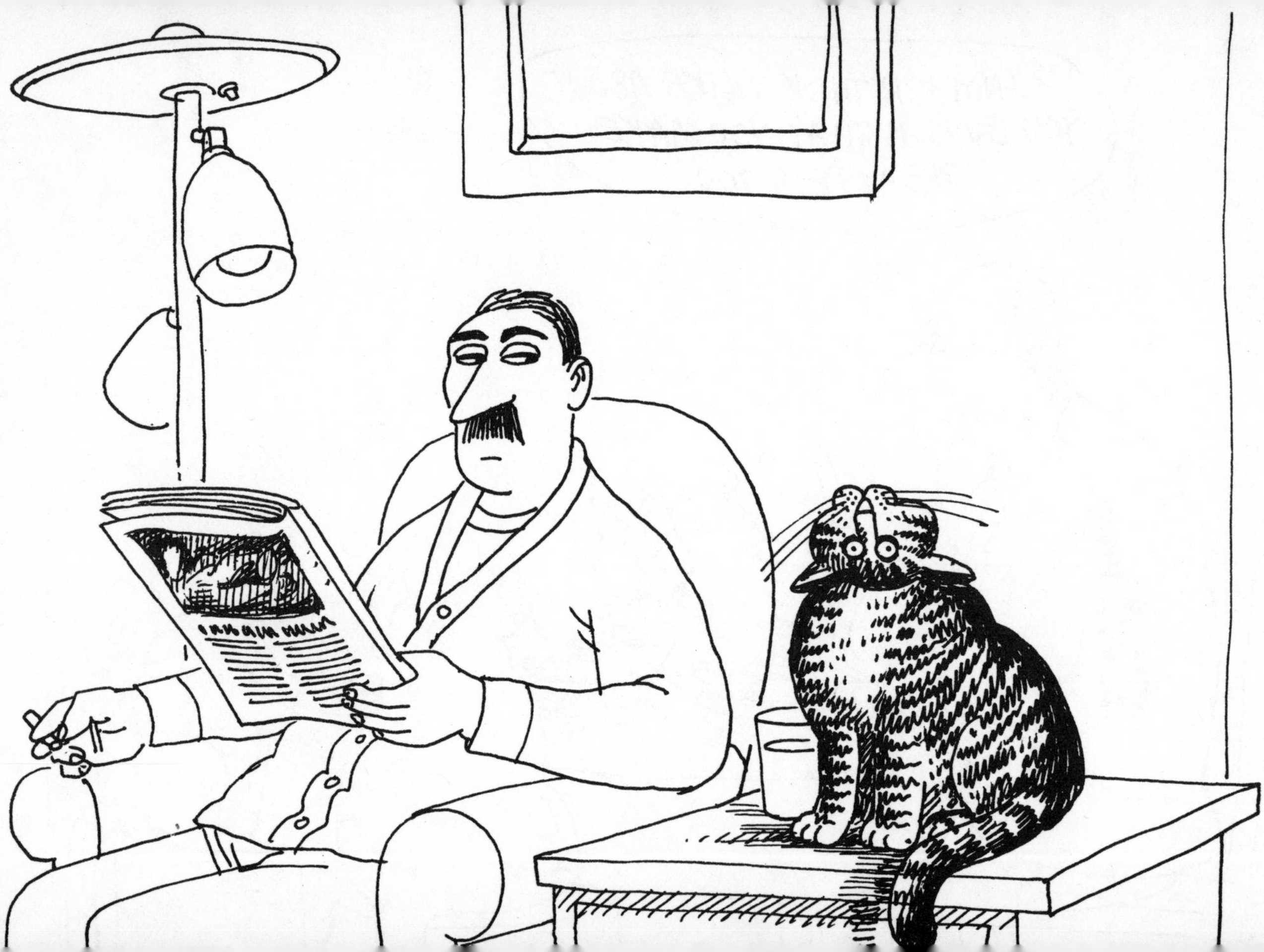

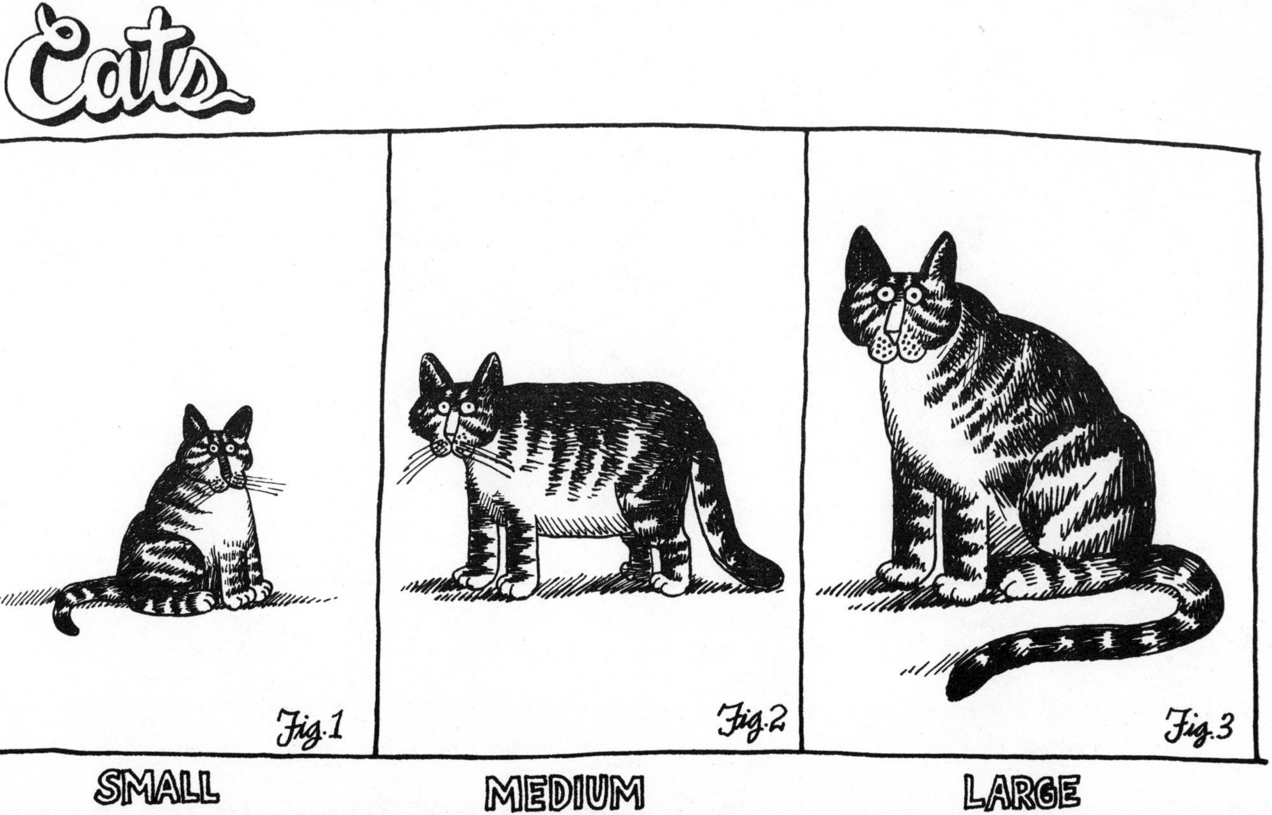
Cats
Fig.1
Fig.2
Fig.3
SMALL
MEDIUM
LARGE

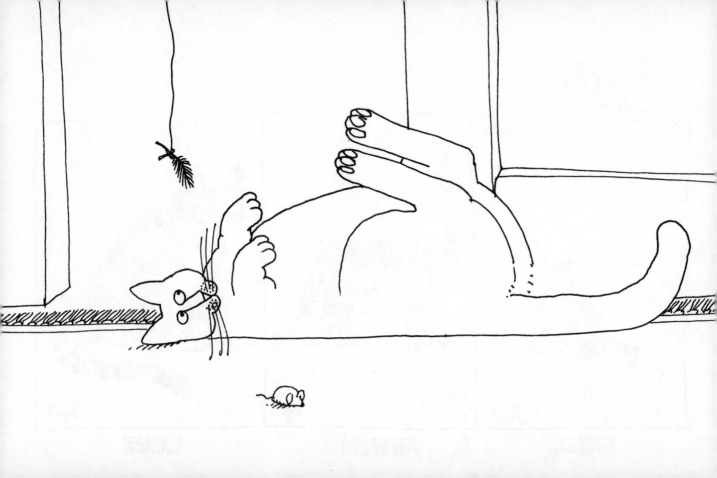

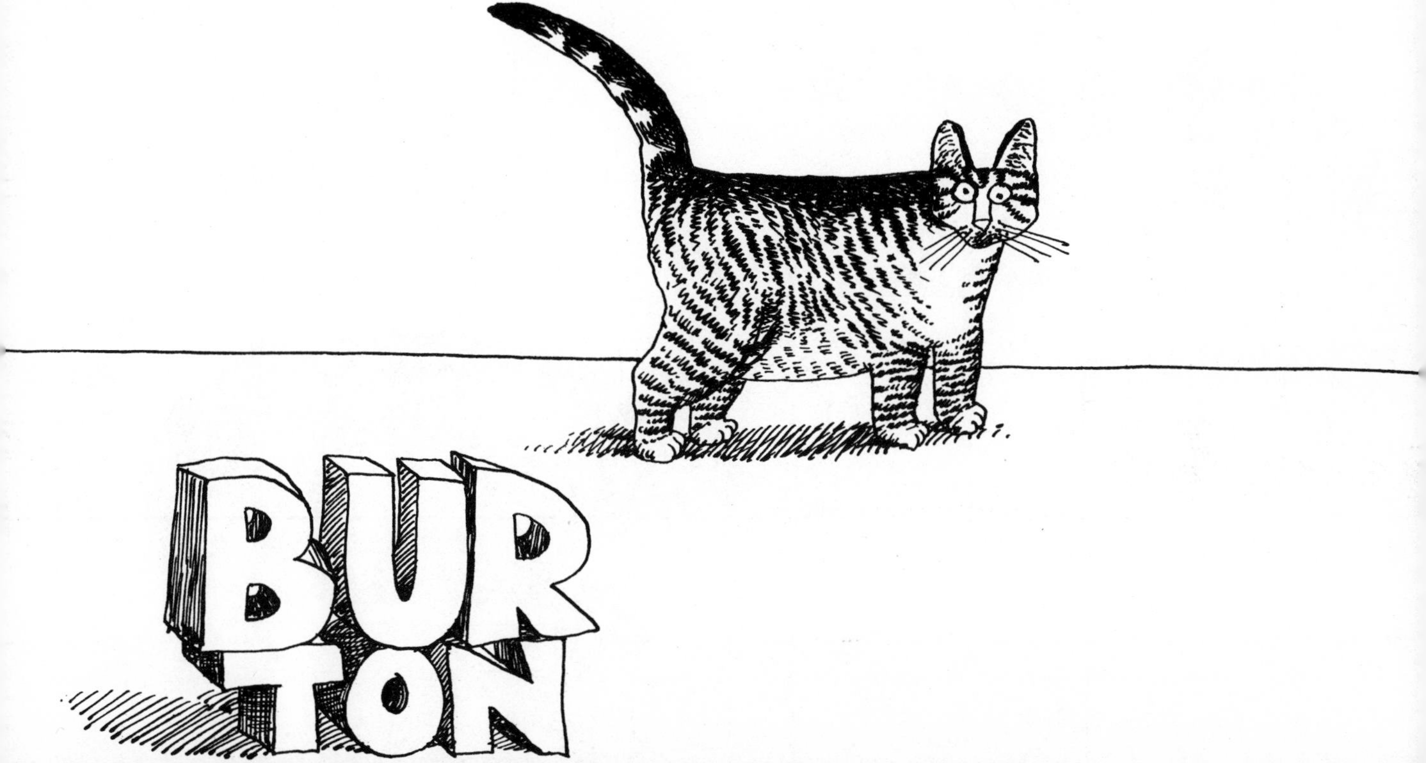
BURTON

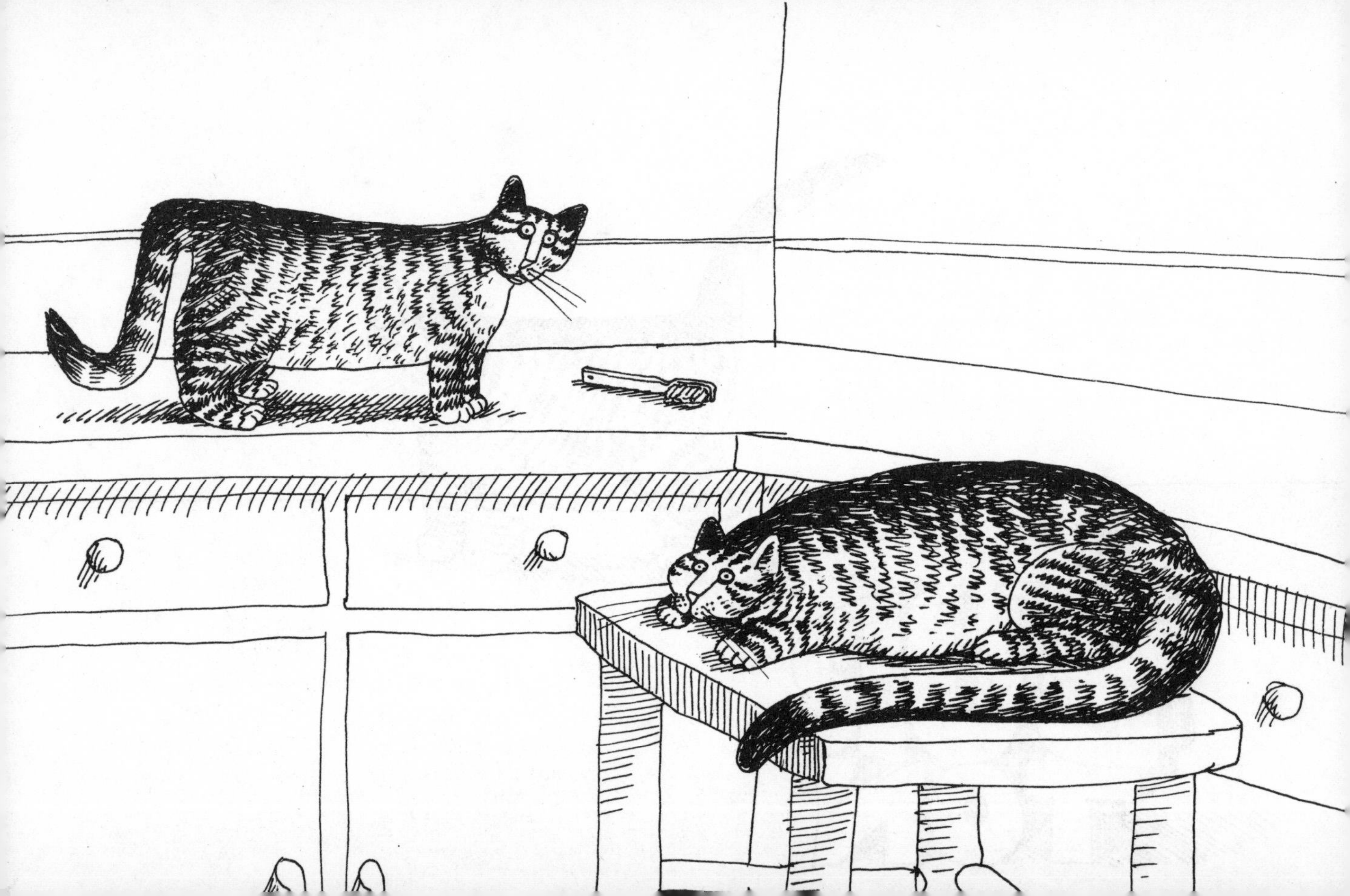

Burton Rustle
20 Apr 74

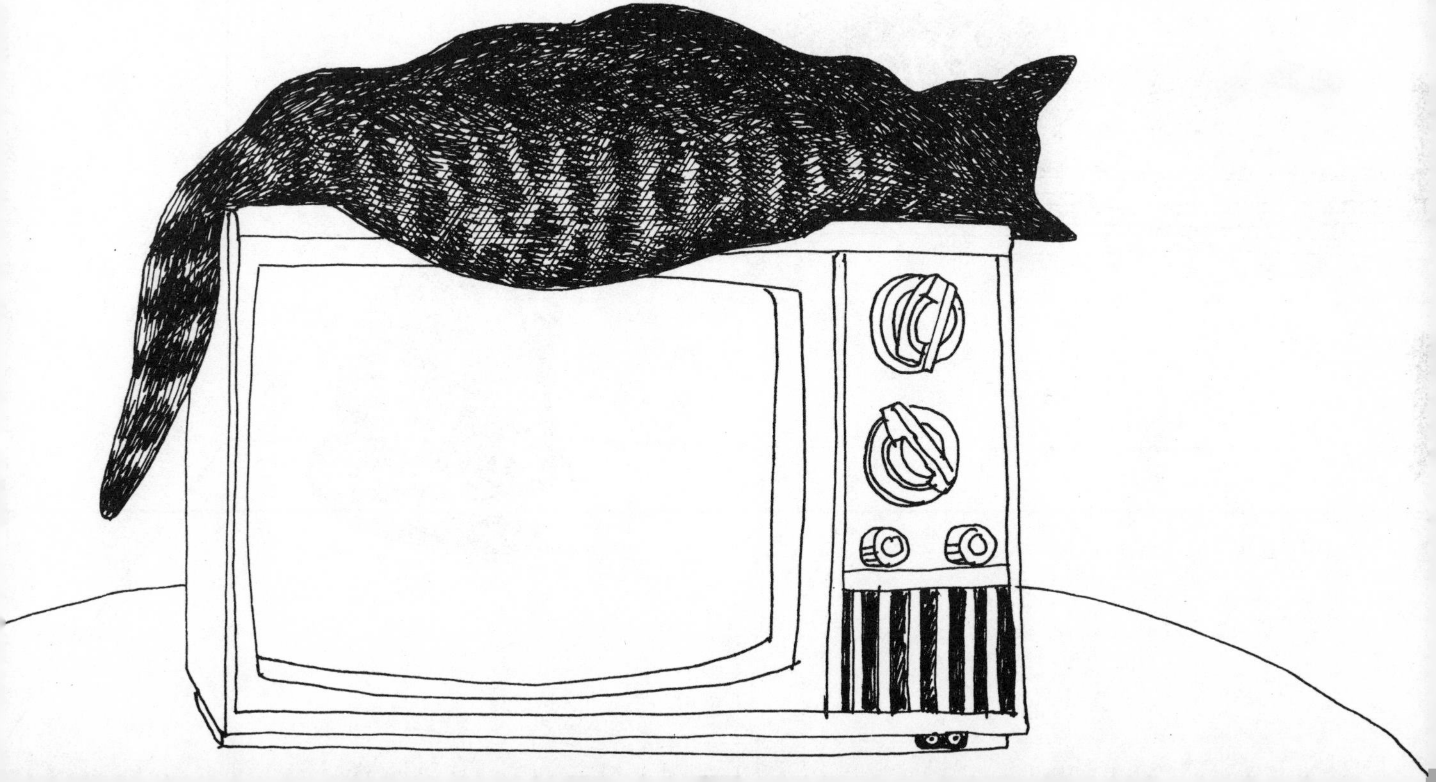

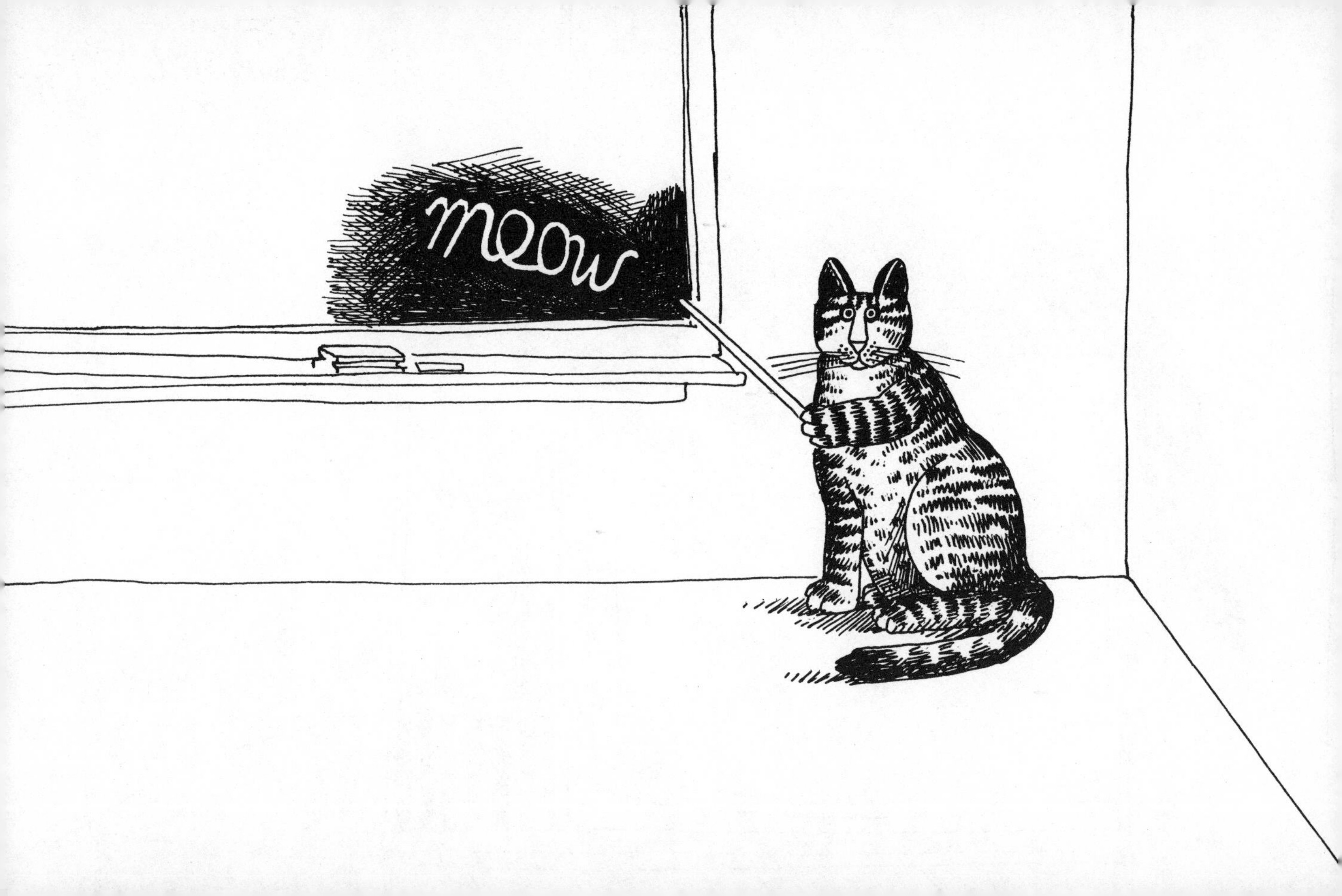
meow

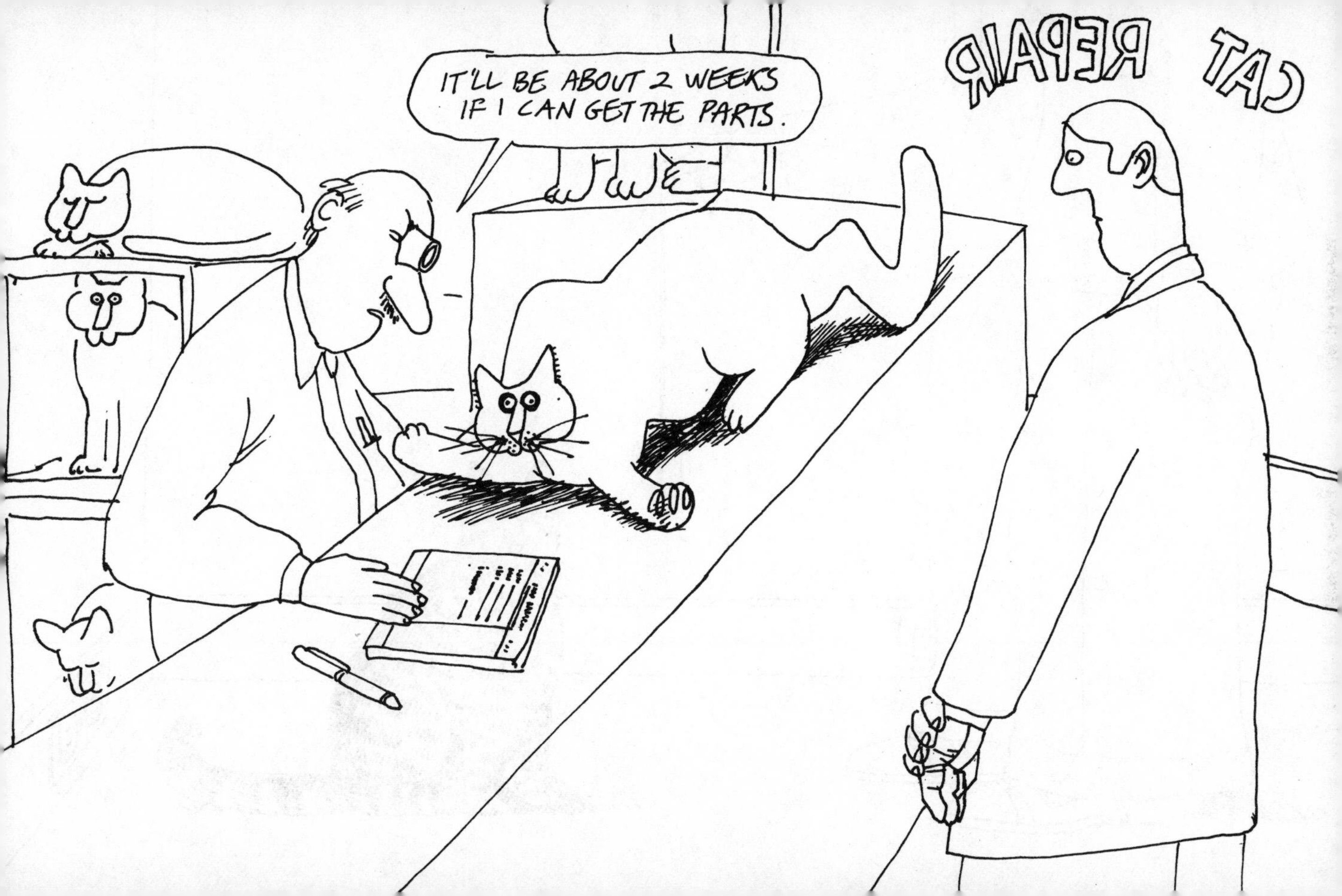
CAT REPAIR
IT'LL BE ABOUT 2 WEEKS IF I CAN GET THE PARTS.

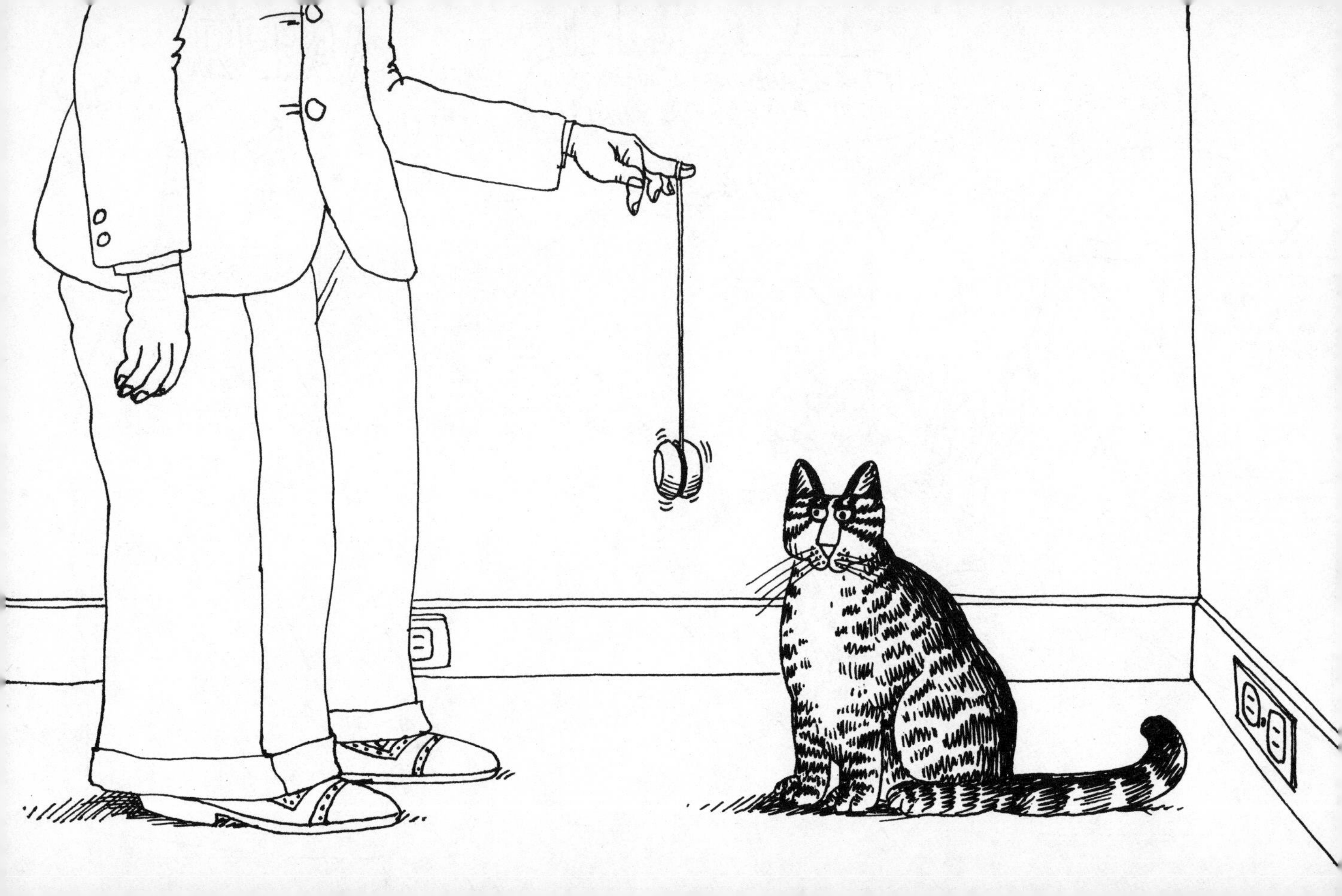

Nit & Burt at the Same Time

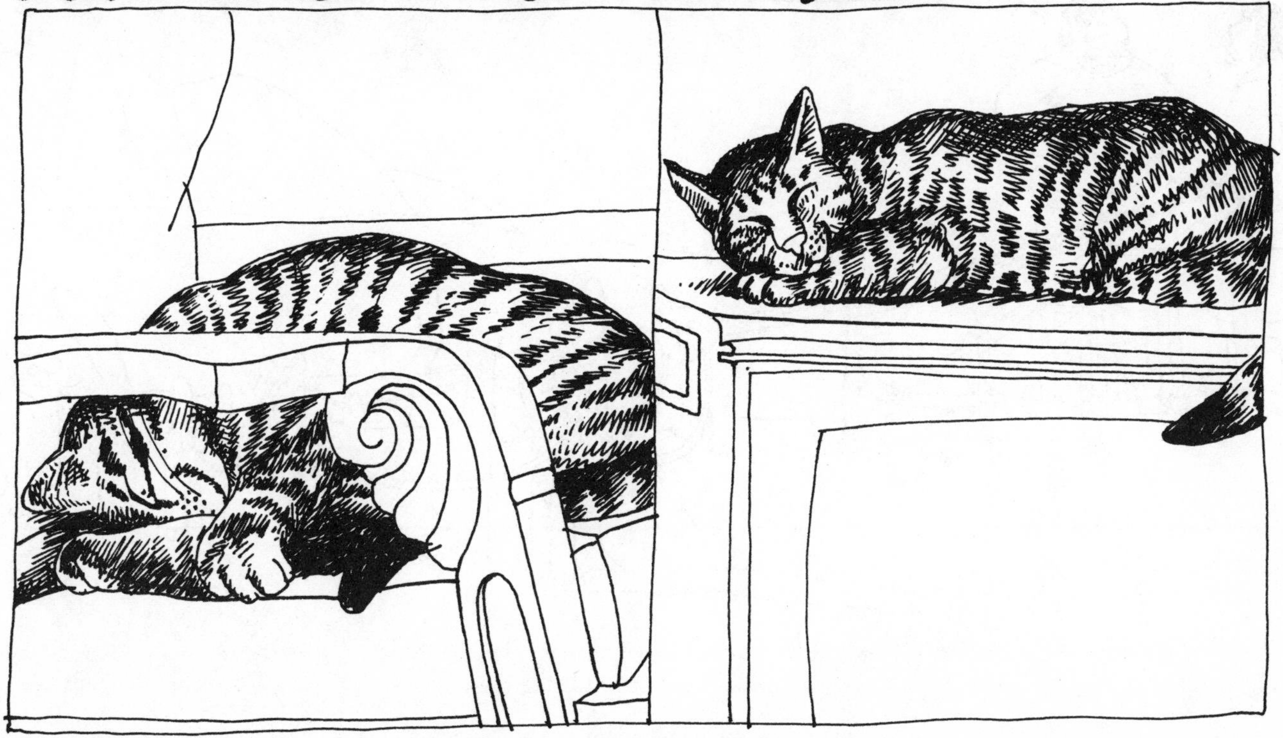

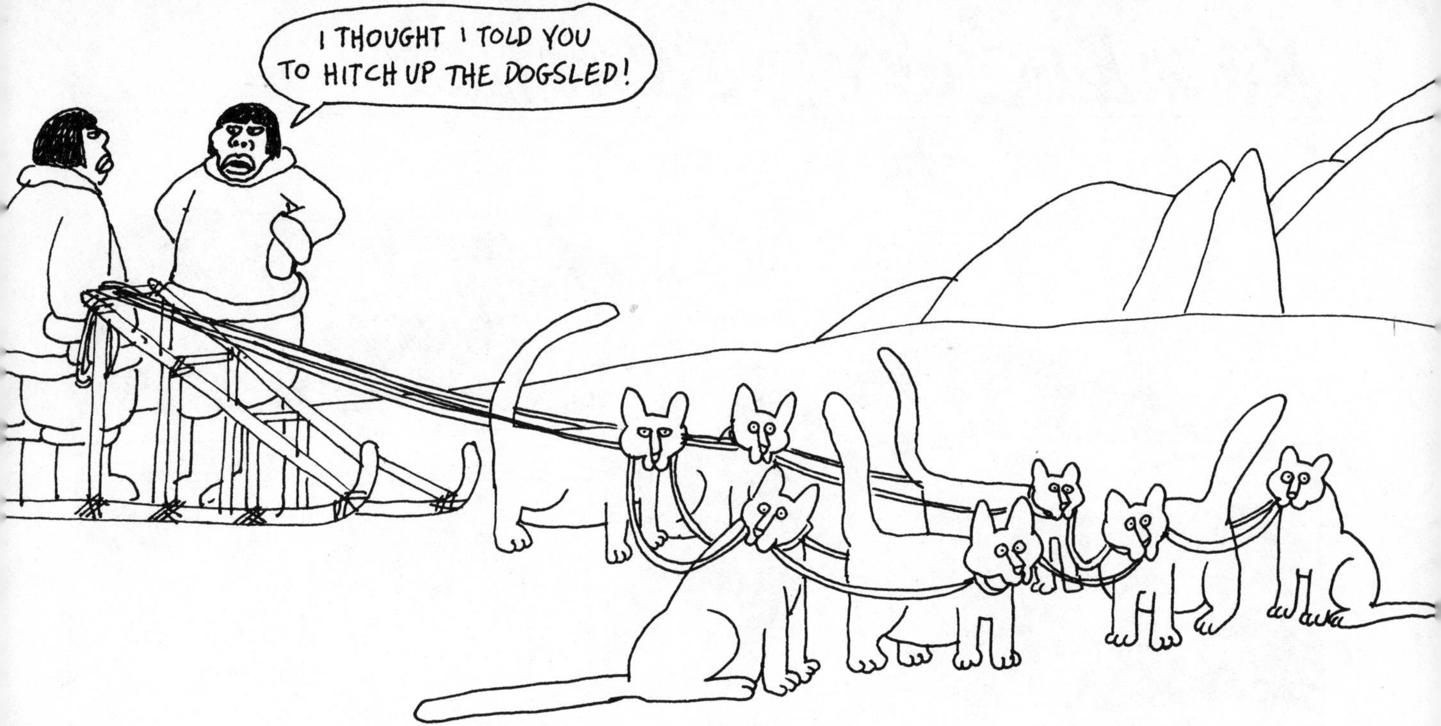
I THOUGHT I TOLD YOU TO HITCH UP THE DOGSLED!

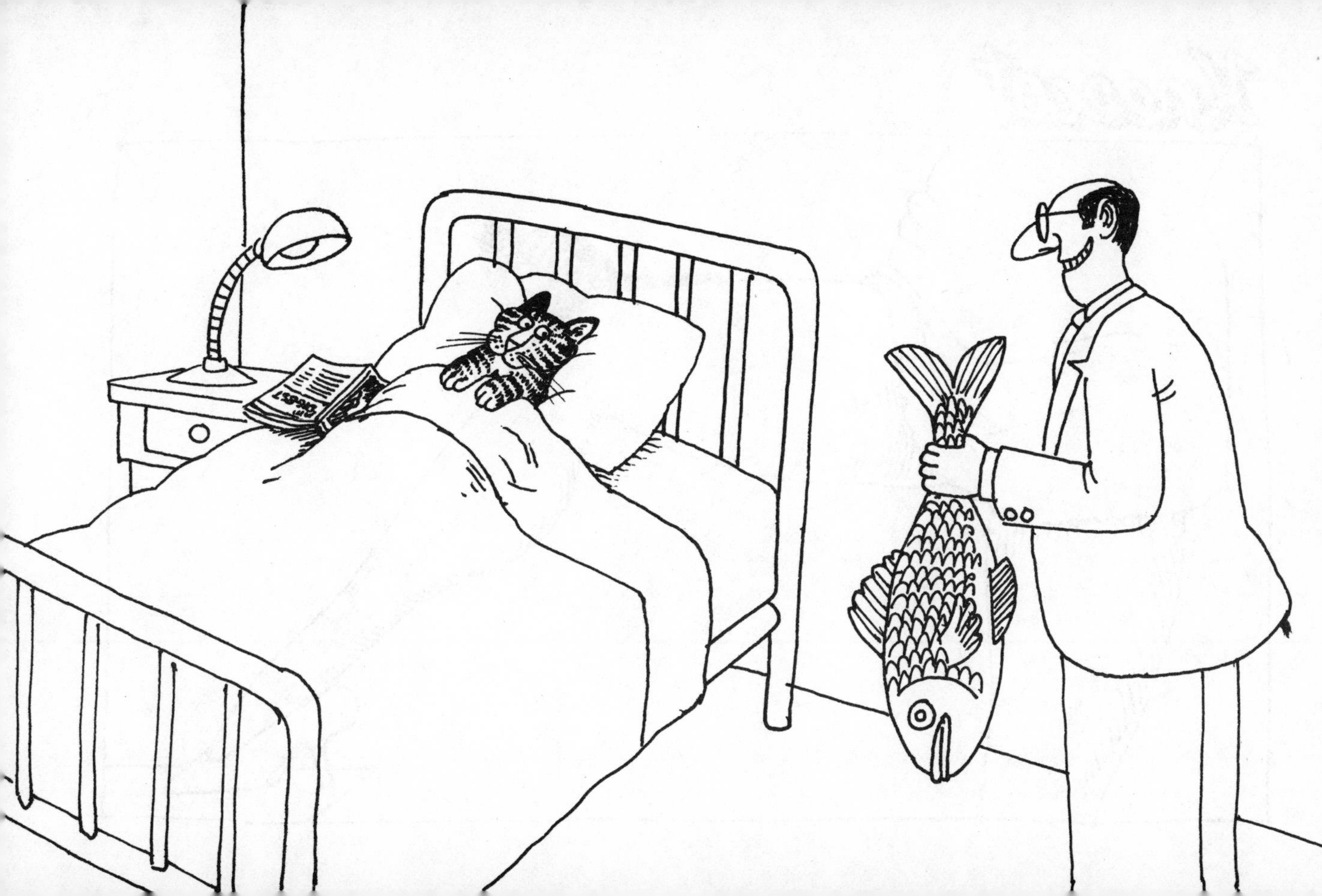

Kneecat

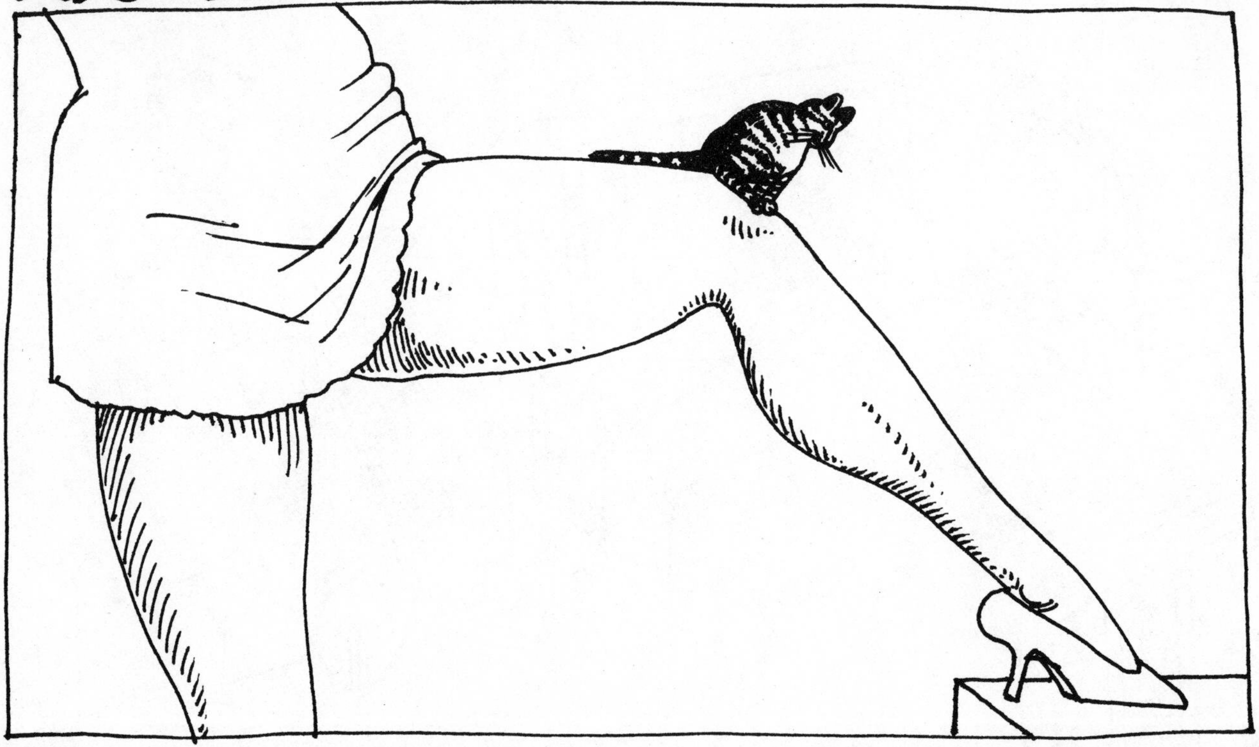

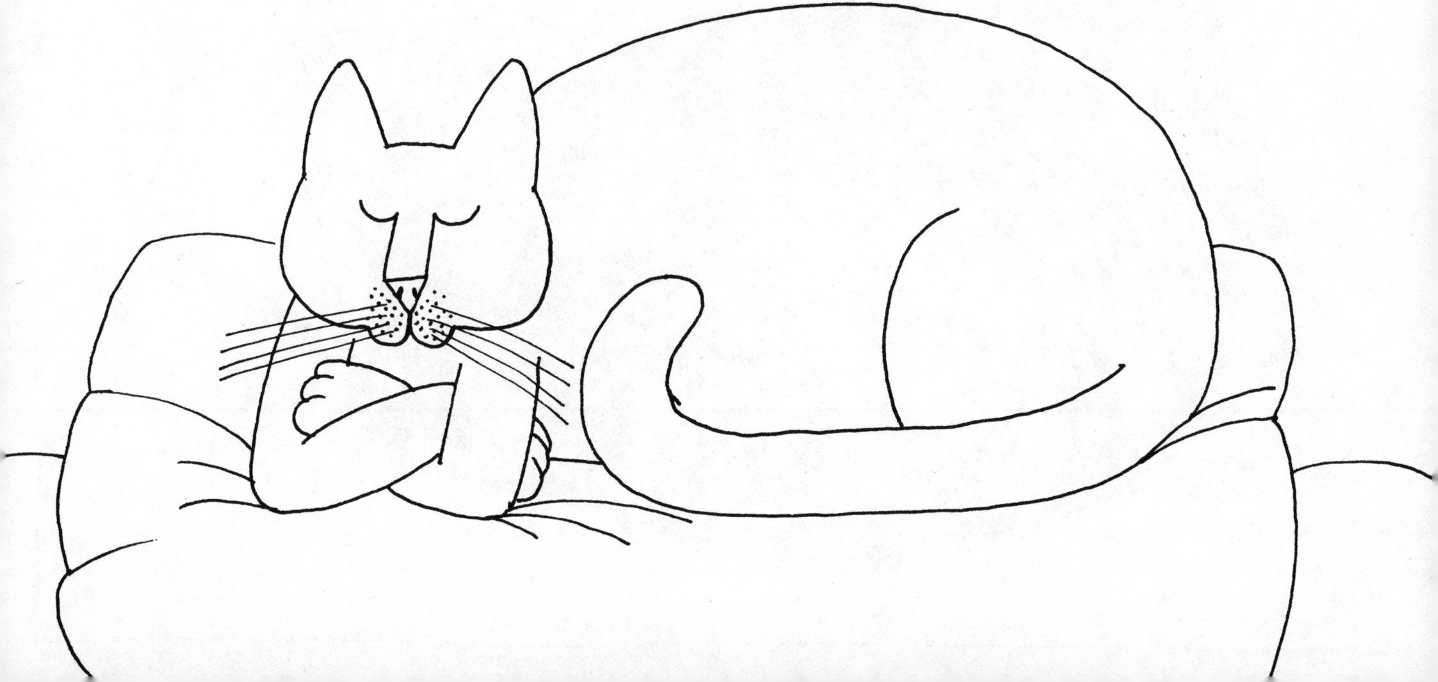

FAT NITTY

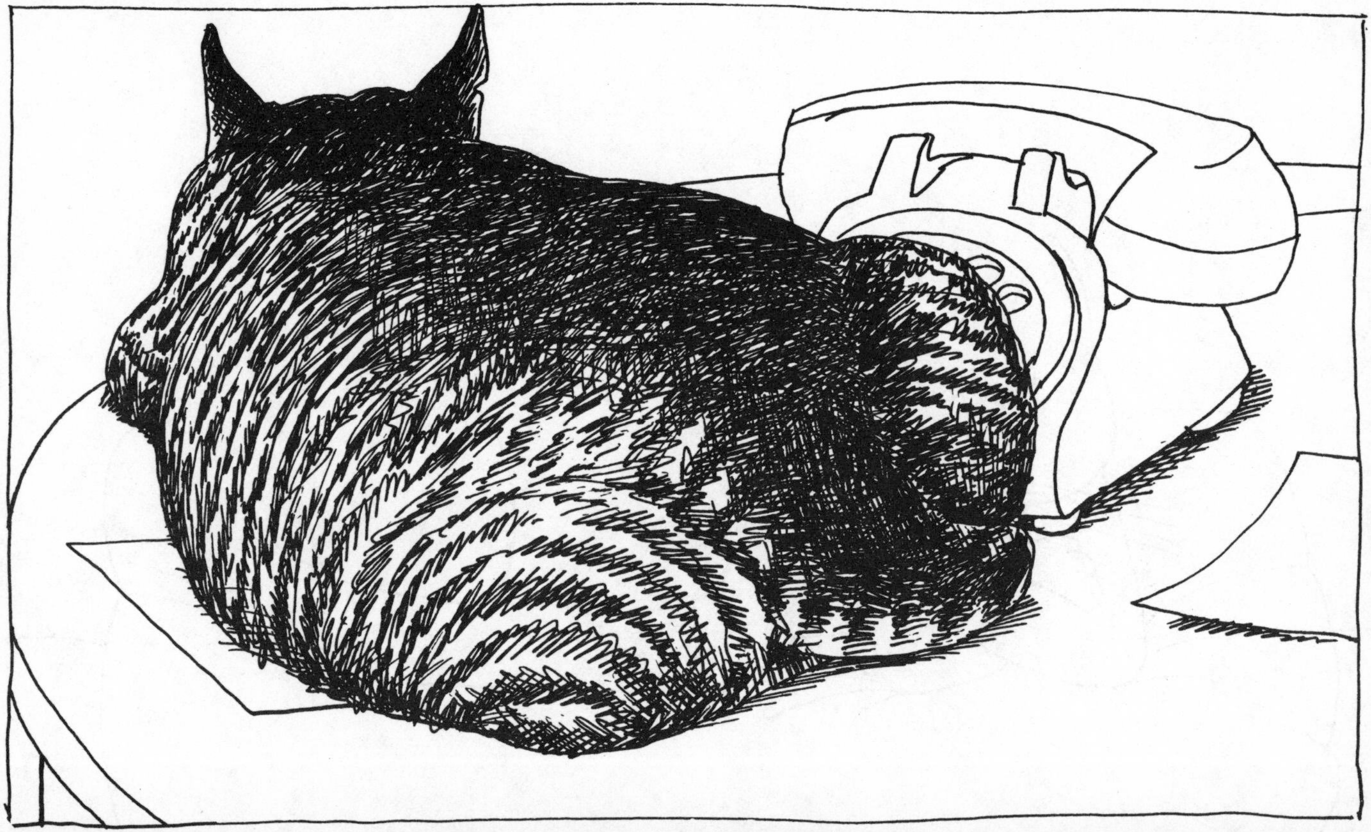

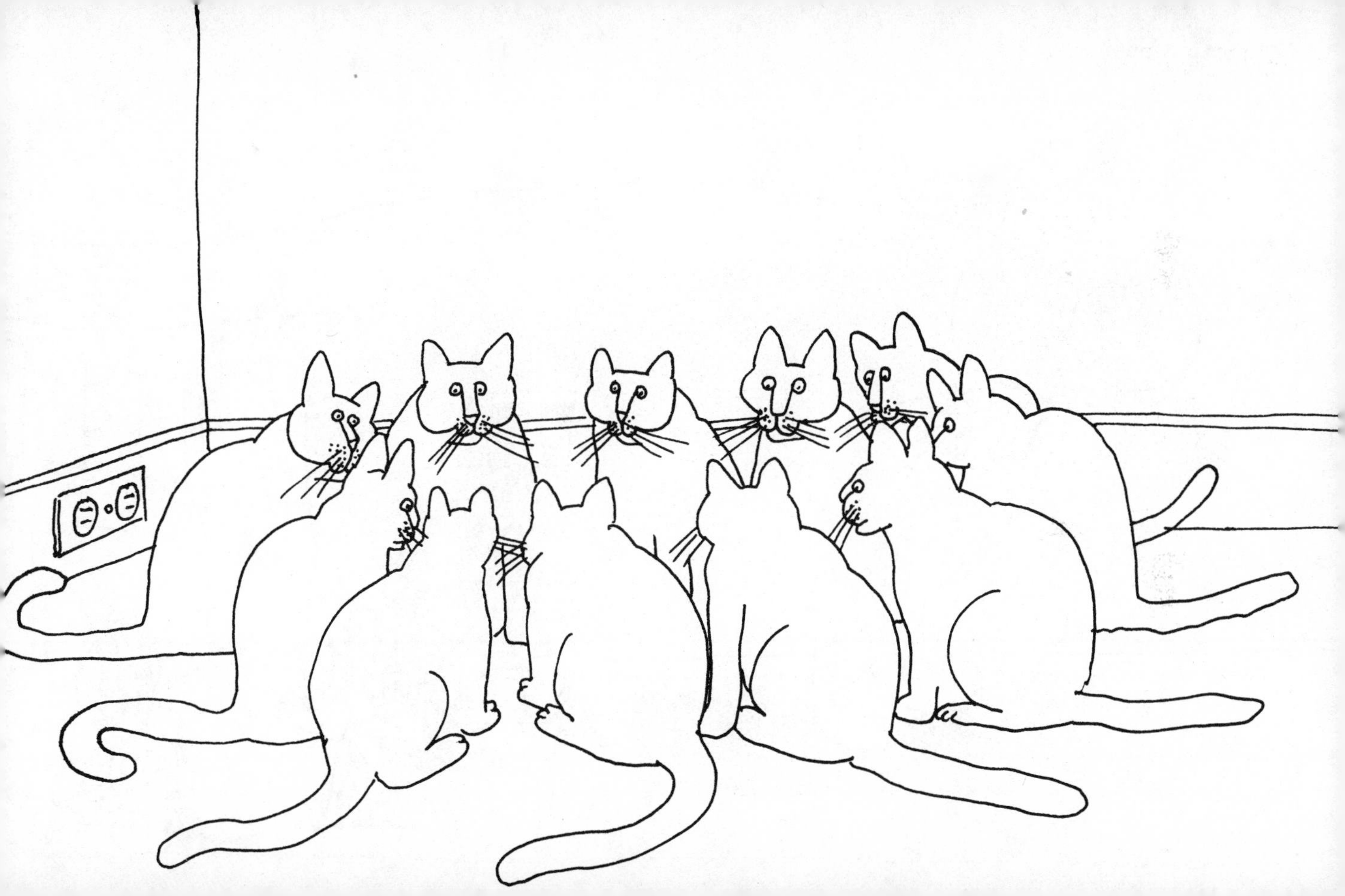

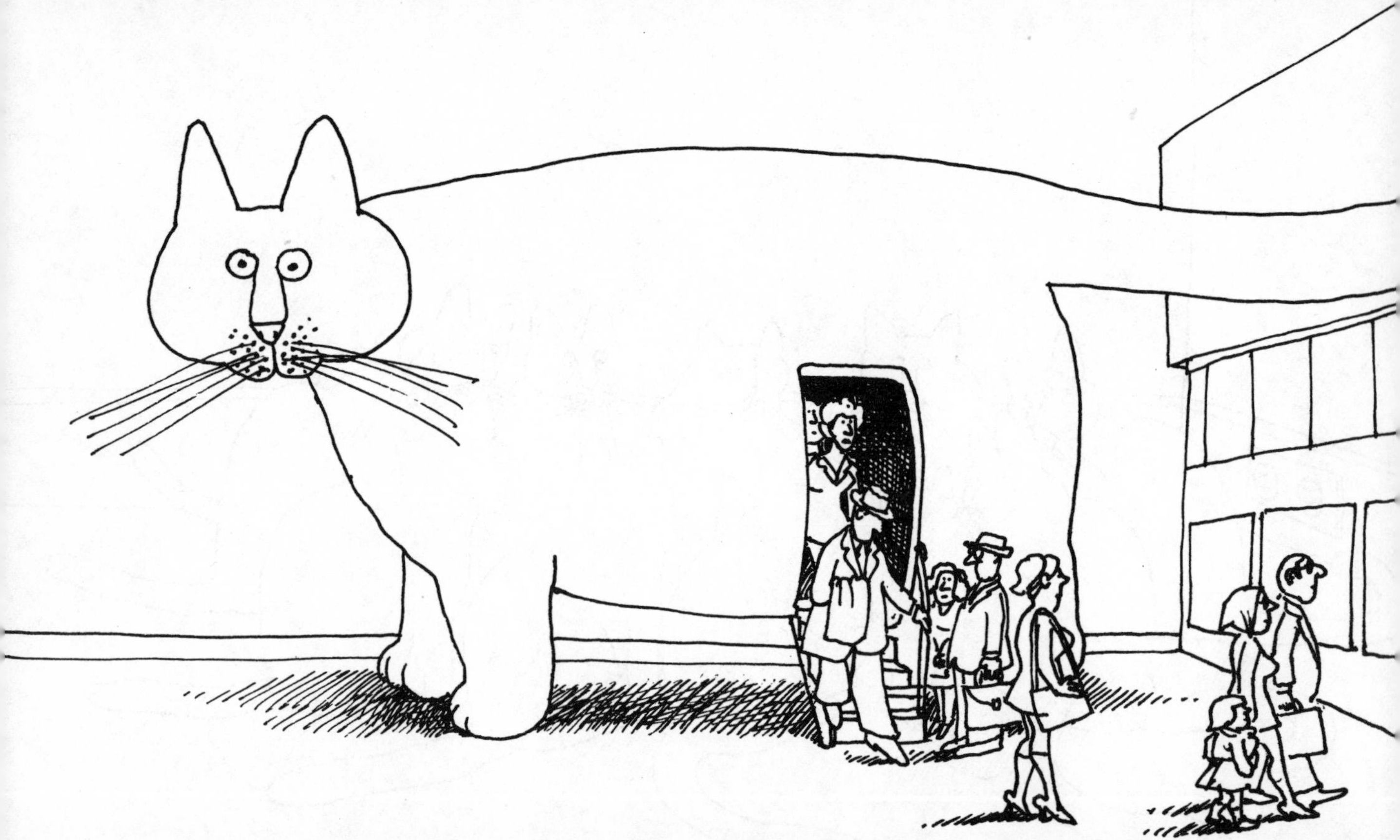

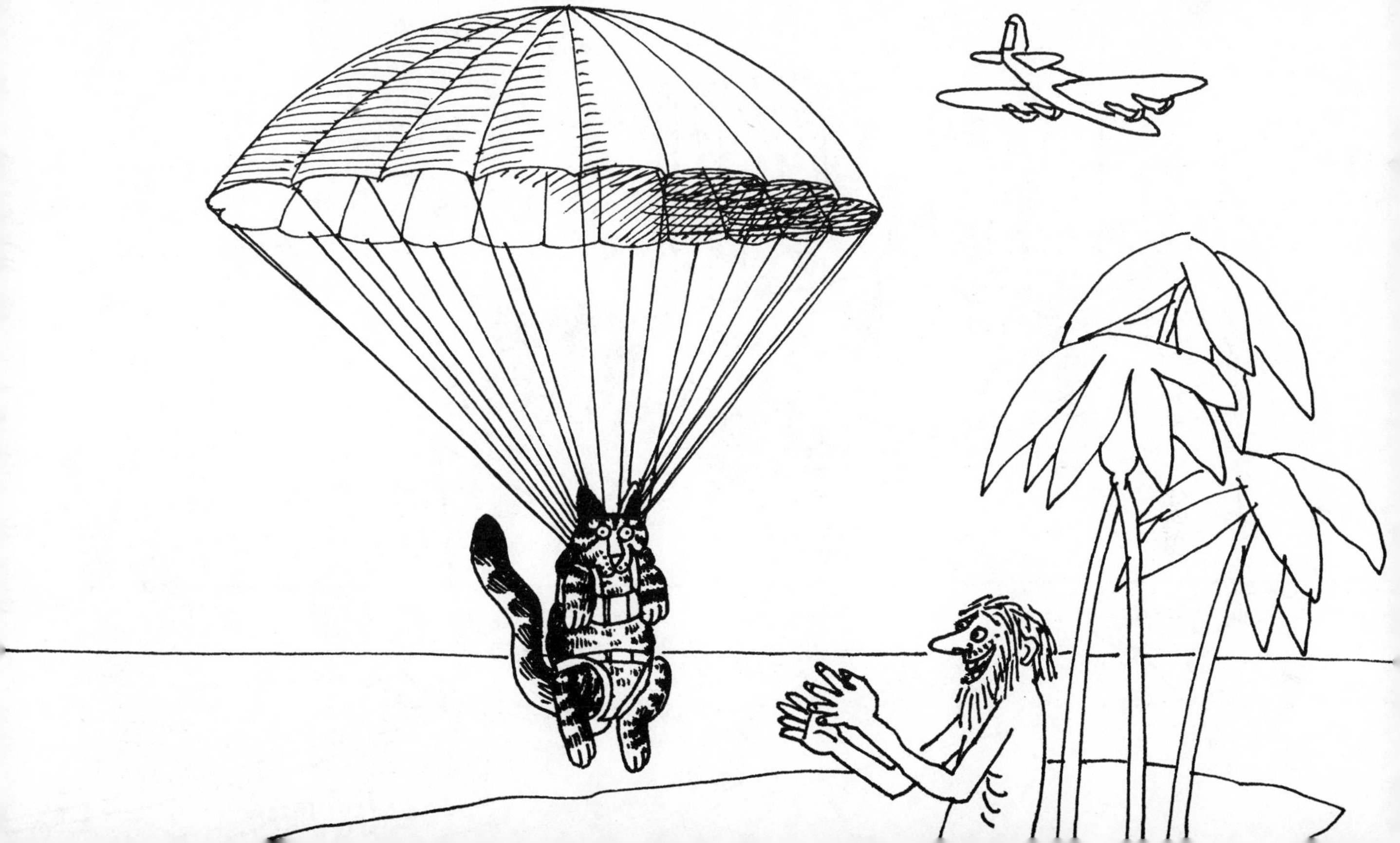

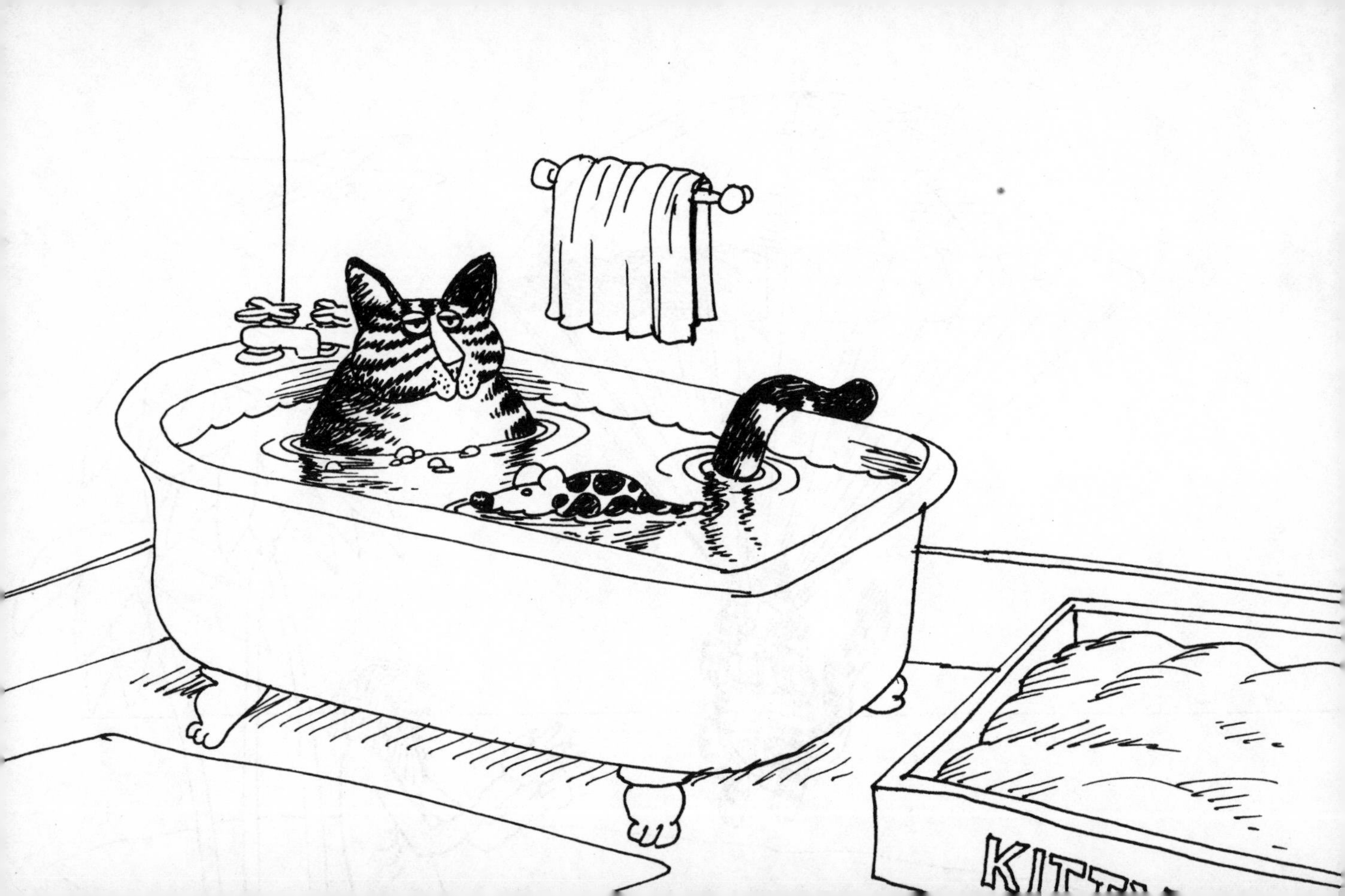

KITT

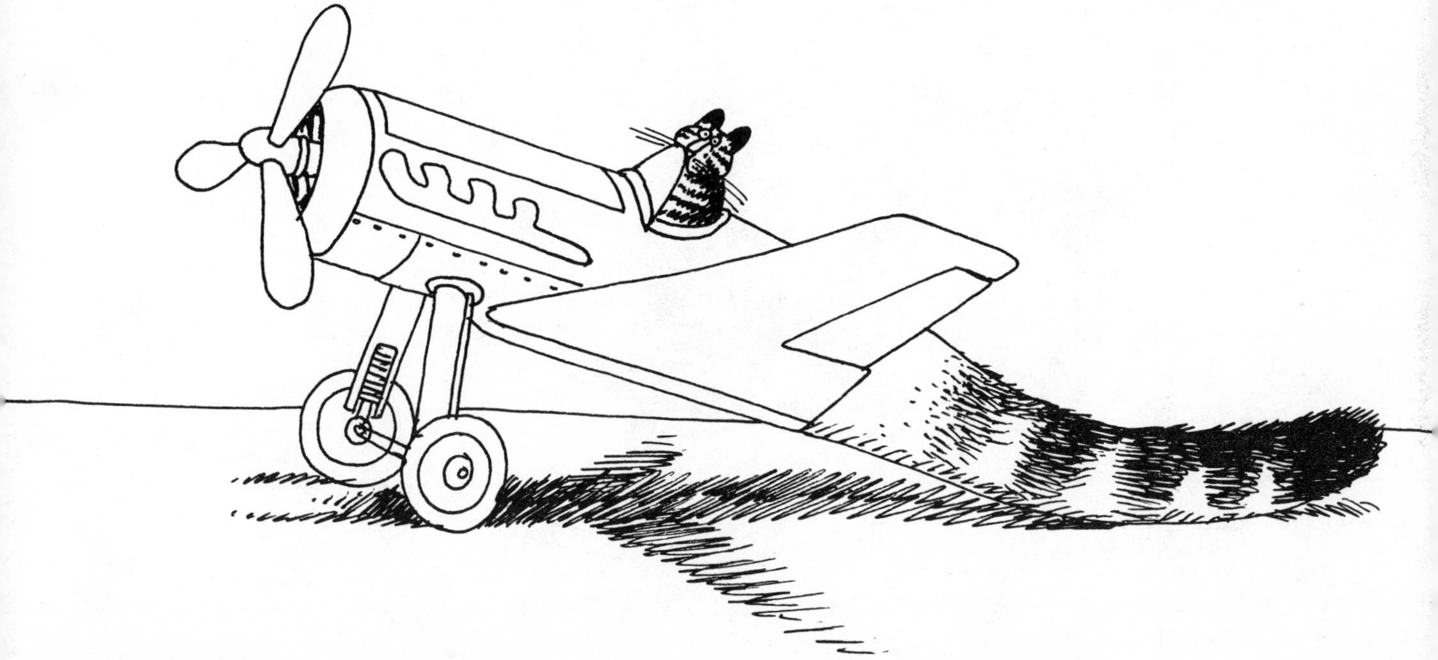

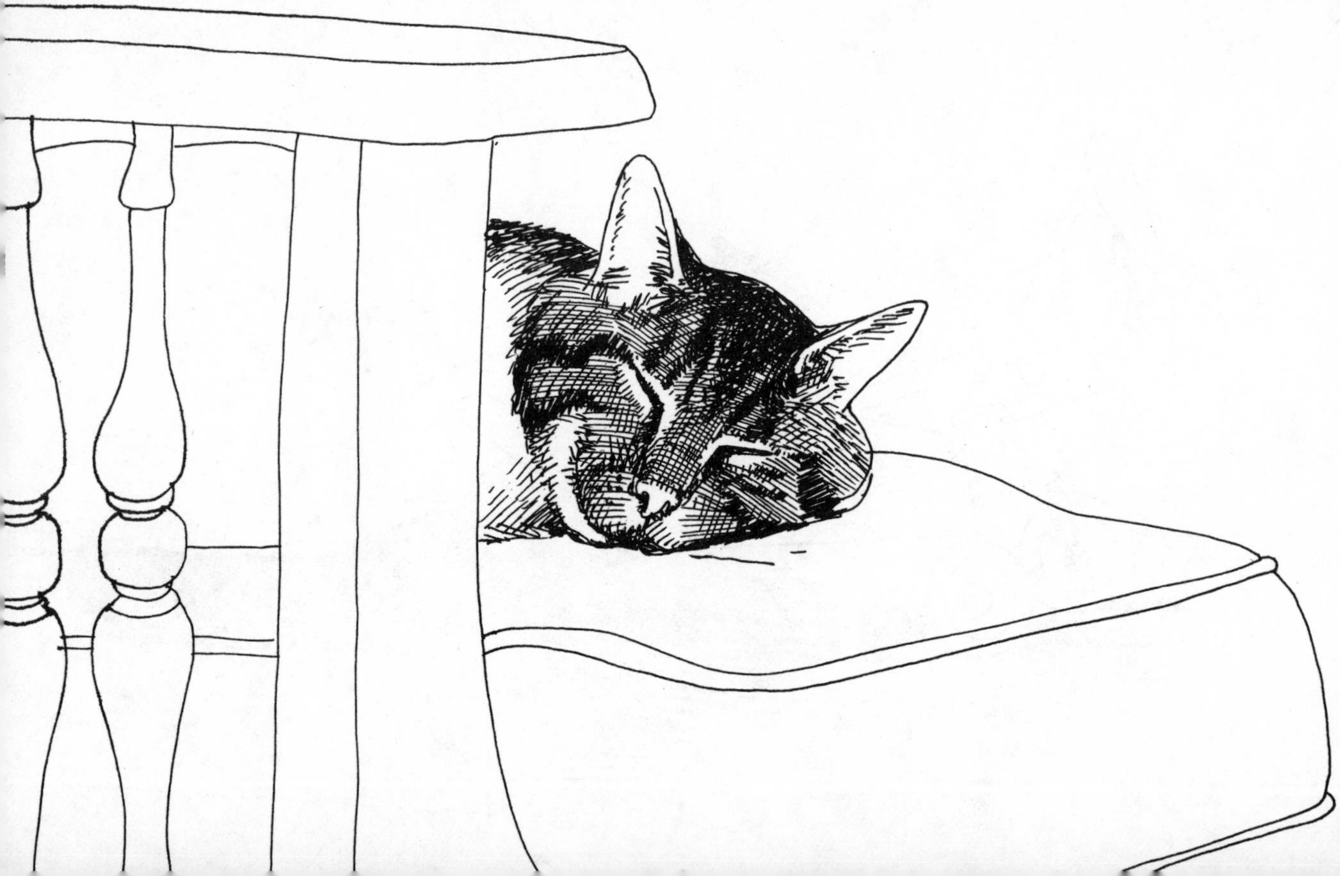

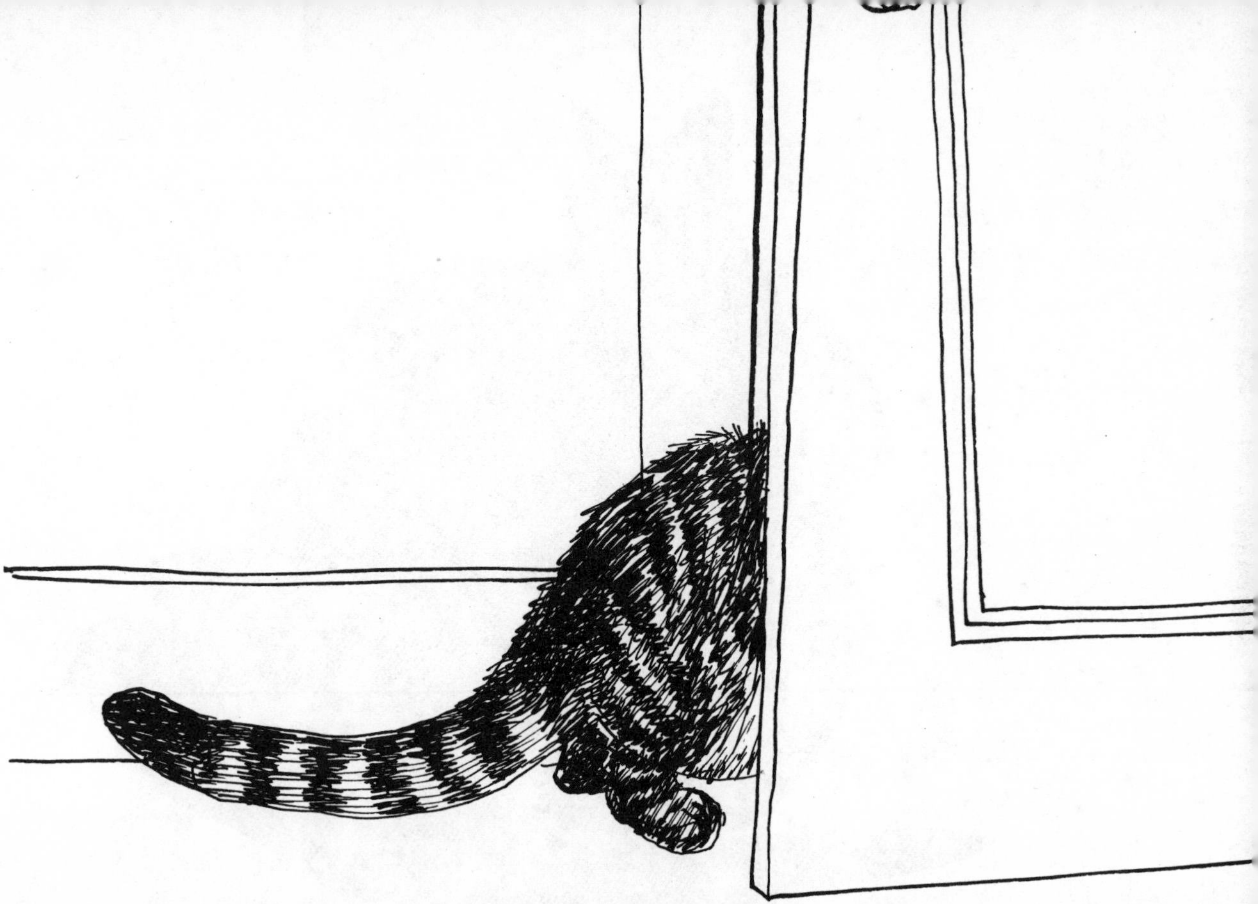

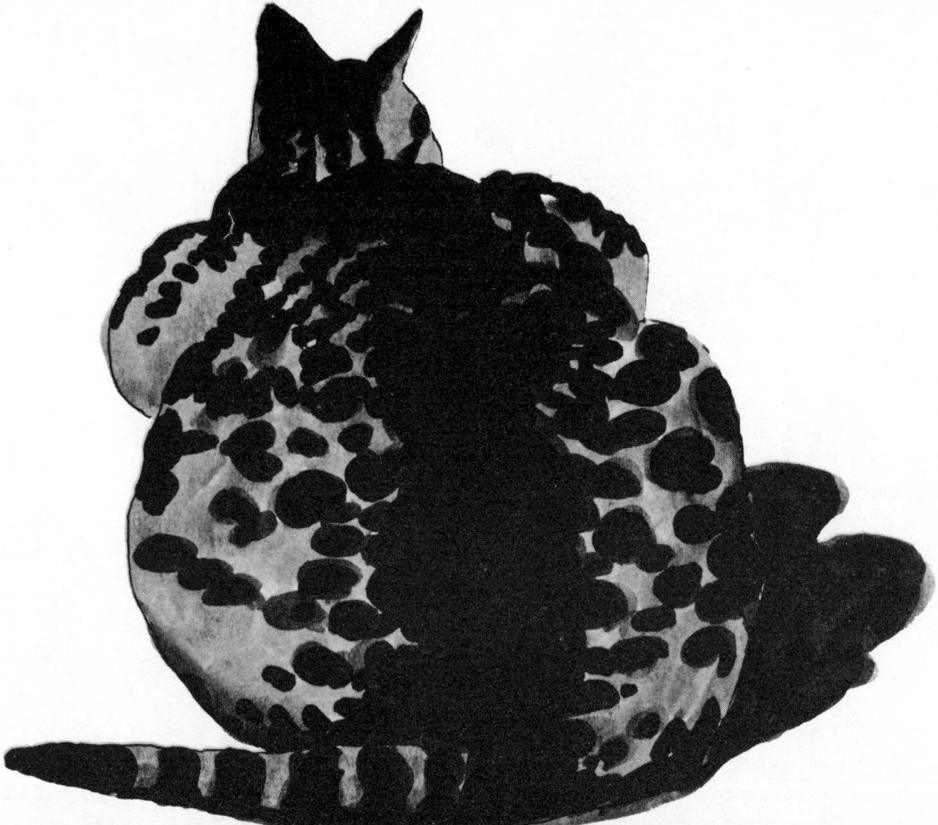

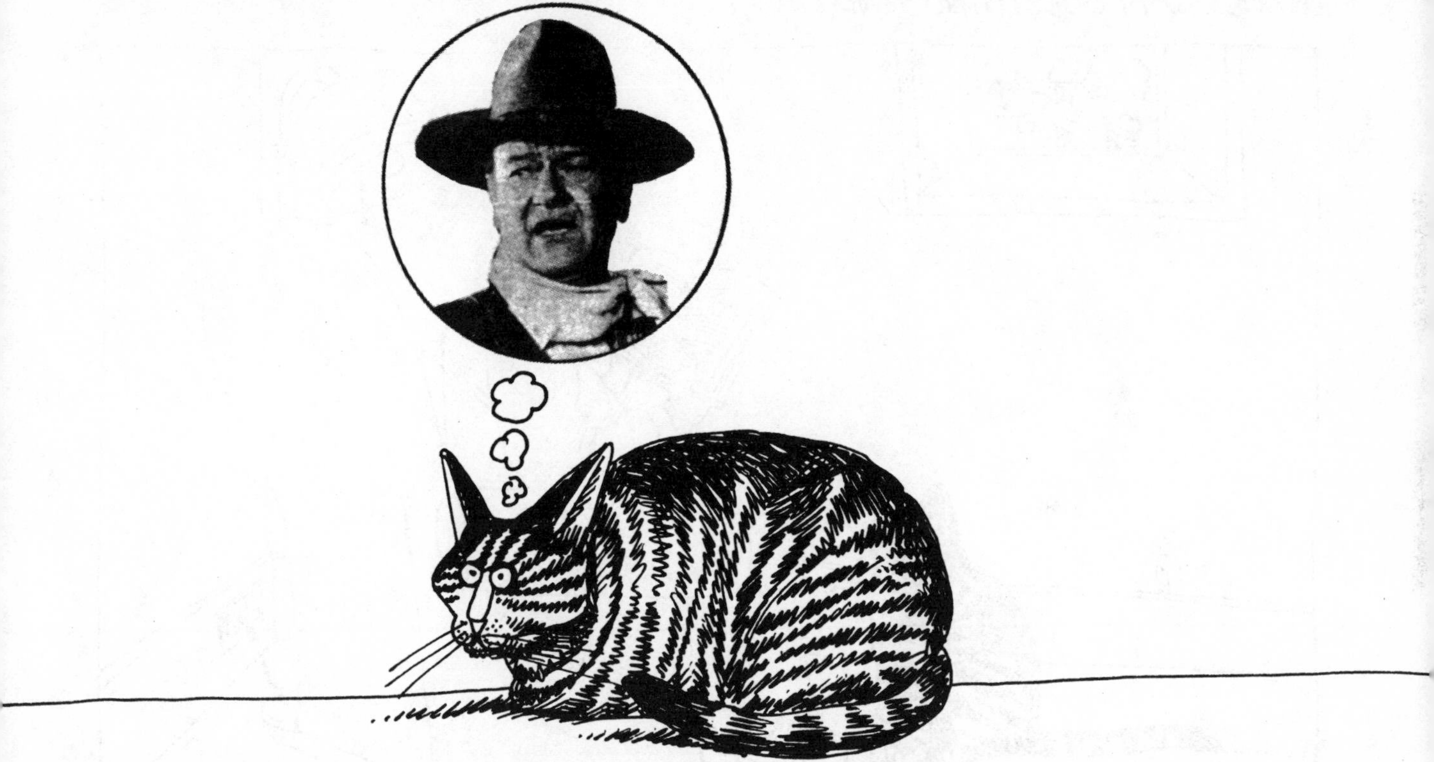

CATS CAN SEE THINGS WE CAN'T

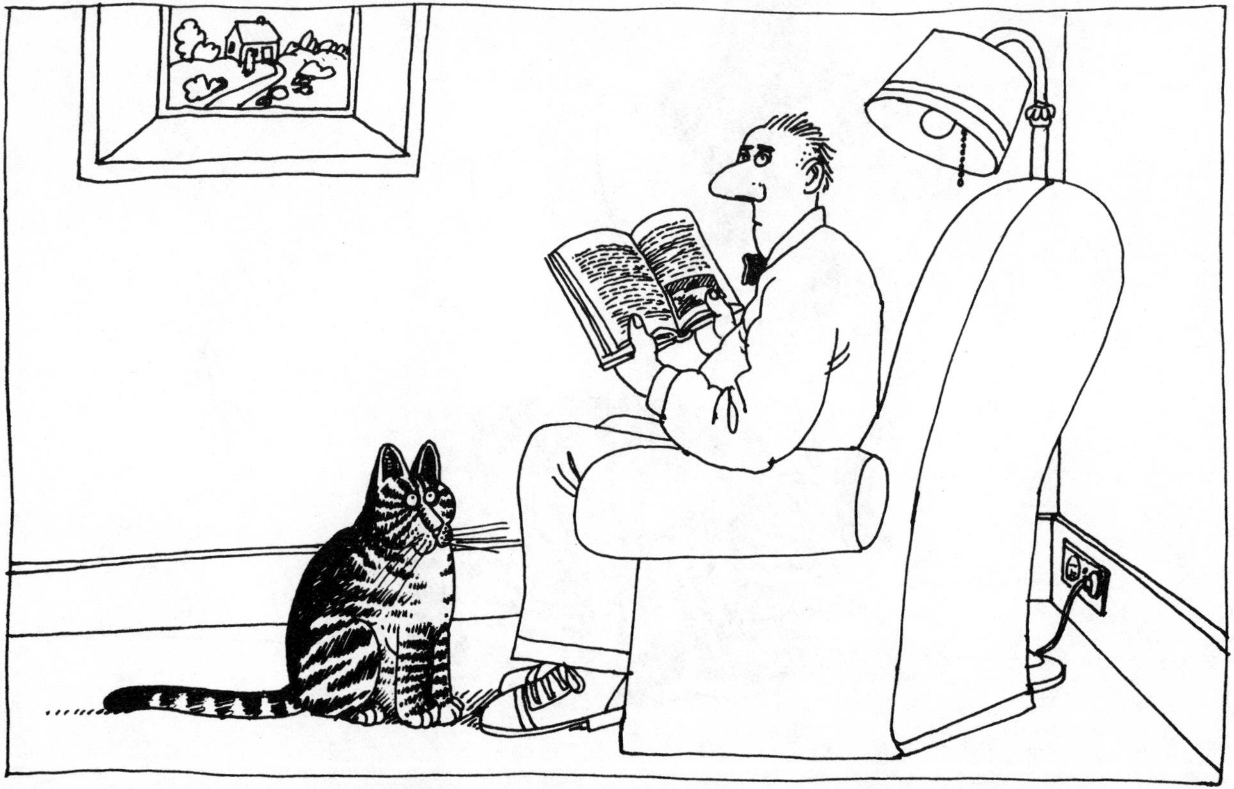

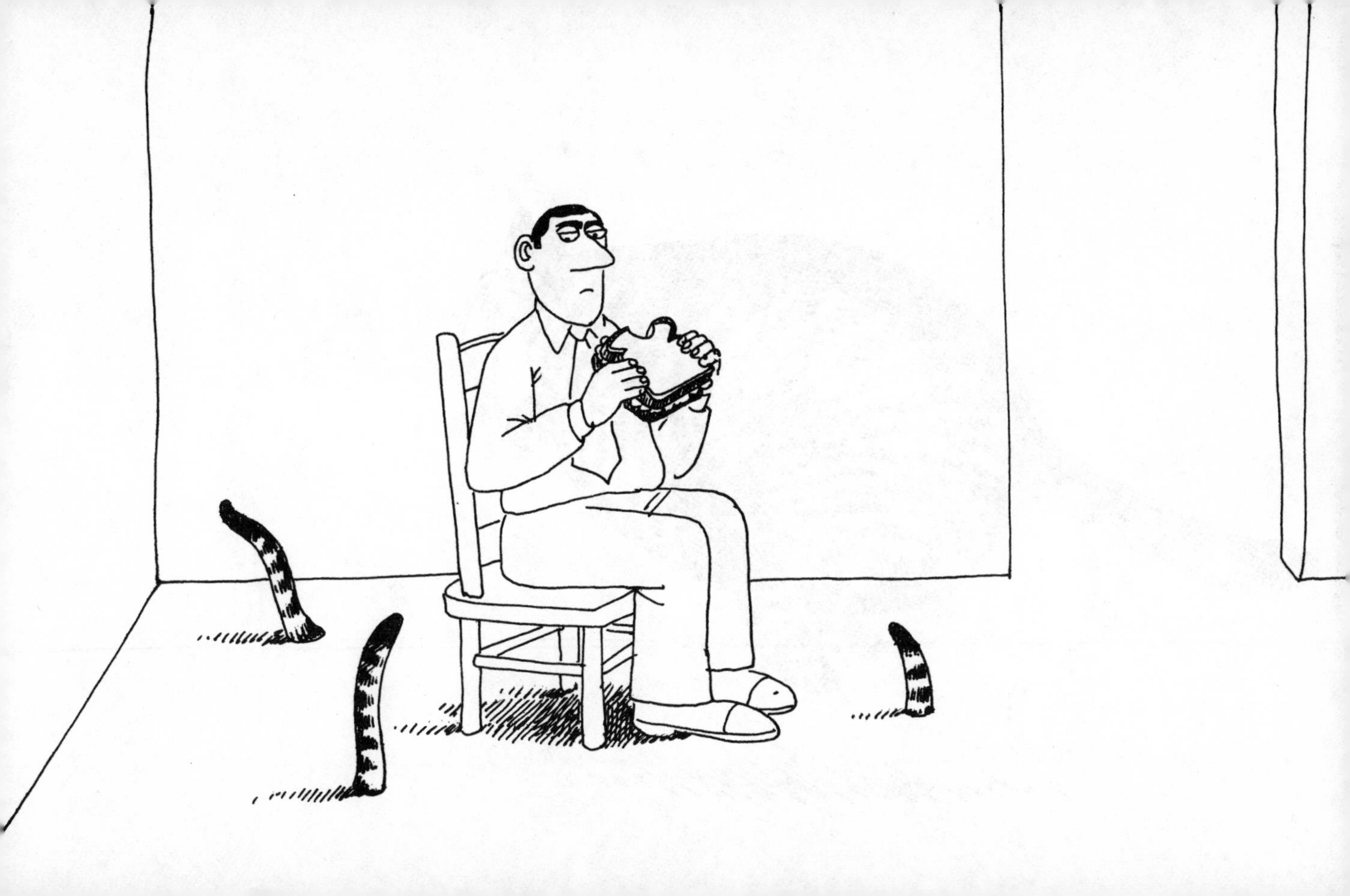

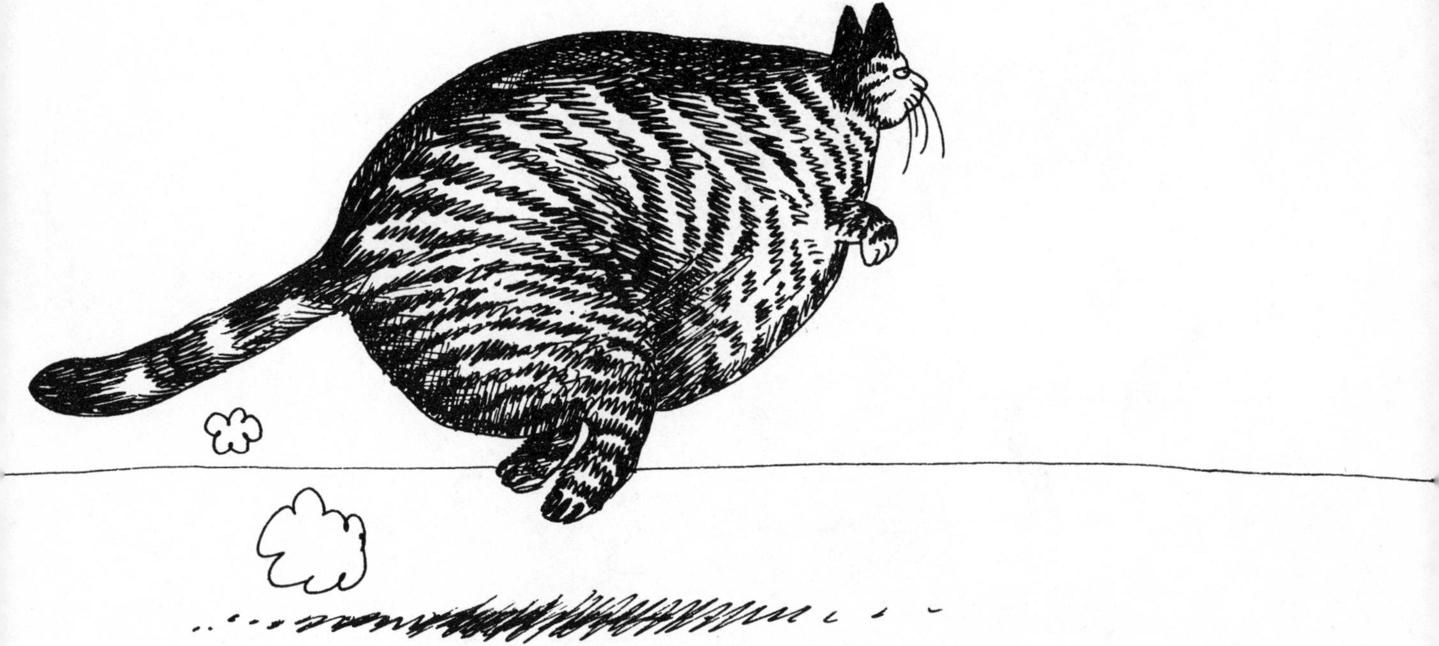

SIAMESE WICKER CAT FIGHTING SUIT

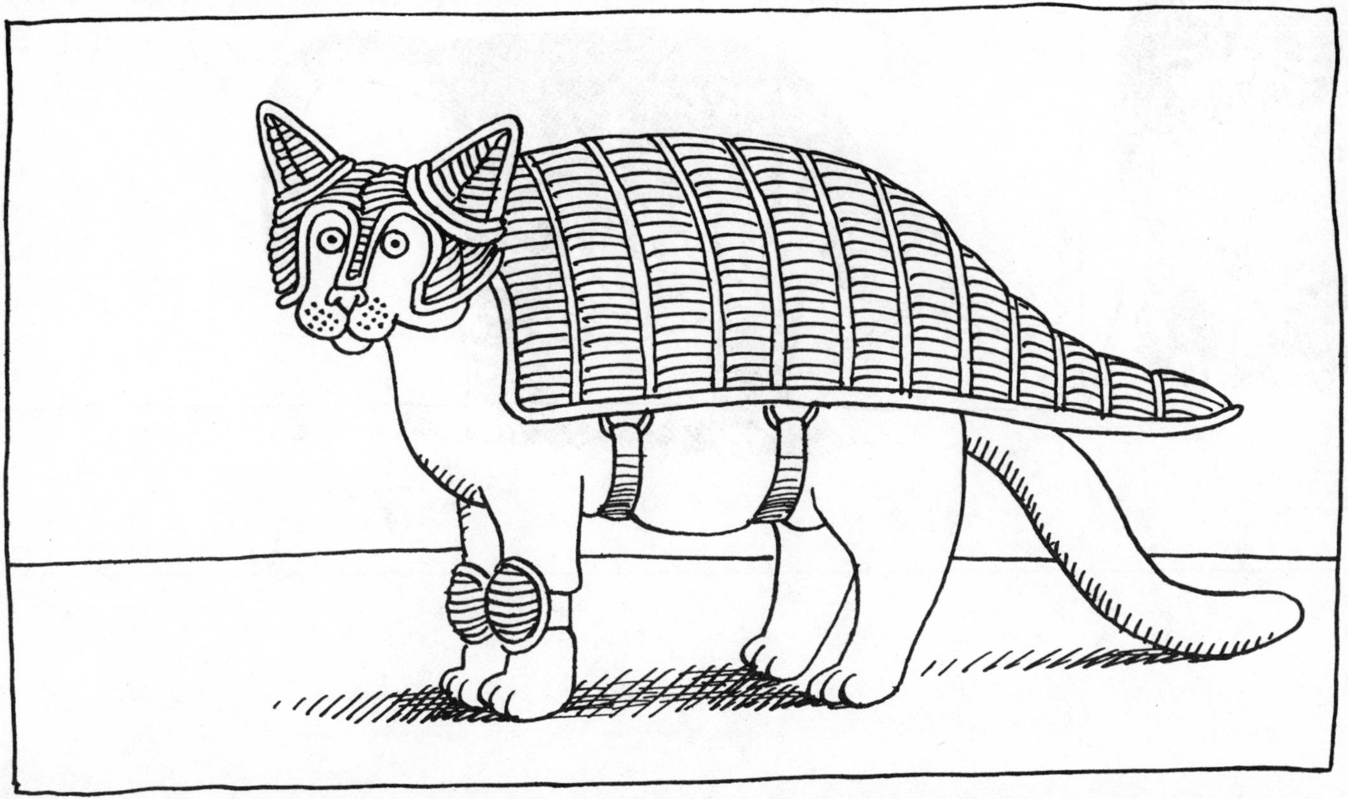

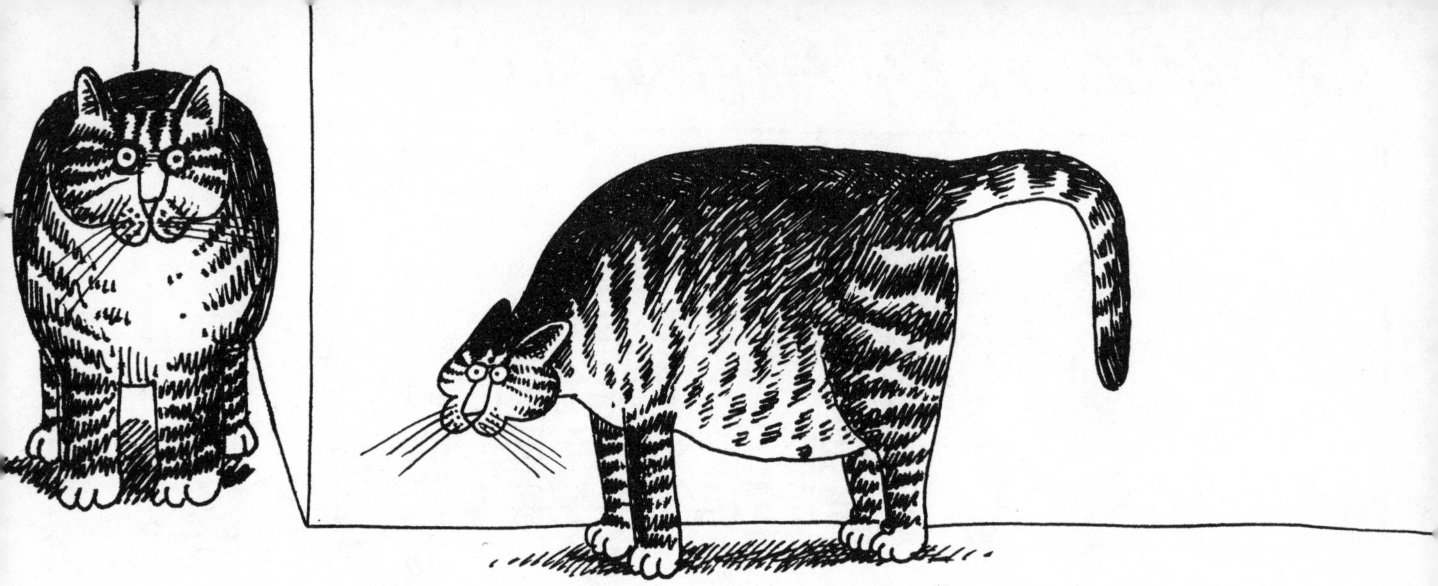

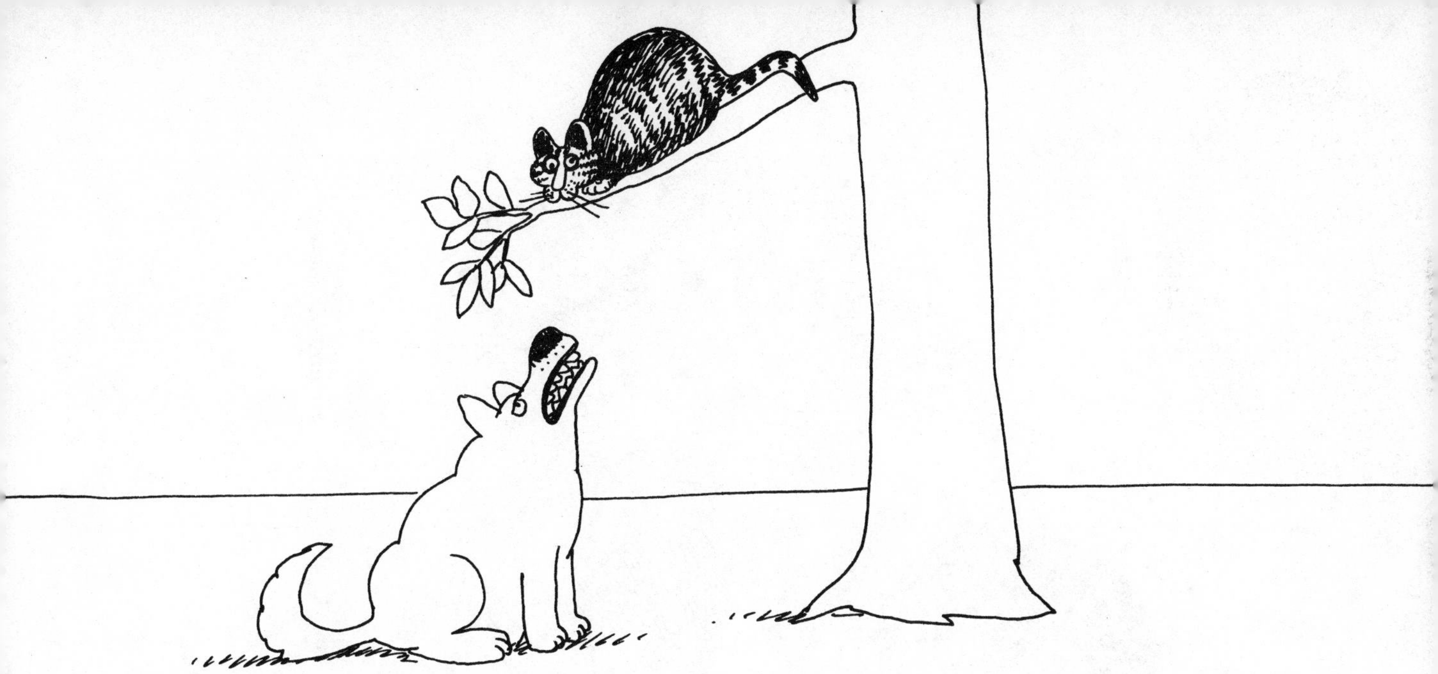

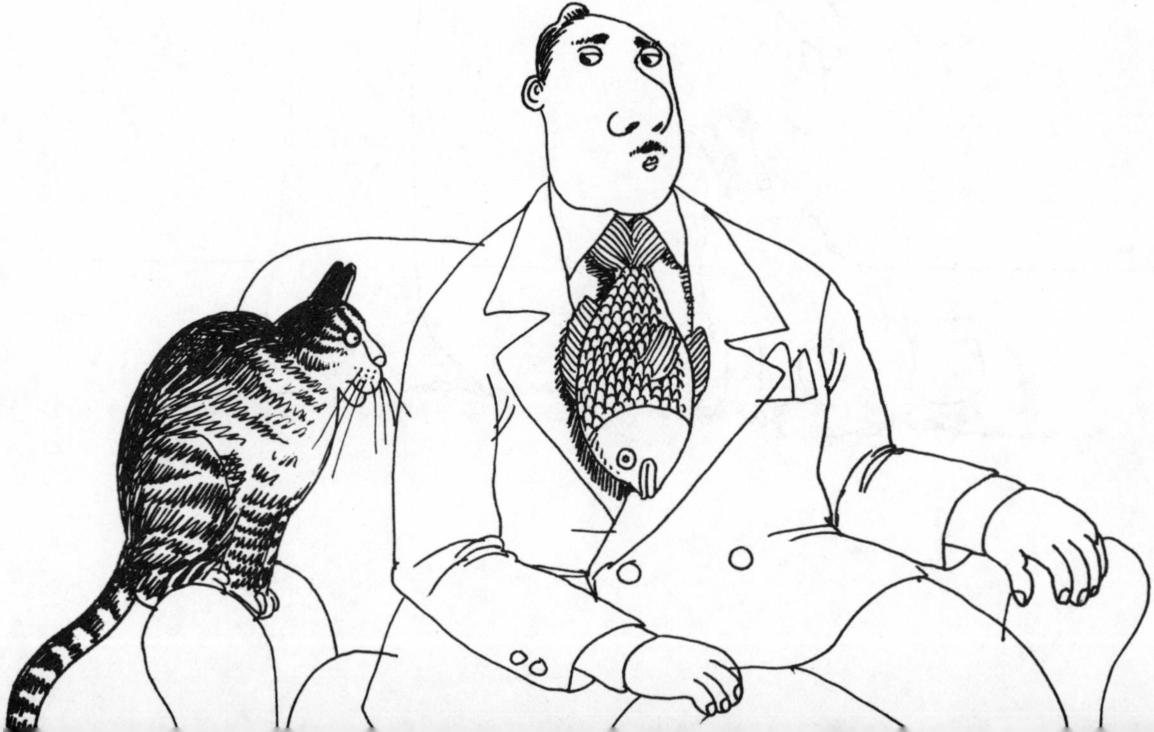

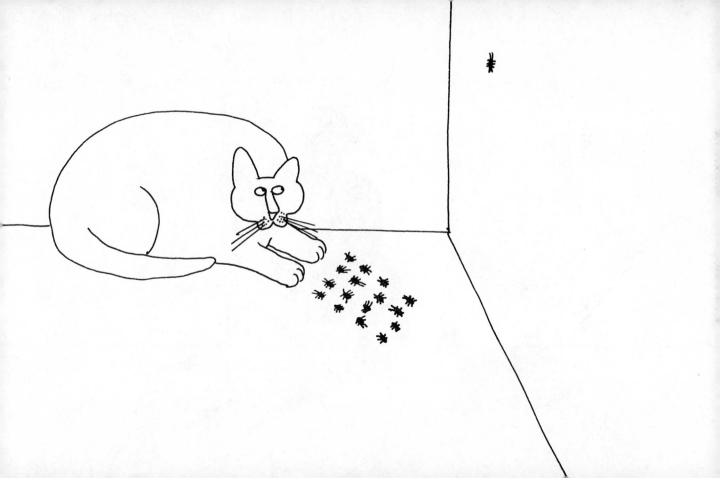

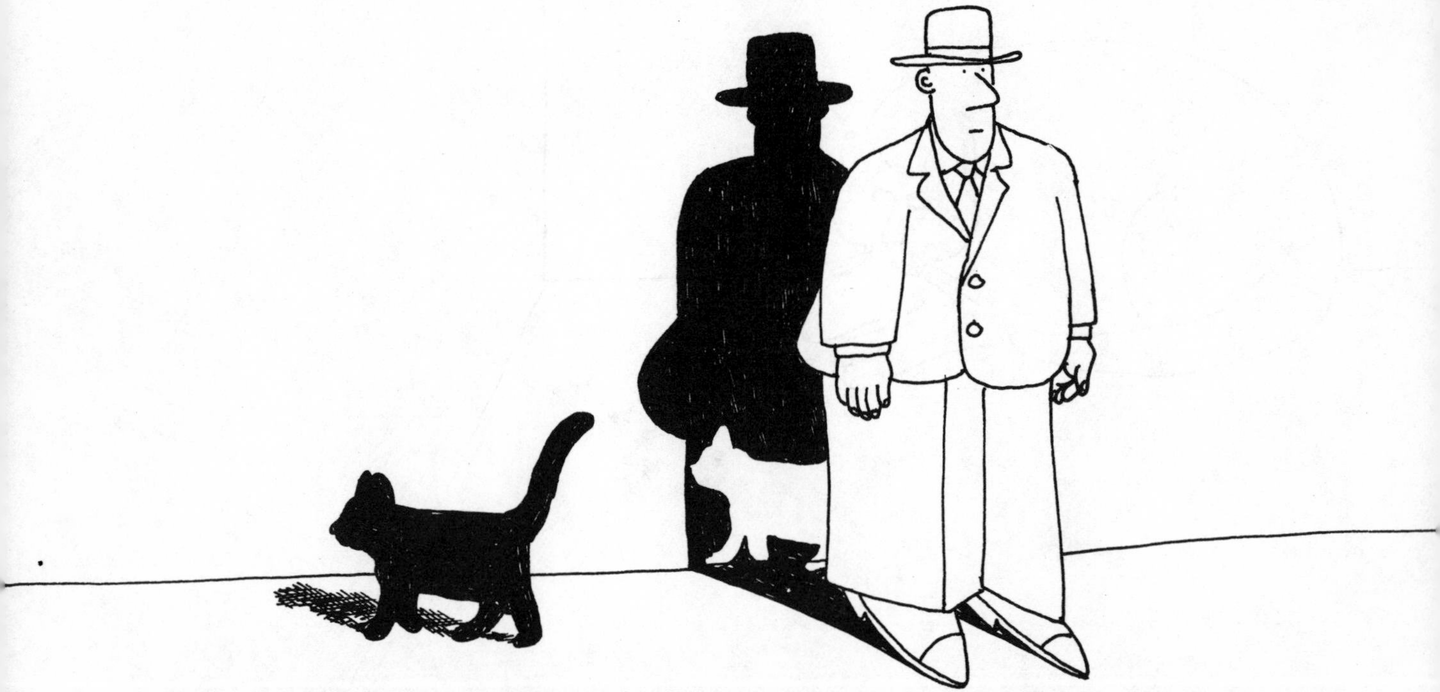

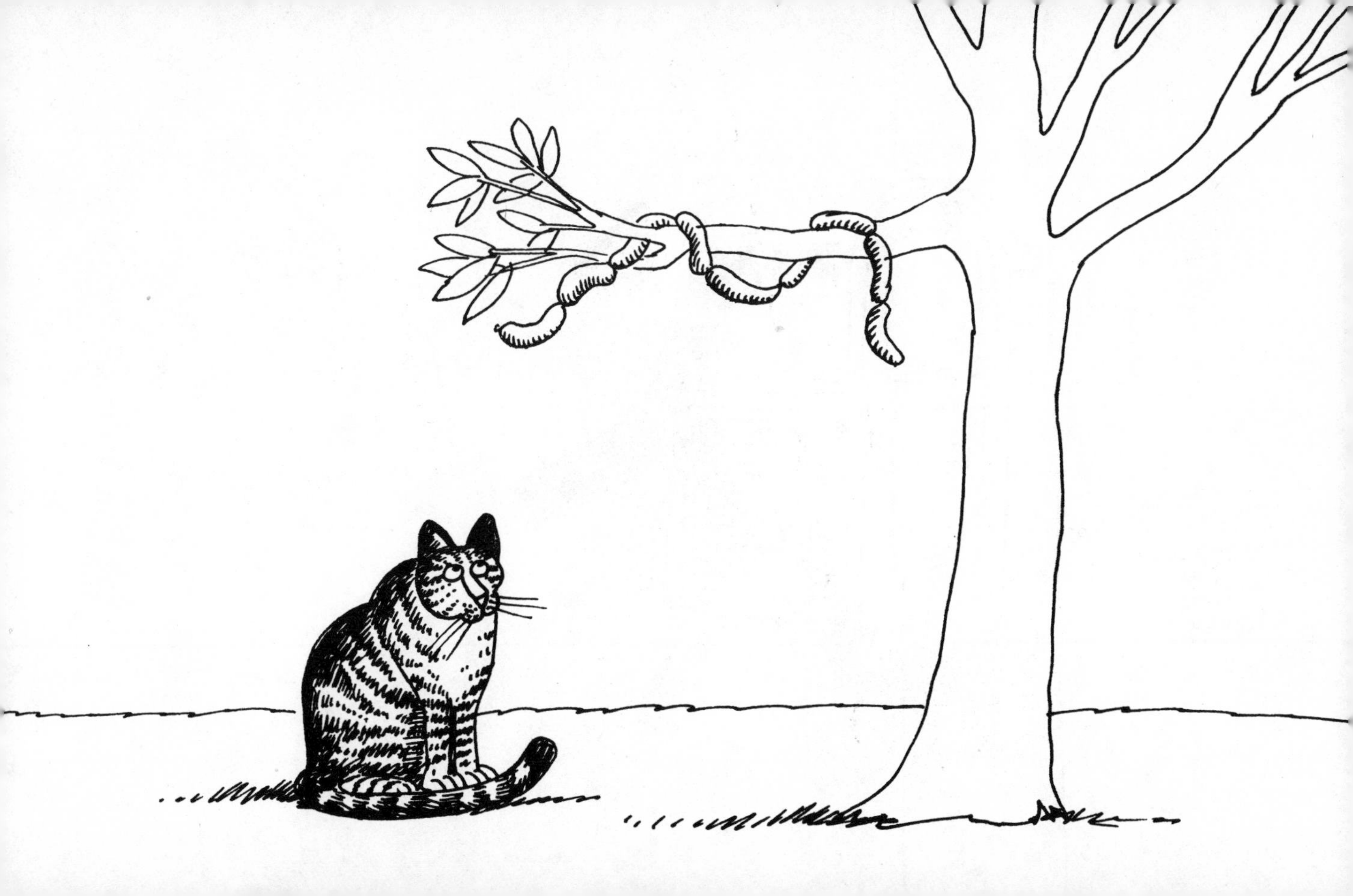

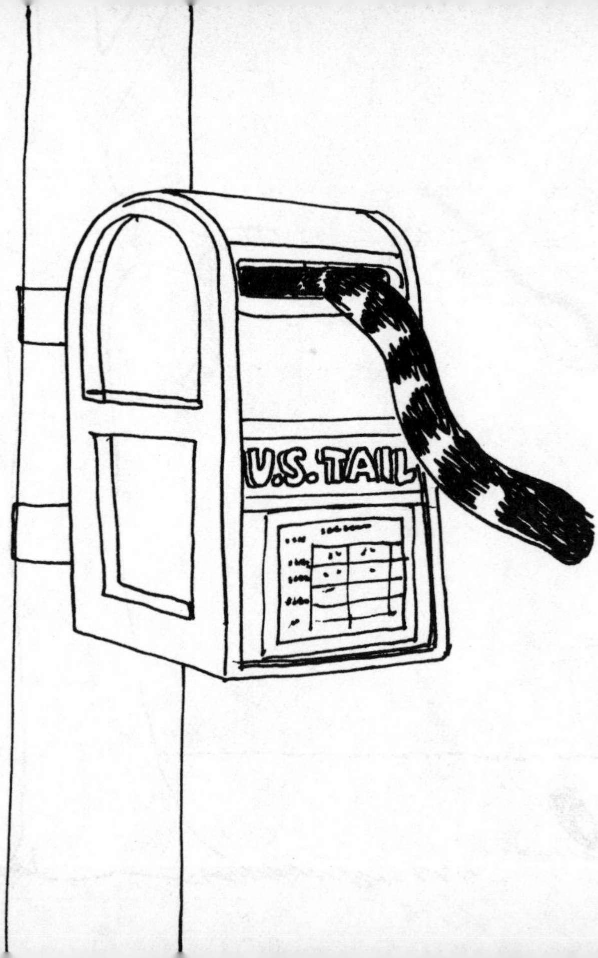
U.S. TAIL

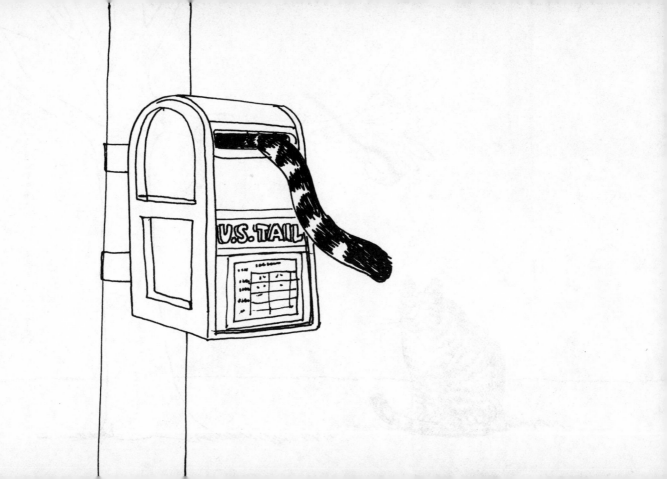

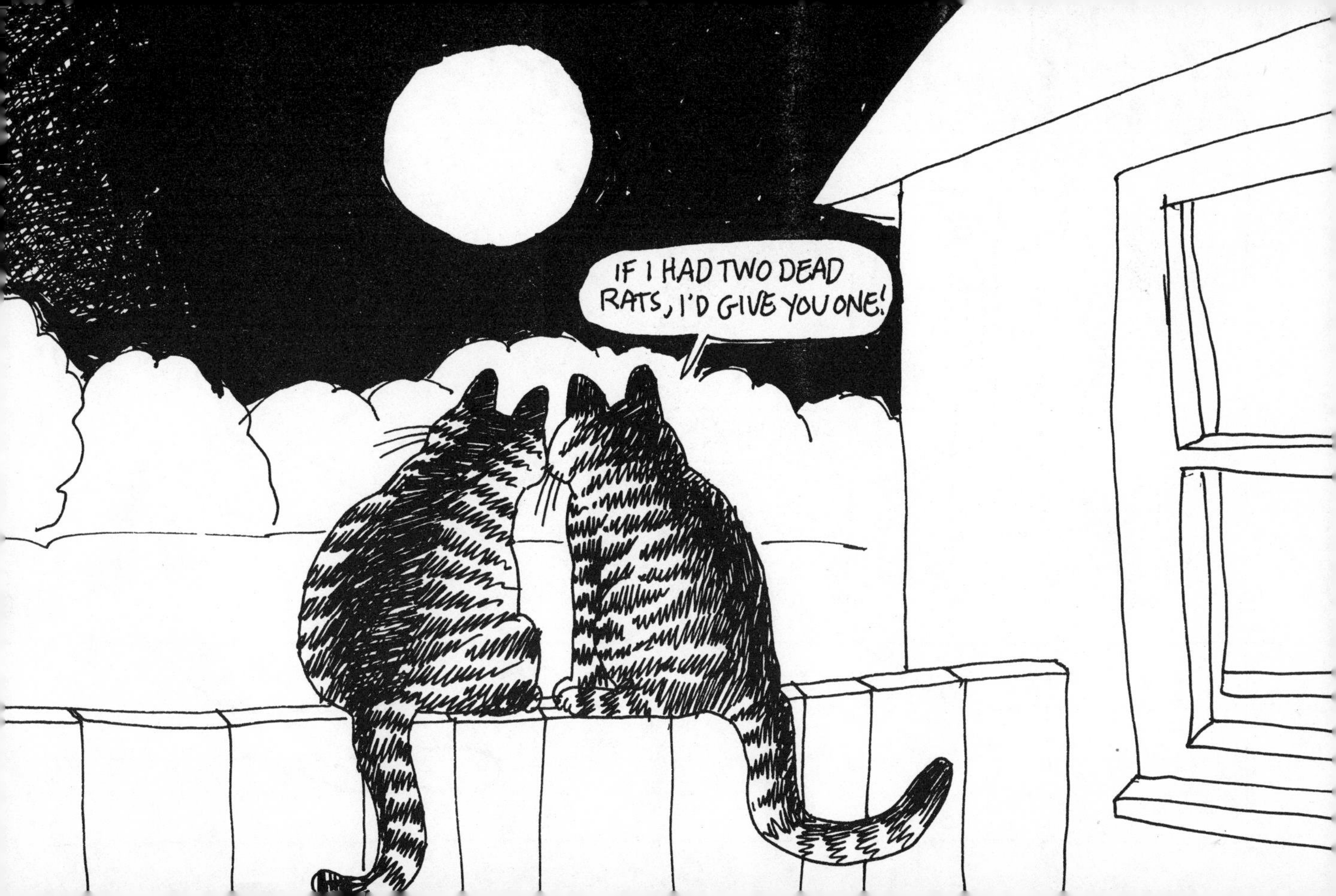
IF I HAD TWO DEAD RATS, I'D GIVE YOU ONE!

How to draw a Qat

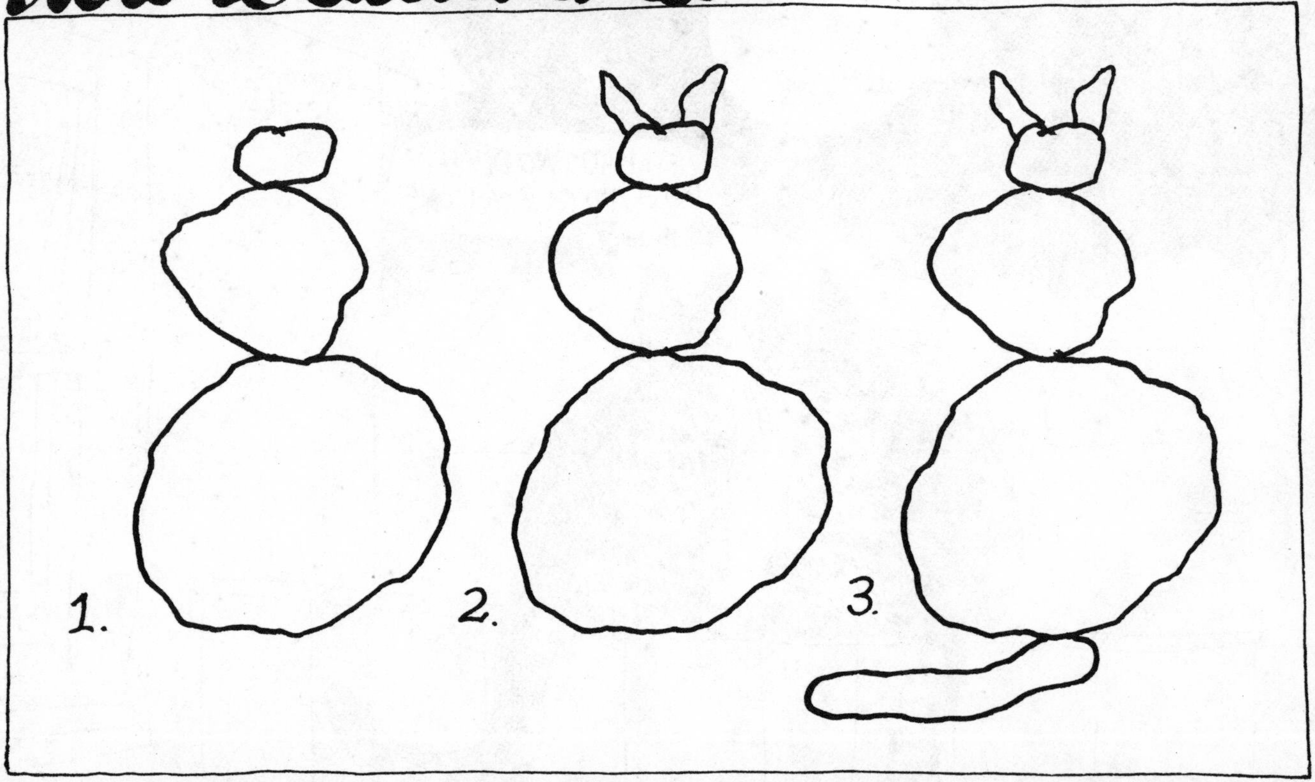
1.
2.
3.